AN

Hawlfraint © Copyright Cyngor Sir Ynys Môn / Anglesey County Council

THE HISTORIES OF WALES
SERIES EDITOR: CATRIN STEVENS

ANGLESEY

THE CONCISE HISTORY

DAVID A. PRETTY

UNIVERSITY OF WALES PRESS
CARDIFF
2005

© David A. Pretty, 2005

British Library Cataloguing-in-Publication Data
A catalogue record for this book is available from the British Library.

ISBN 0-7083-1943-2

Printed in Malta by Gutenberg Press, Tarxien

i Lynwen, Eurliw a Cerian,
i gofio'r hafau ar draethau Môn

CONTENTS

Series Editor's Preface

The concept of *brogarwch* (love of one's region) has always had a special resonance for the people of Wales. It has inspired poets, writers and historians through the centuries and it has enriched our appreciation and understanding of the colourful diversity of our local and regional culture and heritage.

This series, The Histories of Wales, dedicated to these diverse regions, counties, cities and towns, is intended to further enhance ties of loyalty and attachment and to celebrate their individual characteristics and aspirations. The post-war *Crwydro* ... (Wandering ...) and the more recent *Nabod Bro* (Knowing One's Region) series have succeeded to some extent in fulfilling the Welsh speakers' needs for such a series but they have been inaccessible to the non-Welsh language audience. No such venture has been attempted hitherto in English although each region has, of course, been well-served by individual historians, from George Owen, Henllys's *The Description of Penbrockshire* (1603) to John Davies's recent volume on the history of Cardiff, and, in the twentieth century especially, by county history societies, who have produced erudite journals and impressively comprehensive county histories. The Histories of Wales will draw heavily upon the research and expertise of all such amateur and professional historians to produce new histories, which will be both academic in content and accessible to the general public. While each volume has been structured chronologically the authors have been given free rein to interpret this as befits best their chosen regions.

The authors have been selected both for their undoubted scholarship and intimate knowledge of their own particular regions and for their ability to interpret and communicate that knowledge in a lively and concise style to students, scholars and tourists alike. The one encompassing criterion in the selection of authors, however, has been that they fully identify with and love their native or chosen adoptive regions. Thus it is hoped that the histories will be especially acceptable to the inhabitants of each *bro*, whether *brodorion* (native born) or later in-comers. Yet each author is also fully aware that no community or *bro* leads an independent or isolated existence and that regional histories are firmly grounded within the national Welsh experience. Thus, eventually, when the series is complete, each volume will contribute distinctively and uniquely to the composite and fascinating jigsaw, which constitutes the history of Wales.

Aptly, with Anglesey or *Môn* acclaimed the 'Mother of Wales', the first book in the series will explore this fiercely individual and independent county. The author, David A. Pretty, is not only a native of the island but also one of its most prominent historians and he has published widely on Anglesey's political, educational and social history. This volume traces the island's rich history as the last stronghold of the Druids; through its strategic significance during the Edwardian conquest in medieval times; Telford's major achievement in building the Menai Suspension Bridge (1826), to the cultural and linguistic challenges of the late twentieth century. I am greatly indebted to him for undertaking this vast task with such enthusiasm, dedication and scholarship.

Catrin Stevens
Series Editor, The Histories of Wales

Acknowledgements

'Abandon the Anglesey shore – that I cannot', so declared one fiercely partisan medieval poet. More years than I care to count have passed since I left the island to find employment, but Llanfair Pwllgwyngyll and the road to Pwllfanog still provide the best of memories. Again on a personal note, I have good reason to appreciate the opportunities offered by the comprehensive education system as pioneered in Anglesey, entering the secondary school at Beaumaris among the first group of pupils to be freed from the 11-plus examination. Whereas subsequent encounters with school authority were mostly of the non-academic variety, it was my history teacher, Herbert Anthony, who initially inspired me to follow the path that now culminates in a form of personal homage to Ynys Môn.

Tracing the history of Anglesey from the Mesolithic period to the age of the Magnox nuclear power station presented various challenges. I was only able to concentrate on the main themes; it proved impossible to name all the people, places and events that one would wish. Fortunately, the groundwork had been soundly prepared, and my indebtedness to the original research of countless others is readily acknowledged. In the process of synthesis I drew in large measure from the volumes in the 'Studies in Anglesey History' series, as well as the contents of the annual *Transactions* published by the Anglesey Antiquarian Society and Field Club. Whilst I am unable to cite individual contributions, due credit can be paid to the indispensable *Index to Transactions 1913–1985* (1987) compiled by Dewi O. Jones. Gratitude, too, is owed to Dr William Griffith, Charles Parry, M. S. Dolan, Ellis Wyn Roberts and Dr James Scourse for responding to my request for specific information, and to the staff of the Anglesey County Record Office for their help. I would especially like to thank Catrin Stevens, the series editor, who suggested a number of modifications and corrections, and Nia Peris of the University of Wales Press for preparing the work for publication. Inevitably, I often faced contradictory facts, dates and spelling variations; however, the final choice and any inaccuracies or failings that remain are my sole responsibility. The main debt is to my wife, who also mastered the new technology to type and prepare the work as it slowly evolved. Study and story became even more compelling when they reinforced that instinctive need to reconnect with the island of sunlit memory.

David A. Pretty
Tonteg, Rhondda Cynon Taf

I

Prehistoric Times to Middle Ages

Anglesey's prehistory began even before it could be defined as an island with a distinctive geographical identity. Human settlement was precluded during the Palaeolithic period (Old Stone Age) because a slow moving ice-sheet covered the land surface, whose Pre-Cambrian rock outcrops are among the oldest in Britain. Only when the climate improved and the ice began to retreat in the Mesolithic period (Middle Stone Age) did Anglesey become habitable. From about 7000 BC, the first people walked across the exposed central corridor of dry land that lay between two deep river-cut valleys. Drawn by the natural resources and favourable climate, they traversed the low-lying coastal areas to set up temporary encampments in accordance with the seasons. Dense wildwood covered most of the inland region. Nomadic bands existed by hunting, fishing and gathering wild vegetable foods, nuts and berries. Archaeological excavations at Trwyn Du, Aberffraw, the headland site of one of the earliest transient communities, have revealed flint arrow tips used for hunting wild animals such as the red deer and small stone axes that enabled them to cut wood. Glacial and melt-water erosion during the last ice age, later combined with rising sea levels, led to the eventual submersion of the land 'bridge' in the area of Pwll Ceris (the Swellies) around 4000 – 3000 BC. A continuous channel was carved out. And with the creation of the Menai Straits – some 15 miles long and varying in width between 200 yards and two miles – Anglesey finally emerged as a separate island. However momentous an event, its isolation from the mainland had little controlling influence on the movement of people. Subsequent groups of migrants would have readily constructed a log boat or raft to make the short crossing without much difficulty. Indeed, sea travel provided the general means of communication from the outset, establishing routeways with other parts of Britain, Ireland and Western Europe.

Vast swathes of time are telescoped into the earliest prehistoric ages. For thousands of years human activity remained virtually unchanged. A major advance occurred during the Neolithic period (New Stone Age) when there was a perceptible improvement in the life of the people and the degree of social organization. Possessing a greater range of specialized skills they were better able to control their environment, leading to the establishment of agriculture and the domestication of animals. These changes appear in Anglesey about 4000–3000 BC. Gradually, the interior of the island was being opened, and once the woodland had been burnt and cleared for farming, the inhabitants began to live in settled communities growing cereal crops and rearing stock. Barley cultivation predominated at first; with small herds of cattle, sheep, pigs and goats providing much of their basic needs. One site of permanent agricultural settlement has been found at Tŷ Mawr on the footslopes of Mynydd Twr (Holyhead Mountain), the circular hut walls being built of stone. Evidence of Neolithic social life remains elusive but stray finds and archaeological excavations reveal a little of their everyday domestic activities. Items include animal bones, scrapers, flint arrow heads, pins of polished bone or antler, quantities of pottery, and a great number of stone axes, mostly polished end-products from the 'axe factories' at Graig Lwyd, Penmaen-mawr. Their widespread distribution indicates Anglesey's importance in the forging of trade connections.

Linked to these developments was the emergence of religious beliefs, central to which came the idea of an afterlife. While there is no trace of their wooden dwellings, great stone monuments survive to show the care they took in burying their dead. Collective effort made possible the impressive feats of engineering needed to raise the *cromlechi* (megalithic tombs) that served as communal burial chambers. Single upright stones supporting massive capstones (weighing up to 25 tons) were originally covered with a mound of earth or stones, leaving a narrow passage as entrance. At one time over fifty Neolithic tombs could be found in Anglesey, varying in design according to external influences and traditions. As expected, the majority had been erected in the main coastal areas of habitation. Among the best surviving examples are those at Barclodiad y Gawres (Llangwyfan), Bodowyr (Llanidan), Bryn Celli Ddu (Llanddaniel), Din Dryfol (Aberffraw), Prysaeddfed (Bodedern) and Trefignath (Holyhead). Incised decorative patterns and spiral markings on the stones at Barclodiad y Gawres and Bryn Celli Ddu are rare examples of mural art with possible magico-religious symbolism associated with the earth mother goddess that can be stylistically linked to Irish and Iberian influences. Barclodiad y Gawres provides early evidence of a very close tie to Ireland. By the later Neolithic period (*c.*3000–2500 BC) the tombs had become the focus for ritual ceremonies that may have involved ancestor worship.

Of the many advances that resulted from settled life, the changes from stone to metal during the Bronze Age (*c.*2500–1500 BC) and the new emphasis on individual burials are the most significant. Inside the single graves the funeral custom of placing a decorated beaker pot as food vessel for the afterworld signified fresh influences. That the 'Beaker Folk' also included bronze objects underlined the importance now given to the acquisition of material possessions and the status they accorded to a wealthy leader. A complete beaker, together with a bronze dagger and other grave goods, accompanied the crouched skeleton found in the Beaker burial at Merddyn Gwyn, Pentraeth. Occasionally, a *maen hir* (standing stone) marked the gravesite. A mound of earth built around a central stone, such as the round barrow at Bedd Branwen (Llanbabo), became a cemetery where urns containing cremated bodies could be placed. Often the grave goods would include such imported 'luxury items' as jet buttons, necklaces and beads, bronze armlets and bracelets. One can only guess as to the purpose of the other standing stones: perhaps they were for ceremonial use, or as boundary markers. At one time there were sixty-four standing stones in Anglesey. Included among the forty-six still in existence are the stones at Maen Addwyn (Llanfihangel Tre'r-beirdd), Tregwehelydd (Llantrisant) and the two at Penrhosfeilw (Holyhead), both almost 10 ft high.

By the later Bronze Age (*c.*1500 onwards) the pattern of farming settlement had been well established. The economy was thus able to sustain a far more numerous population. Extensive trading contacts had meant that both raw materials and finished metal implements were being imported, with the Irish connection very much in evidence. All the gold objects found in Anglesey – like the bracelets and lock rings found at Capel Eithin, Gaerwen – came from Ireland. There also existed a small-scale native industry. Copper had been extracted at Parys Mountain (Amlwch) from at least 2000 BC, making it one of the earliest mines in Britain, followed by later ore workings on Holyhead Mountain. Certainly, by 700 BC nearby metal-working sites had enabled local bronze smiths, inspired by external influences, to turn out lighter products such as knives and small tools. The hoard found at Cors Bodwrog, near Gwalchmai, included a number of locally made items. Meantime, a growing population had coincided with a period of adverse climatic change that led to the abandonment of upland sites on the mainland. Heightened social tensions put tribal groups on the defensive. Increasingly, there was need for protected settlements and better weaponry. Bronze sword-blades, spearheads and battle-axes of distant origin were among the finds at Tŷ Mawr and Cors Bodwrog.

When the enigmatic Celtic people, with their knowledge of iron, began to exert their powerful cultural influence, an important formative period began *c.*500 BC. The pace of civilization quickened. Superior implements facilitated further progress in agriculture, coupled with an improving climate. Farming prospered in fertile Anglesey, and the population increased. The large enclosed farmstead at Bryn Eryr (Llansadwrn) had granaries for wheat, also space for rearing cattle and sheep. Gatherings of round stone huts with thatched conical roofs signalled the beginnings of small village communities. At the same time the emergence of an aristocratic class of warrior chiefs intensified the bellicose element in tribal society. The burial grave at Gelliniog Wen (Llangeinwen), containing a long broad-bladed iron sword in its scabbard, honoured a pre-Roman warrior of considerable status. Traditional strongholds were refortified and more elaborate structures constructed. Hill forts such as Caer y Twr on Holyhead Mountain offered refuge in times of danger. Located on the highest point on the island – but at 720 ft more a large hill – the rampart walls at Caer y Twr were 13 ft wide. Another seven sites are considered to be Iron Age hill-forts. Built to take full advantage of the local topography they sometimes have an encircling earthwork wall, like Castell Bryn Gwyn (Llanidan), or as in the case of Twyn y Parc (Llangadwaladr), an advantageous position on a rocky coastal headland that could be protected by defensive ramparts on the landward side. By the late Iron Age it appears that Anglesey lay within the tribal territory of the Ordovices, the 'hammer fighters' who would put up such fierce resistance to the Romans.

No better insight has been provided into Iron Age activity in Anglesey than with the remarkable, yet intriguing, chance discovery at Llyn Cerrig Bach, Llanfair-yn-neubwll. When the RAF airfield at Valley was being constructed in 1942–3 it became necessary to dredge peat from around the small lake in order to consolidate land for the runways. In the process a treasure-trove of materials was unearthed; more than 150 pieces altogether. Virtually all of the items deposited are military in character, some embellished with the finest Celtic decorative art forms: iron swords, spearheads, a dagger, and shields with patterned metal boss – which together help create an identikit picture of a Celtic warrior. Also in abundance were the wheel and metal fittings of light battle chariots that represented the advanced military technology of the time. Not only that, there was part of a semicircular trumpet redolent of military ceremonial, a bronze crescent-shaped plaque decorated with a Celtic triskele motif, and two gang chains with neck-rings designed to shackle prisoners of war or slaves. Among those articles of a more peaceful character were the latest in ironware agricultural equipment as represented by the blacksmith's tongs, plough shares and sickle. No doubt, more objects will surface at some future date when circumstances allow further investigation of the site.

Interpreting the significance of this rare collection is even more absorbing. Everything points to a religious explanation. Celtic beliefs, firmly rooted in nature, gave rise to a pantheon of deities. Natural waters were believed to contain powerful spirits who demanded regular sacrifice or the deposit of material gifts; the name of Afon Braint, one of Anglesey's major rivers, is derived from the time of its dedication to the goddess Brigantia. According to authoritative opinion, Llyn Cerrig Bach was similarly associated with a Celtic water-cult that necessitated offerings to the gods of the lake, drawing parallels with other similar European sites.

Most probably they had been thrown into the water from an abutting cliff platform. The fact that several valuable artefacts were deliberately damaged implies they could be war trophies, with perhaps distant origins in other parts of Britain and Ireland. Moreover, the deposition was cumulative, reflecting considerable activity around a sacred shrine over a period of two centuries or more (*c.*200 BC–AD 60), and linked to Druidism. As a distinctive religious caste within Celtic society the mysterious Druids exercised great power, not least as fearsome priestly sacrificers. For them, Anglesey had become a centre of special significance. But with no direct evidence of ritual human sacrifice at Llyn Cerrig Bach (only animal bones were found), it is assumed that such ceremonies took place elsewhere; perhaps in sacred groves where the type of carved stone head discovered at Hendy, Llanfair Pwllgwyngyll – stylistically similar to other Iron Age examples, and said to represent some local Celtic deity – would be displayed. One thing is certain: no further deposits were made in the lake after the first Roman incursion. As it turned out, the Druids and their fate also denote Anglesey's first entry into recorded history.

The Roman Period

Within a few years of the full-scale invasion in AD 43, the Roman army encountered fierce guerrilla resistance in the mountain regions of Wales led by Caratacus (Caradog). On his defeat, the Romans consolidated their military hold before returning to the offensive. This time Anglesey became the direct target of a punitive expedition. So much so that the Roman historian Tacitus recorded the attack on the 'thickly populated' island of Mona in his *Annals*, thus confirming the place name first given currency by Roman writers – although the original Celtic toponym Môn could well have had much earlier beginnings. Suetonius Paulinus, the Roman governor of Britain, had good reason to strike. As well as being the granary of the Ordovices, Anglesey symbolized political opposition to Roman rule, rallied by the Druids. On their island stronghold they provided a sanctuary for numerous hostile refugees from southern Britain, who, in their predicament, conceivably offered the final items to the gods at Llyn Cerrig Bach. Druidism, moreover, aroused deep revulsion because of the practice of human sacrifice. According to Tacitus's graphic account, Paulinus had carefully planned his operation in AD 60, involving the Fourteenth Legion and detachments of the Twentieth. A flotilla of specially constructed flat-bottomed boats ferried the infantry across the Menai Straits, leaving the cavalry troops to either ford or swim alongside their horses. As to the unidentified crossing place, both Traeth Lafan and the narrows between Felinheli and Llanidan have been cited as possible locations.

What confronted them that day momentarily froze even the battle-hardened Roman legionaries. Amid the opposing force rushed frantic black-robed women with dishevelled hair, brandishing flaming torches; Druidic priests screamed blood-curdling curses as they invoked their deity. At this dramatic moment, Paulinus's qualities of leadership were displayed as he summoned his men into action. Having inflicted a total rout, the Romans established a garrison (again unnamed, but possibly sited at Aberffraw) before setting out to eradicate all traces of Druidism. There then followed a savage destruction of the altars and sacred groves where they had held their rituals. News of Boudicca's rebellion in East Anglia forced Paulinus to cut short his stay, and for the next few years the Romans concentrated on regaining control. From the new legionary base at Deva (Chester) the conquest of north Wales was finally achieved under Julius Agricola, commanding the Second Legion (Adiutrix). To complete the task of annihilating the Ordovices he moved quickly towards Anglesey in AD 78 in a mopping up action. With no time to prepare landing craft, Agricola ordered a lightning attack by auxiliary cavalry experienced in fording, thus adding to their aura of invincibility. As the Druids had already been exterminated, the inhabitants promptly submitted.

Situated on the edge of empire, Wales under Roman occupation became a military frontier zone. For the most part, Anglesey, however, remained largely outside the network of strategic forts and road system; the sea-lanes would have provided the most rapid means of ferrying troops and supplies. No longer capable of posing a serious threat, it could be effectively policed from the auxiliary fortress at Segontium (Caernarfon). In time, the inhabitants adapted themselves to the benefits of Roman rule. To counter the growing menace of the Scotti, plunderers from northeast Ireland who disrupted maritime commerce in the fourth century, a frontline coastal defence was set up. Watch-towers at Caer y Twr, Carmel Head and Capel Eithin provided vital links to a system of signal communication with Segontium and Deva. At Caergybi (Holyhead) a small promontory fort was constructed similar to the type found on the Rhine frontier. Thick stone walls and corner turrets protected a harbour used as a fleet base for Irish Sea patrols. Anglesey was certainly a prize well worth defending. Besides having an abundance of corn, the Romans had been quick to profit from its rich mineral deposits. Under their supervision, miners extracted copper from Parys Mountain, and ingots, some officially stamped with Latin inscriptions, were then transported by pack animals or shipped by sea.

Otherwise, the island remained remote from the Roman sphere of influence. As a consequence there is scant archaeological evidence of their presence. Aside from the military structures (the small fort at Aberffraw founded by either Paulinus or Agricola has so far yielded few clues) and copper ingots, fragments of Roman pottery, storage vessels and glass are the most common finds. The supposed remnants of a Roman lady's vanity set discovered near Newborough have proved to be a rare exception. From time to time a number of Roman coin hoards have been uncovered, dating between the first and fifth century AD: a dozen gold coins from the reign of emperor Constantine the Great were found close to the fort at Caergybi; over 300 small coins had been placed in an urn at Trearddur. Most coins were probably issued as payment to Roman soldiers and government officials; others passed into circulation by way of trade.

The Early Middle Ages

Three hundred years of Roman rule seem to have hardly changed the daily lives of the majority of native inhabitants in Anglesey. They still spoke a Brythonic dialect that belonged to the Celtic family of languages. Communities continued to farm the land, rear animals or practice a craft in much the same way as their ancestors had done. Yet there can be no question that the era of Roman peace and stability created the conditions that allowed large native farmsteads to prosper. Din Llugwy near Moelfre, covering a half-acre site, is seen as a fine example of an enclosed rural settlement that flourished during the late Roman period. Circular houses had drystone walls supporting wooden and thatch structures. Evidence of metal-working and traces of imported pottery and glassware have been found on the site. Another substantial farmstead, recently discovered at Gaerwen, possessed a timber granary and corn-drying kiln. Far-reaching changes came with the collapse of Roman power early in the fifth century. It left a void that proved problematic in more than one way. For the historian, the thread of events are difficult to unravel, since very little is known with certainty. Because of the dearth of reliable contemporary sources during the so-called 'Dark Ages', as much accurate information as possible has to be derived from archaeological finds, place names, and the buried truths preserved in Welsh legends, myths, and the 'lives' of the Christian saints.

The withdrawal of Roman troops had created a dangerous power vacuum. The loss of seaboard defences meant Anglesey was immediately vulnerable to attack from across the Irish Sea. During this period of insecurity traditional strongholds were strengthened and hill-forts reoccupied. Caer y Twr incorporated a style of Roman defence, and Din Llugwy was remodelled, probably under the auspices of a tribal leader, into a fortified enclosure with thick stone-enforced walls. Place names bearing the elements *din* (fort) and *wy* (tribe, or tribal land), as found in Dindaethwy, near Cadnant, and Dinsylwy, near Llanddona, are pointers to Celtic tribal forts. How effective they proved to be is not known; neither is it clear how soon after the Irish raids began did they give way to colonization. Some were to settle permanently in Anglesey by the late fifth century, as evidenced by the small number of inscribed stones and territorial toponyms that commemorated Goidelic-speaking Irish chieftains of wealth and standing. One Cunogus (Cunugussus) is honoured on a memorial pillar stone at Llanfaelog, and it was his descendants who colonized the nearby hamlet of Pencaernisiog (derived from Conysiog, or land of Conws – the medieval Welsh form of Cunogus).

To all appearances, there was nothing to equal the Irish settlement in southwest Wales. Yet, their presence seems to have profoundly disturbed the local population, who were only saved by the intervention of other immigrants, this time from the southern lowlands of Scotland led by Cunedda Wledig. Tradition asserts that Cunedda, the heroic warrior chief of the Votadini tribe in the Celtic North, had moved into north Wales (*c.*450) to fight the Irish, and that it was his grandson, Cadwallon Lawhir, who finally expelled the Irish settlers from their last bridgehead on Anglesey, following his victory over the Irish prince Serigi in the battle of Cerrig y Gwyddyl near Trefdraeth (*c.*520). Movement along the Irish Sea routes, either along the coast or via the Isle of Man, had allowed Brythonic kinsmen to maintain close contact, but as with much in the 'Dark Ages' it is a tradition patently lacking historical corroboration. Whatever truths the legends contained, the Brythonic language triumphed (although Irish names persist into the early sixth century), so too did the descendants of Cunedda, allowing Maelgwn, son of Cadwallon Lawhir, to raise the status of his dynasty in northwest Wales.

The emergence of the regional kingdom of Gwynedd in the sixth century was Maelgwn's major achievement. Ruthless in the extreme (his uncle, wife and nephew figure among his victims), he proved to be an astute ruler and brave warrior who tempered his excessive behaviour with acts of Christian charity. Upon his death from the plague (*c.*547) the next ruler of note was Cadfan (d.625). By now the Anglo-Saxon threat from the east had intensified, leading to an English military victory at Chester, and King Edwin of Northumbria's invasion of Anglesey in *c.*629. As a result, King Cadwallon of Gwynedd, Cadfan's son, was forced to retreat to Ynys Lannog (later Ynys Seiriol) prior to fleeing to Ireland. In a change of fortune, he allied with the ruler of Mercia to inflict a defeat on Edwin and pillage Northumbria. All the same, Cadwallon failed to take full advantage of his opportunity to reclaim Brythonic hegemony in Britain, and thus stem the English advance. Within a year it was his turn to die in battle.

Under Cadwallon, the status of Gwynedd as a military power had risen considerably. In the context of medieval Welsh politics, characterized by a patchwork of small independent kingdoms, it claimed a special position, the superiority of its rulers emphasized by such titles as 'great' and 'king of the Britons'. As they set out to consolidate power, the resources of Anglesey underpinned their fierce ambitions. For very good reason, Maelgwn had been designated the 'island dragon'. As a rich natural granary, Anglesey could feed the people and sustain the king's loyal warband. Here the principal seat of government would be located. A *llys* (court) near or on the site of the supposed Roman fort enabled the ruling dynasty to recast Aberffraw as a power centre with symbolic historic authority. And from this time until the close of the thirteenth century it styled itself as a capital, though archaeological work has not yet been able to fix the precise location of the court buildings, now lying beneath the present village. According to one source, it was to Aberffraw that King Edwin's severed head was brought following Cadwallon's victory in 633. In due course, the royal court exuded confidence; with his eulogy to Cadwallon, Afan Ferddig, the court poet, composed what is thought to be one of the earliest Anglesey poems. To affirm itself, the court grandly evoked Byzantine phraseology, as testified by the Latin inscription on the famous seventh-century tombstone at Llangadwaladr church that glorifies Cadfan as 'the wisest and most renowned of all kings'. Named after its founder, Cadwaladr, Cadfan's grandson who died in 664, this royal burial-ground close to Aberffraw also reinforces the strong sense of devotion to the Celtic Church bequeathed by the early Christian missionaries.

The Celtic Saints

Christianity had made significant headway in Roman Britain with conversions in Romanized southeast Wales by the close of the fourth century. Right through the period of heathenism in Anglo-Saxon England, the Christian faith was propagated in the west by itinerant monks and missionaries. Ascetic in character, they evangelized the Celtic lands, turning people away from the old pagan beliefs. Just as the Irish Sea facilitated travel and communication in prehistoric times, traditional seaways were being taken to preach, baptize and set up religious communities. In consequence, the earliest churches and monasteries appear mainly on remote coastal sites. As a prominent landmark it was only to be expected that Anglesey should be directly on the path of such missionary endeavours, bringing it into contact with Brittany, Cornwall, Scotland and Ireland. While evidence suggests extensive travel along the mainland coast, more often than not the sphere of Christian activity was localized. On account of their austere lives, spiritual teachings and moral authority, some of the leading figures were to assume cult status as 'saints', inspiring disciples or followers, perhaps centuries later, to perpetuate their influence by dedicating churches to their name. Almost nothing is known of the early religious communities. Excavations at Capel Eithin have revealed east-west aligned graves that might possibly be associated with the first phase of Christian conversion, but much of the evidence is speculative.

Early Christianity in southeast Wales was strengthened by contacts with western France. As one of the first religious leaders, Cadog became renowned for his travels along the Celtic fringe early in the fifth century, and the dedication of the ancient chapel of Llangadog at the head of Dulas Bay was in recognition of his pioneering missionary work. From Cornwall, Cybi followed the southern sea route a century or so later, as attested by the string of churches to bear his name – the more famous being the monastic settlement (or *clas*) at Caergybi on Holy Island. Where the local ruler was supportive, missionaries gained protection and patronage, although it is a well-established myth that Maelgwn granted Cybi the land inside the deserted Roman fort. From Brittany came the followers of Cadfan: Cristiolus (Llangristiolus), Fflewin (Llanfflewin) and Sadwrn, whose name (Saturninus) has been venerated on a tombstone in Llansadwrn churchyard (*c.*525).

The constant flow of migrations from southern Scotland to Gwynedd, as personified in the story of Cunedda, brought missionaries from the Celtic North to the Anglesey shores of the Menai Straits. Seiriol, reputedly descended from Cunedda, was prominent as a contemporary of Cybi. The cell at Penmon adjacent to a holy well, where Seiriol is said to have baptized his converts, was the origin of a small religious community and monastery. Just off the coast, Seiriol or one of his followers also founded a secluded hermitage on the small island forever associated with his name – Ynys Seiriol – and where a small church was later built. Considerable influence surrounded the cult of Cyndeyrn, another Scottish missionary, and two Anglesey churches in close proximity to each other are dedicated to his disciples Ffinan (Llanffinan) and Idan (Llanidan).

Considering the close contacts with Ireland, it is little wonder that several Anglesey churches should be dedicated to Irish saints – most notably Patrick at Llanbadrig, who had, tradition states, been shipwrecked close by, and Brigid (or Ffraid) of Kildare, at Tywyn y Capel, Trearddur. While it was easier to travel by sea than by land, wandering saints from Powys were able to follow the Roman road system. As the north Wales counterpart to David (Dewi Sant), the cult of Beuno had spread far and wide by the middle of the seventh century. The churches at Aberffraw and Trefdraeth are dedicated to him; Llangwyfan and Llanddaniel commemorate his followers, Cwyfan and Daniel. The Powysian saint Tysilio, in contrast, appears to have taken the sea route when he retreated to Ynys Tysilio (Church Island) in the Menai Straits to live the life of a hermit, and where the church of Llandysilio was founded.

Collectively, the Celtic missionaries had prepared solid foundations for the Christian Church. As many as seventy churches and chapels in Anglesey are dedicated to specific individuals. Cybi and Seiriol remain pre-eminent. The presence of a number of female saints – Ceinwen (Llangeinwen), Dona (Llanddona), Edwen (Llanedwen) and Dwynwen (Llanddwyn) – clearly reflects the prominent status accorded to women within the Celtic church. As Wales's patron saint of lovers, celebrated on 25 January, Dwynwen's shrine became a popular place of pilgrimage. During the Middle Ages lovelorn pilgrims flocked to Llanddwyn with their candles and offerings to seek emotional comfort. Although not always the case, place names that commemorate a saint have the prefix *llan*. At first, it signified an enclosed piece of land with religious connections, perhaps a primitive wooden church next to a cemetery, yet the name of the supposed original founder survived in the locality over the centuries. Of the sixty *llannau* in Anglesey, forty-three are listed as having parish churches traditionally associated with the names of Celtic saints. Inscribed memorial stones provide tangible evidence of early Christianity. The Latin term *sacerdos* that appears on a Llantrisant tombstone commemorates a local sixth-century bishop. A number of cross-marked stones are to be found at Llangaffo, once the site of an important monastery dedicated to the martyred saint Caffo, a disciple of Cybi.

Expansion and Strife

Through good fortune the ruling dynasty of Gwynedd was able to hold on to its inheritance. The kingdom passed from Idwal ap Cadwaladr to Rhodri Molwynog, but friction between his two sons, Hywel and Cynan, created instability in Anglesey at the start of the ninth century. At one time Hywel prevailed; a few years later Cynan had forced his expulsion from the island. Even though Hywel outlived his brother, his death without male heir in 825 meant the extinction of Cunedda's dynasty. At this point, the line of descent was transferred through Cynan's daughter to her son Merfyn Frych from the Celtic North who became, initially, king in Anglesey. New blood was accompanied by new opportunities. Merfyn Frych married the sister of the last king of Powys; their son Rhodri proved equally fortunate in his marriage to the sister of the last ruler of Ceredigion. Such politic marriages were the key to the territorial expansion of Gwynedd. In absorbing both Powys and Ceredigion, Rhodri Mawr became the acknowledged ruler of more than half of Wales, stretching from Anglesey to Gower. Despite his achievements, the union of three kingdoms was once again divided upon his death in 878. Two of Rhodri's sons inherited the greater part of the land: Anarawd, based at Aberffraw, ruled Anglesey and Gwynedd; Cadell held the south.

After Cadell's death, Hywel Dda, king of Dyfed, once again achieved significant Welsh unification when he took possession of Gwynedd on the death of Anarawd's son, Idwal Foel. Hywel Dda's death in 950 was followed by a bleak period of infighting as different branches of Idwal Foel's family claimed kingship. During a dynastic power struggle in Gwynedd, rivals were doomed: murdered, mutilated, exiled or imprisoned. Kings ruled by dint of personal ability and superior forces. When Rhodri ab Idwal was killed in Anglesey in 968, his brother Iago ab Idwal gained authority. Aside from internal intrigues, Welsh rulers also faced well-defined enemies on two sides: the English to the east of Offa's Dyke, and the danger posed by Viking raiders in the west. Both Rhodri Mawr and Idwal Foel had been killed fighting the English. Like Anarawd and Hywel Dda, Iago ab Idwal found it prudent to make peace. In 973, at Chester, he entered an alliance with the English king Edgar to curb the growing Viking menace. Geography determined that this was the greatest external threat to Anglesey.

Viking Raids

Viking expansion began seriously to affect Wales by the middle of the ninth century. Once the Norsemen had secured permanent bases in Ireland and the Isle of Man, the Irish Sea became a theatre for marauding fleets of longships. Only some sixty miles from Ireland, and exposed on all sides to swift plundering raids, Anglesey suffered more than most parts of Wales. Seen as a source of plentiful food supplies and slaves, its wealthy but undefended religious houses also offered rich spoils to the 'black pagans'. The first attack came in 853, followed two years later by an onslaught involving the Danish leader Gorm, later slain by Rhodri Mawr, king of Gwynedd. Displaying strong leadership he was able to check the Viking threat, but final defeat in a famous 'Sunday battle' on the island in 876 forced him into exile. Ingimund's invasion of Anglesey might have led to a temporary foothold at Osfeilion near Llan-faes, but his warband was successfully repulsed and driven out by Hywel Dda's younger brother, Clydog, in 903. For most of the next half century, culminating with Hywel Dda's death, there was a lull in Viking activity. Regardless of the terror they aroused, and unlike other parts of the British Isles, Wales had initially withstood Viking colonization. Instead, Norse raiders resorted to traditional hit and run looting.

The greatest devastation was inflicted in the second half of the tenth century. Their violent attacks were documented in the Welsh Chronicles, with Anglesey once more as the main target. Viking pirates from Dublin ransacked the monastic church of Saint Cybi at Holyhead in 961. Seven years later the royal court at Aberffraw and its neighbouring church suffered a similar fate. Anglesey had good reason to fear the forays of Harald of Man and his sons. In 970 Harald subjugated the whole island. The next year Penmon monastery was pillaged and burnt by Magnus Haraldsson. Only a year after Iago ab Idwal's alliance with Edgar, he was forced to cede power to Hywel ab Ieuaf ap Idwal Foel and imprisoned in 979. In turn, his son Cystennin ab Iago allied with Godfrid Haraldsson, the Viking leader, but was killed in a battle on Anglesey a year later. With no heirs to succeed Hywel ab Ieuaf nor his brother Cadwallon, Maredudd ab Owain ap Hywel Dda, king of Dyfed, successfully imposed his overlordship (986–999) in Anglesey and Gwynedd to reunite the kingdoms as in his grandfather's day. But Viking pressure intensified. Once again, Godfrid Haraldsson launched an expedition against Anglesey, motivated by the acquisition of slaves. Two thousand Welshmen were taken captive and enslaved in 987 – forcing Maredudd ab Owain ap Hywel Dda to pay a ransom of one penny a head to recover his men. Around this time Isle of Man Vikings may well have gained some measure of temporary control in Anglesey. By the end of the tenth century they would resume their destructive raids. On Ascension Tuesday 994, and again in 999, Anglesey was said to have been badly ravaged. No further raids were recorded until late into the eleventh century as Gwynedd had sufficiently powerful kings to deter Viking aggression. By now there was constant Norse involvement in internal Welsh politics. The kings of Gwynedd hired Viking mercenaries to further their own cause, or else to help them resist the Norman threat.

Despite the high level of activity no contemporary source mentions a territorial base in Anglesey. All the same, the Viking legacy endures in familiar coastal place names to this day, not to mention the material evidence. Skerries, derived from the Old Norse *sker* meaning rock or reef, has been identified as a geographical navigation point familiar to Viking sailors who plied the Irish Sea routes in search of booty or trade. Similarly, *holmr*, a Norse term for an island, appears in Priestholm (Ynys Seiriol). Of much more significance is the Scandinavian origin of the name Anglesey itself. Combining *Ongul*, the personal name of a Viking chieftain, and *ey* also an Old Norse designation for an island, the toponym Ongulsey (Ongul's isle) over the years transformed into Anglesey. Its adoption late in the eleventh century is a strong indication that there had been, after all, an earlier short-lived Viking coastal community, perhaps a fortified staging post for cargo ships on the trade run from Dublin to Chester. Taken together, the archaeological evidence gravitates towards the area around the bay at Traeth Coch (Red Wharf). Five Viking silver armlets were discovered at Llanfihangel Dinsylwy. Excavations at Benllech and Llanbedr-goch have revealed possible Viking burial sites. Recent finds of rectangular buildings, silver ingots, lead weights and a hoard of coins at Glyn, Llanbedr-goch, are final proof of Viking-age settlement and mercantile activity within reach of the sheltered haven of the bay. The Vikings in Anglesey, it now seems clear, had been a key part of a wider trading group operating in the Irish Sea.

The Norman Threat

The eleventh century proved to be a period of great change, involving the ruling dynasty and the formidable new threat that followed the arrival of the Normans in England in 1066. The direct descendants of Rhodri Mawr no longer ruled Gwynedd, but kings were often indirectly linked through female lines. As always, power rested not so much on claims of inheritance, as on the personal charisma, ambitions and military attributes of the ruler. Outstanding in this respect were Llywelyn ap Seisyll (d.1023) and his famous son, Gruffudd ap Llywelyn (1039–1063). For a long while Gwynedd was virtually free from Viking attacks. Gruffudd, moreover, pursued an aggressively expansionist policy which brought success against the English and which unified the whole of Wales for the first time. After his death, the country was again divided. Although both successors in Gwynedd, his half brother Bleddyn ap Cynfyn (d.1075) and Bleddyn's cousin Trahaearn ap Caradog (d.1081), were effective rulers, the Norman conquerors, from their base at Chester, had already encroached the northeast coastal plain by the mid-1070s, greedy for land. Only after the death of Trahaearn did the Norman incursions make real headway into the heart of Gwynedd, led by Hugh d'Avranches, earl of Chester, and his cousin, Robert of Rhuddlan.

Trahaearn's obscure claims to kingship brought him into conflict with Gruffydd ap Cynan, scion of the exalted lineage of Gwynedd descending from Rhodri Mawr. Though born in Dublin, and half-Viking (his mother being the daughter of King Olaf), he arrived on the political scene intent on claiming his patrimony. Anglesey was inseparable from the unfolding drama that brought the Welsh, Irish, Norsemen and Normans together in a turbulent mix. Its long-standing links with Ireland are underlined in early Welsh prose tales. In the Second Branch of the *Mabinogi*, the heroine Branwen ferch Llŷr, who had married the king of Ireland at Aberffraw, returns to Anglesey to die on the bank of the river Alaw (though Bedd Branwen, Llanbabo, is a Bronze Age burial place).

Supported by an Irish-Norse fleet Gruffydd ap Cynan landed at the port of Abermenai in 1075 and received the backing of the men of Anglesey. But failure forced his retreat to Ireland. Even when Trahaearn fell in battle, Gruffydd's initial reign in Gwynedd was short-lived. Following his capture in 1081 and long imprisonment at Chester by the Normans, Hugh d'Avranches took advantage of the hiatus in Welsh leadership and overran Gwynedd. To consolidate the military occupation, earth and timber castles were quickly erected by the early 1090s. On Anglesey, Norman control was orchestrated from the motte and bailey castle at Aberlleiniog, near Penmon. Land and revenues in Anglesey then went to fund the new Norman abbey in Chester. Outrage at the scale of Norman oppression triggered Welsh revolts. Even before Gruffydd's escape from prison, the rebellion led by Cadwgan ap Bleddyn (son of Bleddyn ap Cynfyn) in 1094 had resulted in the destruction of the Norman strongholds in Gwynedd, again with Irish-Norse assistance. Aberlleiniog castle was to be burnt to the ground.

In 1098, Hugh d'Avranches, aided by Hugh de Montgomery, earl of Shrewsbury, spearheaded a concerted Norman attack on Gwynedd. Once again, Anglesey became a centre of resistance. Withdrawing to the island Cadwgan and Gruffydd awaited help from a mercenary Norse fleet from Dublin. Their hopes were dashed when the Norsemen treacherously accepted Norman bribes, and both men had to seek refuge in Ireland. The Normans ravaged Anglesey, yet they had little chance to re-establish their presence, because, by accident or by design, a Viking fleet commanded by Magnus Barelegs, King of Norway, appeared off Priestholm. As a Norse poem relates, during the battle of 'Ongul sound . . . where arrows flew quickly' Hugh de Montgomery was killed. The Normans then retreated with their spoils and Magnus Barelegs sailed off (only to reappear in 1102 to steal timber). Saved by Norse intervention, Gruffydd ap Cynan returned to rule over Anglesey in 1099, upon making his peace with Hugh d'Avranches. At the dawn of a new century the Norman threat had been emphatically removed from Gwynedd. Unable to safeguard their supply lines – the Irish Sea still remained a 'Viking lake' – they never again ventured west of the river Conwy. In effect, this allowed Gruffydd a second chance to establish his position as ruler of Gwynedd between 1110 and 1137.

The Age of Independence

Endowed with full kingship, Gruffydd's supremely gifted son, Owain Gwynedd (1137–1170) secured further territorial consolidation after ousting his troublesome brother Cadwaladr and his Norse mercenaries from Anglesey. In general, he was able to exploit political weaknesses in

England, although his conflict with Henry II provoked a major response in 1157. A two-pronged attack on Gwynedd resulted in a seaborne landing on Anglesey, at Tal Moelfre. Here, Owain, *draig Môn* (the dragon of Anglesey), led his men in a ferocious battle, turning the sea red with the blood that was spilled. The area around Llanbedr-goch and Llanfair Mathafarn Eithaf was badly ravaged and churches despoiled, but the invaders also suffered a heavy price before retreating. Further English hostilities fared little better. A pragmatic acknowledgement of Henry's overlordship enabled Owain Gwynedd to weld his kingdom into an independent feudal state. As an indication of his ambitions, he no longer styled himself king of Gwynedd but 'prince of the Welsh'. This period of national awakening was accompanied by a striking literary revival that celebrated princes, patriotism, piety and passion. The royal court at Aberffraw enjoyed a cultural florescence led by the most prominent bardic family of medieval Wales. Like his father Meilyr Brydydd, *pencerdd* (chief court poet) to Gruffydd ap Cynan, Gwalchmai ap Meilyr was generously rewarded with a gift of land in Anglesey by Owain Gwynedd – hence Trefeilir and Trewalchmai. Before he fell from favour with his patron, Gwalchmai had boasted of being a loyal warrior with the rousing words:

> *Gwalchmai y'm gelwir, gelyn y Saeson*
> *Er lles brenin Môn ymosodais mewn brwydr*
> (Gwalchmai they call me, enemy of the English
> For Anglesey's king I have lunged out in battle).

As so often in the past, Owain's death was followed by an ugly internecine struggle for dynastic succession. His eldest son, the poet-prince Hywel ab Owain Gwynedd fell victim to his half-brothers, Dafydd and Rhodri, at the battle of Pentraeth in 1170: 'the eagle of the battlefield' killed with a spear. Dafydd ab Owain Gwynedd took the lead. Three years later he expelled another brother, Maelgwn, who held all or part of Anglesey. When Dafydd and Rhodri fell out, the latter was imprisoned but managed to escape. In a complete reversal Rhodri ab Owain Gwynedd became ruler of Anglesey and gained the upper hand in western Gwynedd, only to be ousted by his nephews, Gruffydd and Maredudd ap Cynan in 1190. With help from the king of the Isle of Man he briefly recovered Anglesey, but was again defeated by his nephews, who had been joined by another grandson of Owain Gwynedd, Llywelyn ab Iorwerth. Crossing the Menai Straits, Llywelyn won the battles of Porthaethwy and Coedana in 1194. Rhodri ab Owain Gwynedd died the following year and was buried at Caergybi. After a savage conflict, which saw a succession of rulers vie for mastery in Anglesey, Llywelyn ab Iorwerth emerged as the dominant personality in Gwynedd at the turn of the century.

During his reign Llywelyn ab Iorwerth displayed great statesmanship and military prowess in his bid to restore national unity. Secure in Gwynedd, he, too, was able to take advantage of his opponents' debility to promote his political leadership, albeit with the English king as overlord. Adopting the unique title 'prince of Aberffraw and lord of Snowdon' in 1230, Llywelyn had signified his expansionist claim to supremacy over his fellow rulers in Wales. It was envisaged that they owed special allegiance to the prince of Aberffraw, and that he alone would pay homage to the king of England. Accordingly, the court at Aberffraw gained ascendancy over the other two principal seats at Mathrafal (Powys) and Dinefwr (Deheubarth). Court poets consciously elevated Aberffraw's superior status. To Llywarch ap Llywelyn, *Prydydd y Moch*, Llywelyn Fawr (the Great) was *Brenin gwych Aberffraw* (Aberffraw's splendid king). In keeping with its reputation as an *eisteddfa arbennig* (special seat), the hall and chamber buildings were of high quality oak, adorned with sculptured stones. Mead was drunk from gold goblets. In turn, Aberffraw gave added symbolic significance to the island already noted for its fertility, enabling it, as regional breadbasket, to supply other parts of Wales at times of crop failure. And it is Llywarch ap Llywelyn who makes the first reference in poetry (*c.* 1213) to *Môn, mam Cymru* (Anglesey, mother of Wales). Llywelyn Fawr's ambitious legacy, however, was immediately threatened following his death in 1240. Dafydd ap Llywelyn's short reign as self-styled 'prince of Wales' saw a decline in the influence of Gwynedd. Moreover, his strained relations with Henry III culminated in an English offensive in 1245, with a royal force from Ireland, 3000-strong, taking Anglesey by storm, destroying the harvest crop during a three-week rampage. A partition of Gwynedd came after Dafydd's death the following year, and it took another decade before Llywelyn Fawr's grandson, Llywelyn ap Gruffydd, was able to reassert its hegemony.

Since the time of Gruffydd ap Cynan, Gwynedd had remained for the most part largely undisturbed. During a century and a half of relative peace the native rulers vigorously promoted the essential features of a feudal state, not merely to emphasize their superior status in Wales, but also to gain wider political recognition in England and beyond. They followed Anglo-Norman patterns in exerting their authority and strengthening the keystones of power. Within the principality this meant the development of an extensive administrative apparatus, revised codes of law, taxation, economic regeneration, support for the church, and strong defensive measures.

Whereas political power and decision making remained the prerogative of the prince, he also became increasingly dependent on a small corps of counsellors and officials to ensure effective governance, dispense justice, and act as negotiators and diplomatic envoys. Anglesey men figured prominently in the service of the rulers of Gwynedd. Maintaining a

distinguished family tradition, Einion ap Gwalchmai, the son of
Gwalchmai ap Meilyr, became one of Llywelyn Fawr's leading ministers,
combining the role of *ynad llys* (judge of the court) and household
poet. His son, Einion Fychan, in turn, served Llywelyn Fawr, Dafydd ap
Llywelyn and Llywelyn ap Gruffydd. Privileged members of this
ministerial élite were often allocated lands on the island. As *distain*
(steward), the chief official of the royal court, Ednyfed Fychan was
rewarded with extensive territory that included the township of
Penmynydd. With possibly three of his sons, Gruffydd, Goronwy and
Tudur, following him in this office, the ancestor of the Tudors had
prepared the foundations of a family power base.

The main administrative units were already well established; sometimes
following clearly outlined river boundaries. Perhaps from as early as the
post-Roman period, Anglesey had been divided into the three *cantrefi*
(hundreds) of Aberffraw, Cemais and Rhosyr. By the twelfth century
their subdivision into six *cymydau* (commotes) produced, respectively,
Llifon and Malltraeth; Talybolion and Twrcelyn; Dindaethwy and Menai.
Within each commote the prince maintained a *maerdref* (royal manor) as
administrative centre, five of which are known: Aberffraw, Cemais,
Penrhosllugwy, Llan-faes and Rhosyr. Each had its own timber-framed
hall and associated buildings; recent excavations near Newborough have
revealed a substantial royal complex at Llys Rhosyr. In the interests of
good government the royal court was itinerant. Aided by other officials,
the *rhaglaw* (bailiff) and *rhingyll* (sergeant) managed the royal estate
ready for the visit of the prince and his retinue. Though again of ancient
origin, it was not until the twelfth century that the *trefi* (townships) also
came into widespread use as the basic unit of human settlement. Gerald
of Wales, who made a brief stop at Porthaethwy during his famous tour
of the country in 1188, put the number of townships at precisely 363 (the
true figure was little more than 200). Each township then consisted of
family holdings, inhabited by two different social classes: the bondmen
and freemen.

Tenants on royal land were obliged to render food dues as well as
provide labour service. Those at Tre Feibion Meurig in Llifon maintained
the hall and chamber of the court at Aberffraw; others operated the
princes' mills, that were particularly numerous in Anglesey. It was
ancestry, above all, that gave the small groups of freemen their status,
privileges and hereditary lands. From the twelfth century further
agricultural expansion and permanent settlement was being deliberately
promoted by the princes with the creation of more free townships. Many
were set aside for royal kinsmen, court poets or favoured servants and
their descendants, principally Llywarch ap Bran and Hwfa ap Cynddelw,
two officials in Owain Gwynedd's court. As in the case of the commote

centres and bond hamlets, most of the large prosperous sites were located on fertile soil close to the coast, thus allowing easier access. In addition, royal grants of land to both freemen (including colonists from the mainland) and bondmen encouraged the agrarian exploitation of the underdeveloped interior of the island. The result was a more productive arable and pastoral economy. Communications with the mainland improved when organized ferries came to provide regular access. Under the control of the princes, ferries operated from Llan-faes, Porthaethwy and Abermenai. In addition, the bishop of Bangor owned the Porth yr Esgob ferry, with its terminal at Cadnant.

Profound change accompanied the transition to a cash economy during the thirteenth century. To meet the growing financial requirements of the princes, the customary dues of the freemen were being commuted into money payments. For the same reason, commercial activity was being stimulated in the commote centres. Chief among them was the royal manor of Llan-faes (where archaeological work has revealed a large number of silver medieval coins). Well placed at the northern entrance of the Menai Straits, its bustling port, market and fairs gave rise to the largest and wealthiest urban settlement in Gwynedd. About thirty ships a year entered the port; by the 1290s this number had risen to eighty. Among those involved in trade were butchers, bakers, shoemakers and brewers, who produced almost 3,000 gallons of ale annually. A charter issued by the princes, granting borough status and special privileges, enabled them to regulate economic life to their advantage. Revenue from the herring fishery, land rents, fair tolls, trading licences, ferry tolls and customs duties (levied on such exports as wool and hides; and imports like French wine) generated a good-sized income for Llywelyn ab Iorwerth – but nothing to match the resources of the English king. Advances in the economy had an effect on all spheres of life. For one thing, the growth in population that accompanied these years of peace and prosperity revitalized the religious dimension.

Of all the Celtic lands, Wales had been the last to accept the supremacy of the Pope. Roman Catholic doctrines and observances became official in north Wales in 768, sanctioned by Elfodd, 'archbishop of Gwynedd', an alumnus of the monastery at Caergybi. Only when Anglesey was finally free of the Viking menace did the church flourish under royal patronage. At a time of growing prosperity in the twelfth century, Gruffydd ap Cynan reportedly 'built many churches'. Instead of the old wooden structures new stone churches were built, some provided with towers and decorated fonts. Saint Seiriol's Romanesque priory church at Penmon, erected during the reign of Owain Gwynedd, remains the best example. By 1250 the most valuable churches were Llan-faes and Amlwch. Collaterally, the parish had evolved as the ecclesiastical unit of organization, incorporating the territorial boundaries of individual or groups of townships. Sustained by the tithes, the resident priest would devote himself to the pastoral and spiritual needs of his parishioners. In all there would be seventy-four parishes on the island, with as many parish churches, grouped into the diocese of Bangor.

Change also came to the monastic movement, aided by the benefaction of the princes. The old Celtic *clasau* at Caergybi and Penmon had survived the Viking onslaught. Penmon was rebuilt between 1120 and 1170. Over the centuries various rulers had given grants of land; on his deathbed Gruffydd ap Cynan directed that money be paid to both foundations. Yet, the native monastic tradition was on the wane. A European revival inspired by religious orders such as the Augustinians, Cistercians and Franciscans brought much needed reform to monastic life. The *clas* at Caergybi was redesignated as a collegiate church. Under Llywelyn Fawr's patronage, Penmon was transformed into an Augustinian house and granted to the prior of Priestholm in 1237. In addition, he introduced the Franciscan order into north Wales, setting up a friary in the town of Llan-faes. It was here that he buried his English wife Joan (Siwan) in fine style, as shown by the decorated carved grave-lid bearing her effigy, now in Beaumaris church. Princely generosity towards the Cistercian order resulted in their abbey at Aberconwy being liberally endowed with estates on the island. But the greatest religious landowner by far was the bishop of Bangor.

As the commander of the prince's armed forces, the *penteulu* was accorded high status in the royal court. Traditionally, every freeman rendered military service. But to strengthen the fighting force some bondmen were also recruited, and township lands granted in return for military service as in the case of the tenants of Bodffordd and Grugor in Malltraeth. Castle building, likewise, had become an integral part of Gwynedd's security by the time of Llywelyn Fawr. Partly to safeguard the fertile lands in Anglesey – whose abundance so impressed Gerald of Wales – formidable stone castles were erected to control the main mountain routes through Snowdonia's natural barriers. No such defensive structure was built on the island itself. As had been brutally demonstrated from Roman times, the Menai Straits could hardly be considered a natural moat against invaders. Anglesey's vulnerability to a maritime assault was again exposed both in 1157 and 1245. It remained the 'soft underbelly' of Gwynedd. With only a few ships at their command, the rulers of Gwynedd knew full well that little could be done to prevent an attack from the sea. Even the prestigious palace complex at Aberffraw, almost entirely a timber structure rebuilt after the Viking raid of 968, remained open and unfortified. Bereft of a strong maritime tradition, Welsh rulers had no answer to English naval supremacy.

The Edwardian Conquest and Settlement

Surmounting family rivals, Llywelyn ap Gruffydd had seized power in Gwynedd by 1256 as a prelude to exerting control over most of Wales. His *pencerdd*, the sword-wielding poet Dafydd Benfras of Anglesey, met his death (*c.*1260) on one campaign in the south. Once more, a single-minded leader of vision and ability had come to the fore. Acknowledged 'prince of Wales' by other Welsh rulers, and Henry III in 1267, he was soon in a position to surpass the achievements of his grandfather, Llywelyn Fawr. During the following decade Llywelyn ap Gruffydd robustly expanded the structures of state already in place. Though Aber on the mainland, directly opposite Llan-faes, had become his favoured residence, the poets still instinctively identified him with Aberffraw: in the words of Gruffudd ab yr Ynad Coch he was *Gwir freiniawl frenin Aberffraw* (The true and regal king of Aberffraw). But Llywelyn's political fortunes changed following deteriorating relations with the English crown. His repeated failure to pay homage to the new king was soon being overshadowed by the imperialistic designs of Edward I. Undermined by internal opposition and defection, Llywelyn's ill-fated actions spelled disaster for Gwynedd.

The first war came in 1276–7. Mindful of past campaigns in Gwynedd, Edward's military strategy was to besiege Snowdonia by land and sea. Led by the king himself, an army from Chester made its way along the coast, but the early capture of Anglesey proved the key to success. Now that Norse ships no longer had command of the Irish Sea, a fleet of sixty ships was able to cut off Welsh supply lines in the rear by blocking the Menai Straits. Once in control of the island, a large group of reapers who accompanied the 2,000 soldiers commandeered the harvest for their own benefit, thus depriving Llywelyn of vital grain supplies. Faced with the prospect of starvation, not to mention a possible attack directed at the mainland from Anglesey, he capitulated. The terms of the Treaty of Aberconwy added to Llywelyn's humiliation. He retained only those lands that were his before 1256, and in addition to the heavy fines, he was allowed to hold Anglesey subject to an annual payment of 1000 marks (later remitted). One section of the treaty relating to Anglesey cut to the quick: if Llywelyn should die without heir the island would revert to the English crown.

Discontent at the arbitrary nature of the settlement did not take long to provoke a Welsh rebellion. For Edward I the war of 1282 was to be the final solution of the Welsh question. As in the previous campaign, the military objective was to isolate Llywelyn in Gwynedd, and detailed preparations were made for the invasion of Anglesey. From the naval base at Rhuddlan a large fleet carried crossbow-men and archers for the amphibious attack. By mid-summer the island had been captured and garrisoned under the command of Luke de Tany. Llan-faes now became the main base for further military operations. Again the islanders were deprived of their harvest; only this time a bridge of boats, largely preconstructed, was placed across the Menai Straits near Bangor in readiness for the final co-ordinated assault on Snowdonia. But disregarding the current peace negotiations, Tany launched a precipitate attack in November, which ended in catastrophe. Having crossed the pontoon bridge at low tide, the troops and horsemen were soon overwhelmed by a superior Welsh force. In the course of their hasty retreat the bridge broke under the excessive strain, and among the hundreds that drowned was Luke de Tany himself.

Although this success provided a psychological boost for the Welsh side, Llywelyn ap Gruffydd's own death at Cilmeri the following month, followed by the execution of his brother Dafydd in 1283, brought the age of independence to a tragic end. Gwynedd, the part of Wales that had shown the longest resistance to alien domination, was finally subjugated. English troops remained stationed on Anglesey, supervising food supplies, and guarding the repaired pontoon bridge, before it was finally dismantled to allow shipping through the Menai Straits. For Edward I the capture of the island had both a strategic and symbolic importance. During July and August 1283 he made a victory tour, visiting Rhosyr, Llan-faes and Aberffraw, now firmly in his grip. In different ways the fate of some Anglesey men had already been decided. Dafydd ab Einion Fychan, of the line of Gwalchmai ap Meilyr, Llywelyn's *distain*, was killed in south Wales fighting for his prince. Iorwerth Foel of Aberffraw, who had sided with the English king in 1277 (only to suffer when Llywelyn took his revenge: he lost horses and corn, and his houses were burnt), could look forward, like others with an eye to the main chance, to his reward.

To strengthen his military domination Edward encircled Snowdonia with a ring of massive fortresses. Funds did not allow the building of a castle on Anglesey as intended at this time, so it was Conwy and Caernarfon castles that guarded each end of the Menai Straits. In their shadow stood the borough towns, colonized by English settlers, whose economic activity generated the wealth that supplied the castle with provisions. An imposed settlement, the Statute of Rhuddlan (1284), completed the political annexation in its administrative and legal aspects. Llywelyn's lands were taken over by the crown and placed under the Justice of North Wales, who acted as royal viceroy at the head of the new machinery of government centred at Caernarfon. (Aberffraw's eclipse in the mid-fourteenth century was foreshadowed when 198 pieces of timber from the Welsh princes' hall and other buildings were dismantled in 1317 for reuse in construction work at Caernarfon castle.) The principality was then divided into shires on the English pattern and superimposed on the existing system of *cantrefi* and *cymydau*. Anglesey, naturally enough, formed a self-contained county. Each county had a sheriff, who was the principal royal official responsible for law and order, administration, and the collection of all revenues. Within each commote, the *rhaglaw* and *rhingyll* remained the chief officers.

After years of violent conflict the regime of the conqueror, inevitably, was characterized by its harshness. Resentment amongst the Welsh intensified under the twin burdens of oppressive officialdom and extortionate taxation. Roger de Pulesdon, tyrannical sheriff of Anglesey and tax collector, became a figure of hate. The most serious challenge to the Edwardian settlement came in 1294–5, led by Madog ap Llywelyn. A distant cousin of Llywelyn ap Gruffydd, he could claim descent from the dynasty of Gwynedd. Though connected to Merioneth, he also had lands in Anglesey. As it happened, the restive island became one of the centres of a widespread revolt. Because of its English element, the town and church of Llan-faes were put to the torch. When the borough of Caernarfon suffered a similar fate, Anglesey men lynched Roger de Pulesdon. The English military response repeated previous successful operations. Naval supremacy was established; a squadron of 12 ships and 500 men patrolled the Menai Straits to gain a hold on Anglesey's grain supplies. In April 1295 the island was quickly taken and Edward I returned again to direct the reconquest from his headquarters at Llan-faes. A number of Anglesey hostages, including the descendants of Ednyfed Fychan, were temporarily imprisoned at Shrewsbury and Hereford. Already, he had commissioned the last of his great fortresses.

Beaumaris castle was built to keep Anglesey pacified and bolster permanent English rule. Accessible from the sea, it would dominate the northern approaches to the Menai Straits. On a flat marshland site (the name is derived from the French *beau marais*, or beautiful marsh) close to Llan-faes, Master James of St George, the king's architect, put his genius to work when he designed the perfect concentric castle. Around 400 stonemasons and 2,000 labourers drawn from various English counties were employed in its construction, using stone quarried at Penmon and Benllech. Escalating costs added to the sense of urgency, as Master James pleaded with the Exchequer for more money to pay his workforce. All the while he needed to keep a close watch on the Welsh. By 1298 the castle could be defended; its first constable, William de Felton, commanded a garrison force of 130 men. Two rings of walls, surrounded by a moat, had the added feature of a small dock that enabled supply ships to sail directly from the Menai Straits up to the castle gateway. Over £14,500 would be spent between 1295 and 1330, yet it still proved too expensive to have the project completed to the original plan. An unfinished masterpiece, Beaumaris castle is nevertheless regarded architecturally as the 'most technically perfect' medieval fortress in Britain. Today it is a UNESCO World Heritage Site.

The attached borough received its charter in September 1296. In order to lure English settlers into a racially hostile environment the townsmen received grants of land and exclusive commercial privileges, enabling them to appropriate the trade of Llan-faes. Moreover, the Llan-faes ferry was transferred to the constable of the castle in 1302. As the new official port and centre of commerce, its population grew rapidly. Though the colonists at Beaumaris outnumbered those in the other north Wales boroughs, financial constraints meant that the town could not be provided with any kind of defensive wall – in contrast to Conwy and Caernarfon. What remained of Llan-faes after Madog ap Llywelyn's revolt was deliberately demolished and most of its inhabitants uprooted and ethnically shunted some fourteen miles across the island to Rhosyr. Despite the protestations, led by Einion the local doctor, Llan-faes had been largely vacated by 1303. In May of that year the reluctant evacuees at Rhosyr were compensated with a borough charter, and at their request the settlement was renamed Newborough. In no time it had grown and flourished as a serious trading rival to Beaumaris. Newborough's very Welshness attracted country people to the weekly cattle market and twice-annual fair much to the irritation of burgesses at its alien counterpart. But already the great storm of December 1330 had provided a dire portent; wind-blown sand threatened the long-term prosperity of the town, whose inhabitants, beer and wine would inspire Dafydd ap Gwilym's eulogy to 'Niwbwrch': *cefnither nef yw'r dref draw* (that town is heaven's own cousin).

Coexistence and Conflict

How to reward supporters, and integrate those Welshmen who had comprised the old governing class, was another task that faced Edward I. For his loyalty Iorwerth Foel received lands in Aberffraw, making him one of the richest taxpayers. Most of the *uchelwyr* (native aristocracy) thought it wise to submit to the crown; collaboration offered the best chance to preserve their social standing and further family self-interest. In the event, a small number were given administrative positions as middle-ranking or lesser officials below Englishmen. Descendants of Ednyfed Fychan had been quick to transfer their allegiance; some had even fought on the side of Edward I in 1282. One man who epitomized this spirit of loyal co-operation was his great-grandson, Sir Gruffydd Llwyd of Tregarnedd, the first Welshman to act as sheriff of Anglesey in 1305–6. Another eight

Welshmen were trusted to serve as sheriffs of the county during the fourteenth century. Einion ab Ieuan proved his fidelity in 1320 when Edward II faced troubles with his barons, unlike the English sheriffs of Caernarfon and Merioneth who revolted against the king. Other prominent Anglesey clans also showed political realism; descendants of Llywarch ap Bran and Hwfa ap Cynddelw were among the numerous Welshmen appointed *rhaglaw* or *rhingyll*.

Another way to channel Welsh energies was through military service in Scotland and France. Five hundred soldiers from Anglesey were recruited in 1298 to fight for Edward I in Scotland. The eminent royalist Iorwerth Foel led seventy archers in the abortive 1310 campaign. As the king's chief military recruiter in north Wales, Sir Gruffydd Llwyd raised forces on a number of occasions; he was probably present at the battle of Bannockburn, which heralded Scottish freedom. But archers and spearmen from Gwynedd were fighting England's battles. Hywel ap Llywelyn ap Gruffydd, of the lineage of Hwfa ap Cynddelw, led an Anglesey contingent that fought in France. For his service in France, Goronwy ap Tudur of Penmynydd was appointed constable of Beaumaris castle in 1382. With Anglesey open to attack by Scottish or French sea-rovers, home defence was always a prime concern for the English government, compounded by the fear that local inhabitants might side with the invader. The danger of Scottish intervention was highlighted in 1315 when Thomas Dun's fleet entered the port of Holyhead and seized one of the king's ships. Interestingly, a hint of complicity surrounds the actions of Tudur ap Cynddelw, the local *rhingyll* later accused of official incompetence. In the face of such threats watching the coasts became an obligation, and the garrison at Beaumaris castle was reinforced. Still, this did not prevent the Scottish raid on the town in 1381, when a number of houses were destroyed.

Beaumaris might have been planned as an English outpost, but there was an active Welsh presence in the borough from the outset. Most remarkable was the way certain individuals rose quickly to the top. Dafydd ab Einion, formerly of Llan-faes, and who may have served Llywelyn ap Gruffydd before 1282, turned out to be the richest burgess in 1305. Another enterprising Welshman was Einion ab Ieuan, the sheriff of Anglesey, who held office as bailiff. Mindful of their privileges, the resentful English element – drawn mainly from Cheshire – made frequent attempts to debar the Welsh. Even when this was largely achieved by the 1350s ancient hatreds persisted, occasionally bursting into violence on market or fair days. One such commotion, a century later, is remembered as 'Y Ffrae Ddu yn y Bewmares' (the Black Affray of Beaumaris), when Dafydd ab Ieuan ap Hywel, the *rhingyll* of Twrcelyn, was slain.

A strong current of hostility to English rule was never far from the surface. In seeking the forgiveness of seven Anglesey brothers whom he had offended, the poet Gruffydd Gryg in the mid-fourteenth century encapsulated the extent of their loathing with the phrase *a'm casaodd fel Sais* (who hated me like an Englishman). Whereas a small minority might have fared well in the post-conquest period, discontent among others could easily break into open rebellion. Madog ap Llywelyn had served an early warning in 1294–5, putting the authorities forever on their guard. Tension turned to real fear when anti-English members of the squirearchy perpetrated violence. By the reign of Edward III the natural leaders of the native community were being purposely shunned. Even the descendants of Ednyfed Fychan became alienated. Tudur ap Goronwy of Penmynydd and his brother Hywel (a clergyman) were the ringleaders of an armed band who murdered Henry de Shaldeford, the royal attorney in north Wales, while on his way to Caernarfon in 1345. Both spent time in prison yet suffered no permanent losses. On the contrary, of all the leading Welsh *uchelwyr* the Tudor family of Penmynydd, either through intrigue or bravado, would provide the drive for the restoration of Welsh independence. All the while they had remained custodians of native culture, praised by their household poet Gruffudd ap Maredudd ap Dafydd – whose love of Anglesey could outweigh the passion for the women in his life. There is every likelihood that the Tudors had a guiding hand in pushing the claims of Owain ap Thomas ap Rhodri, the great-nephew of Llywelyn ap Gruffydd. In one overtly patriotic ode, Gruffudd ap Maredudd ap Dafydd roused old warrior loyalties in support of Owain.

Better known as Owain Lawgoch, he had gained a reputation as an outstanding mercenary captain in the service of the king of France. Though born and brought up in England, Owain was the last descendant of the house of Gwynedd. When he began to plan a French-backed invasion to claim his rightful inheritance the authorities moved swiftly to quash any nationalistic stirrings. Evidence of plotting gave them good cause to be alarmed. In 1370 an Anglesey freeman named Gruffydd Sais was convicted of being an adherent of Owain Lawgoch and deprived of his land. Among the band of Welshmen known to be serving in Owain's 'free company' of soldiers abroad were two from Anglesey. Less certain, however, is the extent of their contact with supporters at home or the degree of Tudor involvement. Expectations, as expressed in vaticinatory poetry, were high. Llywelyn ap Cynwrig Ddu o Fôn later wrote poignantly of those who had been watching the shore, their horses and weapons at the ready, only to be consumed with grief at news of Owain's assassination (in 1378) by a nefarious English agent. He had never set foot on the island, but he was revered as *Y mab o'r Berffro ym Môn* (the son from Aberffraw in Anglesey).

The Revolt of Owain Glyn Dŵr and its Legacy

Welsh political aspirations received fresh impetus with the revolt of Owain Glyn Dŵr. This time the house of Penmynydd was directly implicated from the start. The uprising began in September 1400 when alien English boroughs were attacked and Glyn Dŵr proclaimed 'prince of Wales'. How it happened across the whole of north Wales can only be explained by the degree of pre-planning and co-ordination under local leadership. If not the actual instigators, the surviving sons of Tudur ap Goronwy (d.1367) were certainly key players with influence, military experience and a network of family contacts. As first cousins of Glyn Dŵr, Gwilym and Rhys ap Tudur, *ben ymwanwyr Môn* (chief fighters of Anglesey), also received the enthusiastic support of the Franciscans of Llan-faes. (Their eldest brother, Goronwy ap Tudur, who drowned in Kent in 1382, had been buried in the friary.) When the royal army under Henry IV swept through north Wales towards Anglesey to quash the insurrection, it was Rhys ap Tudur who marshalled a Welsh force on the high moor at Rhos Fawr, Llanfair Mathafarn Eithaf, to fend off the attackers. This did not prevent the despoliation of the eastern side of the island, nor the retaliatory razing of the friary at Llan-faes. Once order had been restored, English rule was tightened: legislation in 1401 prevented Welshmen from holding property or office in the boroughs. Although a general pardon was issued, it excluded Glyn Dŵr, Gwilym and Rhys ap Tudur.

Numerous factors had contributed to the initial revolt. All around, the symbols of conquest and enforced settlement reminded the Welsh of their loss of independence. Anti-Welsh sentiments within the boroughs, and at the highest levels of state and church administration, fed the deepening frustration. Many church livings had gone to Englishmen or absentees; clerical taxation bred much resentment. To add to this mood of national despair there was widespread social distress. The decline in population following recurrent outbreaks of bubonic plague (1349, 1361 and 1369) had severe economic consequences for both the labour market and trade. The Anglesey commotes were no exception. In the face of great losses, the poet Gruffudd ap Maredudd ap Dafydd of Talybolion begged for God's mercy. Both freemen and bondmen suffered badly; farms remained unoccupied; labour was scarce; people were unable to pay the cash rents, feudal dues and heavy taxes. The Extent of Anglesey, a new official survey compiled in 1352, took account of the straitened circumstances in a traumatized society. Hardship and poverty inflamed much of the discontent that existed in the country. In the minds of many Welshmen rebellion raised expectations of a great change to come.

Failure to secure a pardon provoked Gwilym and Rhys ap Tudur to respond in spectacular fashion. Heading a small band of men they captured

Conwy castle on Good Friday 1401 in a daring precision raid while the main garrison attended service at the parish church. Why Conwy was chosen rather than Beaumaris is not immediately clear; but soon most of Wales was plunged into a war of national independence. To strengthen his position Owain Glyn Dŵr looked for allies in Scotland, Ireland, and France. As interpreted by the bards, the fiery comet that appeared in the sky 'high over Anglesey' in the spring of 1402 offered an excellent omen. A French naval squadron assisted in the siege of Beaumaris castle the following year, and in their savage attack on the town the Welsh also had Scottish support. French ships blockaded the Menai Straits for a time. Relieved by sea from Chester, the garrison stood firm. Yet, when a company of troops ventured out in January 1404 under the command of the Welsh deputy sheriff of Anglesey, Maredudd ap Cynwrig of Porthaml, it was ambushed by a combined force of some 200 Welsh and French soldiers. As a result Maredudd ap Cynwrig defected to the liberation cause. Though positive evidence is lacking, a reference to the recapture of Beaumaris castle suggests that it did fall into Welsh hands for a short while during 1404–5. Newborough, too, had become exposed to the ill effects of war; several houses and lands were burnt. By this time Anglesey was certainly free of English control.

The years 1405–6 were the apogee of Glyn Dŵr's power. As prince of Wales, his coat of arms was the royal arms of the princes of Gwynedd (four lions rampant). But in 1405 he also suffered a major reversal in Anglesey. It had not been a principal battleground in the revolt; most of the military action took place on the mainland where the mountainous terrain most suited guerrilla warfare. Yet, strategically, as in the campaigns of Edward I, the island was seen as the essential stepping-stone to the conquest of Gwynedd. Once again, the English exploited their sea power to the full. A large Anglo-Irish naval force under Stephen Scrope arrived from Ireland in a surprise raid on Anglesey in June 1405. Heavily outnumbered, the local Welshmen could offer little resistance in open battle at Rhos-meirch. The town and castle of Beaumaris were retaken. In the face of an avenging army, many islanders fled to the protection of Snowdonia with their livestock. After wreaking large-scale devastation, the Irish eventually left but took with them, as a battle trophy, the shrine of Saint Cybi from Holyhead to be displayed in Dublin cathedral. For Anglesey this intervention had marked a decisive turning point; it shattered morale. To all intents the rebellion here was at an end well before the famous Pennal declaration of March 1406, containing Glyn Dŵr's visionary programme for an independent Welsh state.

Royal control was reasserted during 1406. Under John Mainwaring, sheriff of Chester, the process of pacification gathered momentum and as before Beaumaris castle came to symbolize English military domination. Troops dispatched to the island patrolled the Menai Straits in order to prevent any contact between the cowed inhabitants and Glyn Dŵr partisans on the mainland, so depriving them of food supplies. At the end of the year a general fine of £537 7s was imposed on the community 'for rebellion in Anglesey'. Listed under the six commotes are the names of the 2,121 people who submitted to the commissioners at Beaumaris. They include most of the householders outside the boroughs of Beaumaris and Newborough. Not all had necessarily been active participants, but it is possible to identify Glyn Dŵr's adherents in Anglesey. Included are a number of key local officials who had served as *rhingyll* and sheriff, as well as a significant section of the clergy, among them the archdeacon of Anglesey, the canon of the collegiate church at Holyhead, the rector of Aberffraw and six members of the Franciscan friary at Llan-faes. A minority refused to surrender. Einion Sais of Bodorgan became an outlaw, losing some of his lands. True to character, Gwilym and Rhys ap Tudur remained unrepentant, though there were no further audacious military exploits to record. Also listed among those who did not submit was their younger brother Maredudd and a kinsman, Gwilym ap Gruffydd ap Gwilym. Among the hundred or so islanders who had sacrificed their lives was Gwilym ap Gruffydd ap Tudur Llwyd, a wealthy landowner, who died fighting in front of Beaumaris castle.

Against this background, English rule was quickly re-imposed. As his reward, one of the commissioners, Robert Parys, received land at Mynydd Trysglwyn, that would later bear his name as Parys Mountain. Early in 1407 Mainwaring became military commander of the island, backed by Thomas Bolde, the constable of Beaumaris castle. So confident were they of the situation in Anglesey that the garrison unit of two men-at-arms and twenty archers could be halved by August. Rather late in the day, the relieved townspeople were granted £10 towards the cost of raising defensive earthworks (a stone wall was built by 1414). As the tide of revolt finally turned, leading to its final collapse, so too came the day of reckoning. Captured at Welshpool after an ill-fated Shropshire raid, Rhys ap Tudur was executed at Chester in 1412. Gwilym ap Tudur fared better; he seems to have been pardoned in 1413, the same year that the county of Anglesey obtained (at a price) a charter of communal pardon. Maredudd ap Tudur severed his personal connections with Anglesey. His son Owain, who became, surprisingly, a courtier at Windsor, gained subsequent historical notice as the grandfather of Henry Tudor, the future king Henry VII. In stark contrast, the house of Penmynydd lost its glory; in placing a greater value on their nation than on their family the Tudors sacrificed almost all of their lands and prestige. Only the rump of Goronwy ap Tudur's descendants was to remain at Penmynydd.

The war had exacerbated the problems associated with depopulation and poverty. Large tracts of land still remained untenanted and uncultivated, with rents unpaid. Many bondmen had taken advantage of the social turmoil to escape from their feudal obligations. After the death, destruction and misery, the next decades saw a very gradual recovery. Agricultural life in Anglesey, characterized by its open fields and mixed farming, began to display former resilience. Many of the mills were repaired or rebuilt; the island's famed millstones continued to be in demand both at home and abroad. The extensive damage at Beaumaris and Newborough was slowly put right; markets and fairs revived economic activity; ferries across the Menai Straits were resumed. With royal approval, the Franciscan community at Llan-faes had been re-established in 1414, but on condition that no more than two of the eight friars would be Welsh. Militarily, the authorities continued to be on their guard. Many Welshmen, it is true, again went abroad to fight for the crown in the course of the 'Hundred Years War' – Owain ap Maredudd ap Tudur was in France in 1420. But in view of the potential French or Scottish threat to the Anglesey coast, the garrison at Beaumaris castle was periodically strengthened. Bitter experience had taught English settlers to be wary. In 1442 the burgesses of Beaumaris petitioned parliament to enforce those laws designed to prevent the infiltration of Welshmen into English boroughs.

The rise of individual *uchelwyr* families had been a significant feature of the Later Middle Ages. By acquiring land, wealth, political influence and marriage alliances they became the masters of local society. As has already been noted, the descendants of Hwfa ap Cynddelw, Llywarch ap Bran and, above all, Ednyfed Fychan, were conspicuous by their presence. But it took some deft action during, and immediately after, the Glyn Dŵr revolt to maintain their predominance, helped by a forgiving king. Maredudd ap Cynwrig of the line of Llywarch ap Bran had shrewdly submitted in November 1406 and paid five pounds, one of the highest fines. It was well worth it. In terms of land and offices he could celebrate his speedy rehabilitation as the top figure exercising power in Newborough and the commote of Menai in a manner befitting one famously partial to imported Spanish wine. If the house of Penmynydd had been the chief casualty of the rebellion, Gwilym ap Gruffydd ap Gwilym was the archetype of unscrupulous opportunism and ambition. First married to Morfudd ferch Goronwy ap Tudur, he had quickly made his peace with Henry IV, putting him in the ideal position to profit from the acquisition of land forfeited by Gwilym and Rhys ap Tudur and other rebels. In this way he laid the foundations of the mainland Penrhyn estate.

Around the Gruffydd family of Penrhyn revolved many of the developments leading to the creation of gentry landed estates in

Anglesey. Gwilym Fychan, Gwilym ap Gruffydd ap Gwilym's son through his second marriage, purchased the lands that would form the nucleus of the Plas Newydd estate. Unfailingly loyal to the crown, he sought to be legally 'made English', anglicizing his name to William Griffith. Aspiring individuals of purely English origin also knew where best to nurture relationships. From Cheshire stock, the first William Bulkeley (d.1490) to settle in Beaumaris held the office of deputy constable of the castle. An astute marriage to one of the daughters of Gwilym ap Gruffydd ap Gwilym assured future success, as did his accumulation of land and public offices. Commensurate with their social pretensions, the golden couple erected Henblas as the family mansion – the largest house not only in Beaumaris but the whole of Anglesey (its demolition in 1869 now leaves the recently restored Hafoty, Llansadwrn, as a splendid period example of gentry residence). By the end of the fifteenth century most *uchelwyr* families were well integrated into the new order. Their co-operation and active participation in royal service, moreover, enabled them to gain control of the machinery of government in north Wales when the crown was at its weakest during the Wars of the Roses.

II

The Tudor Period

The dynastic struggle for power during the Wars of the Roses necessarily involved the participation of Welshmen on opposing sides. From the first, Anglesey gentry were loyal to Henry VI and the Lancastrians. When duke Richard, the Yorkist leader, arrived at the port of Beaumaris in 1450 on his return from Ireland, local officials including William Bulkeley had made an abortive attempt to prevent him disembarking. Deteriorating relations between the king and duke Richard led to open conflict in 1455. During the years of war the garrison at Beaumaris castle was reinforced, but for the most part the main battleground would be the Welsh borderland. What remained of the Tudor family in Anglesey allowed events to pass them by. Tudur Fychan, the son of Morfudd and Gwilym ap Gruffydd ap Gwilym, who eventually took over Penmynydd after the latter's death, evinced no interest in the feud between the Lancastrians and Yorkists; unlike his uncle, Owain ap Maredudd ap Tudur, now plain Owen Tudor, whose allegiance to the Lancastrian cause through marriage to the widow of Henry V led to his execution in 1461. Jasper Tudor, his surviving son, made great efforts to mobilize further support in Wales during the reign of the Yorkist Edward IV before he was eventually forced to flee abroad. Rumour had it that he planned to land at Beaumaris to start a rebellion in north Wales. When his fortunes fell further, Jasper took refuge in Brittany with his young nephew Henry Tudor.

Thanks to Welsh poets, Henry Tudor had become the focus not merely for Lancastrian hopes, but the aspirations of a nation. Vaticinatory poetry presented him as a *mab darogan* (son of prophecy) who would free Wales from tyranny. Being of the line of Ednyfed Fychan, he was celebrated by Dafydd Llwyd o Fathafarn as 'the eagle from Anglesey'. Though Henry never set eyes on the island, he had doubtlessly been made aware of his own place in history during his upbringing at Raglan castle with its strong bardic associations. After Edward IV's death in 1483 he was the main Lancastrian claimant. By manipulating Welsh nationalism, bardic propaganda zealously prepared the ground for his return from France. A flood of poems kept Welsh expectations in ferment. By now the epithet 'black bull' was being solely used to designate the Tudors, so that Dafydd Llwyd looked to the *tarw o Fôn* (bull from Anglesey) for deliverance. In the same spirit of optimism, Robin Ddu o Fôn declared:

Y mae hiraeth am Harri
Y mae gobaith i'n hiaith ni
(There is a longing for Harry
There is hope for our nation).

Landing near Milford Haven in 1485, Henry Tudor rallied Welsh support under the red dragon standard of Cadwaladr. From Anglesey, Rhys ap Llywelyn ap Hwlcyn of Bodychen, Bodwrog, led a company of foot soldiers to join him in mid-Wales and fight on Bosworth field. Another partisan, Llywelyn ap Heilyn would return to Bodorgan the blade of his two-handed sword bent in battle.

After victory Henry VII lost little time in rewarding his leading Welsh supporters. Rhys ap Llywelyn ap Hwlcyn was appointed sheriff of Anglesey and, by grant of denizenship in 1486, accorded the same rights as Englishmen. The political situation did not allow any immediate change in Wales; Henry's first concern was to secure his crown in the face of would-be supplanters and insurgents. When the Cornish rebelled against a tax imposition in 1497, the warrior qualities of Owain ap Meurig of Bodeon in suppressing the revolt excited the poet Lewys Môn to gruesomely describe the remains of flesh on his gloves. (Kneeling, in full field-armour, with sword at his side but *sans* gloves, Owain is commemorated in the splendid fifteenth-century glass window at Llangadwaladr church.) By the close of his reign, when he was in a better position to turn his attention to Wales, Henry VII granted a series of charters removing the restrictions imposed upon Welshmen during the Glyn Dŵr revolt. As well as equal rights, they sanctioned the English system of land inheritance whereby estates could be transferred to the eldest son. The charters of liberties issued to the counties of Anglesey, Caernarfon and Merioneth in 1504 and 1507 were not so much for altruistic reasons as the payment of £2,300. Predictably enough, the award of equal privileges did not go down well with the English settlers in Beaumaris.

Among further concessions to Welsh sentiment, Henry VII employed genealogists to trace his Tudor ancestry and welcomed Welsh gentry to the royal court. In one way or another he would learn more of his Anglesey pedigree. His distant relative, Owain Tudur Fychan, who was granted denizenship in 1495, moved to London to serve as Esquire of the Body. Otherwise, the family that remained on the small Penmynydd estate did not seek to take advantage of this prized kinship to restore their former standing in society (after a modest recovery, the last male heir died in 1669). In his elegy to the first Tudor king, Dafydd Trefor praised the benefits brought by Maelgwn's descendant in leading his own people out of 'bondage'. Henry might have gone a long way to please the ambitious gentry class, keen to acquire office and expand its landed estate, but not everyone had reason to join in the euphoria. The Welsh, lamented the Glamorgan bard Llywelyn ap Hywel, were in thrall to Henry and Jasper:

> *Gweision gan wŷr Môn ym ni*
> (We are servants of the men of Anglesey).

The Tudor ruling family, he went on, preferred the counsel of Englishmen. Nationalistic idealism and political realities had proved irreconcilable. But it went further than this. Never again would Anglesey be directly linked to a royal line. From the Early Middle Ages the *llys* at Aberffraw had accorded the island a paramount historic status, evoked by the kings of Gwynedd and the princes of Wales. Now, ironically, Môn was being uttered within a context confirming that Wales's destiny would henceforth be entrusted to the rulers of England.

Political union came in the reign of Henry VIII. At first, the king showed little interest in Wales, even if Welshmen still found a niche in court circles. Rhydderch ap Dafydd of Myfyrian, Llanidan, served as a footman. Meurig ap Llywelyn, the son of Llywelyn ap Heilyn, rose to be Captain of the Guard and was rewarded with the manor of Aberffraw. Instead of the patronym ap Meurig, his son Richard, living at Bodorgan, anglicized the surname to Meyrick. Characteristically, the Bulkeleys of Beaumaris were already well positioned to advance their family interests. Rowland Bulkeley, who undertook leadership on the death of his father William, withstood the hostility of the Griffith family of Penrhyn, prior to the profusion of outstandingly able Richard Bulkeleys. Sir Richard Bulkeley I (d.1547), his son, began his rise to prominence as Esquire of the Body in the royal household before gaining the confidence of Thomas Cromwell, the king's chief minister. By cultivating contacts at court he was able to fend off the persistent opposition of the Penrhyn and Glynllifon families on the mainland, who resented the overbearing power of an 'Englishman'. He acquired the post of constable of Beaumaris castle and chamberlain of North Wales. By amassing public offices, property – particularly in the commote of Dindaethwy and the town of Beaumaris – and considerable wealth, Sir Richard Bulkeley I gained a pre-eminent position in society.

Equally, Bulkeley, as confidant, served Cromwell's interests in north Wales during the momentous events of the 1530s. Religious changes had precipitated Cromwell's policy of administrative reform in Wales. A petition from the burgesses and landowners of Beaumaris, Anglesey and Caernarfon supported the extension of English laws and rights. With Henry VIII as Supreme Head of the Church of England, he initiated a radical political settlement whereby Wales was merged with England according to the Acts of Union of 1536–43. Following the appointment of justices of the peace there were a number of far-reaching political measures which aimed at uniformity under English law. Existing counties, including Anglesey, were retained and new shires created. Equality also meant parliamentary representation at Westminster: one member for the county, and another for the borough that was a shire town.

Politics became the preserve of the gentry, who were at loggerheads if rival factions contested a seat in pursuit of social power and family prestige. By mid-century two hostile groups appeared in Anglesey. On the eastern side there was the ultra-ambitious Bulkeley family determined to exercise control over political life. Ready to challenge them were the native Welsh gentry in the west of the island, together with their allies among the less wealthy English immigrant families. William Bulkeley, Llangefni, younger brother of Sir Richard Bulkeley I, sat as the first MP for the county seat in 1542. On his death seven years later he was replaced by his nephew Sir Richard Bulkeley II (d.1572), regarded as the main architect of Bulkeley supremacy. Initially, as will be seen, he came under a cloud at the start of Mary's reign, allowing opponents to take full advantage. In a rare contested election in 1553 William Lewis of Prysaeddfed was returned to the Commons through the connivance of a biased returning sheriff. Bulkeley, who had gained the majority of votes, legally proved his case, but the incident further poisoned relations between the leading gentry families. That said, the Bulkeley family consolidated its political power. Sir Richard Bulkeley III (d.1621) represented the prestigious county seat in three parliaments.

Because the county court had been transferred from Beaumaris to Newborough for some unknown reason in 1507, as the new shire town it was here that parliamentary elections were held. It transpired that only its burgesses returned the borough member and supported him financially. Consequently, the first members came from Welsh gentry stock; Owen ap Hugh of Bodeon, MP in 1545, was one of the leaders of the anti-Bulkeley faction. Newborough, however, was now little more than a rapidly decaying village threatened by shifting sand dunes, while Beaumaris prospered. Due to the influence of Sir Richard Bulkeley II, Beaumaris regained its status as the shire town in 1549. Faced with increasing impoverishment, the burgesses of Newborough were then released from their financial obligation. Beaumaris alone would return the borough member, a privilege confirmed by the charter of 1562. Once again, the Bulkeleys with their connections at court had pulled the right strings. Political control was vested in a corporation of only twenty-four electors, and as the dominant family, owning half the town's property, the Bulkeleys soon had Beaumaris snugly in their 'pocket'. Family members or close associates monopolized the constituency.

The distinguishing feature of the Tudor period would be the ambition, greed and opportunism shown by the Bulkeley family. Their fortunes in Anglesey blossomed as succeeding generations or close relatives filled the premier administrative, political and church posts. Yet another Richard Bulkeley (brother of Rowland) had earlier served as archdeacon of Anglesey. Understandably, their increasing wealth and influence continued to arouse the jealousy of less fortunate neighbours. Sir Richard Bulkeley III, a court favourite of Elizabeth, successfully fought off a coalition of minor squires in Anglesey to strengthen this supremacy and emerge as leader of Gwynedd gentry.

Henry VIII's great need for money led to the dissolution of the monasteries between 1536 and 1540. First, commissioners, among them Sir Richard Bulkeley I, compiled a survey of their wealth, followed by visitations to seek out abuses. Deficiencies within the Welsh religious houses – the small number of monks, their moral failings and poverty – had already contributed to their spiritual decay, aggravated by secular involvement in monastic affairs. These defects were apparent in Anglesey as in other places. On the eve of their demise there were only two monks at Penmon, and four at Llan-faes. In 1504 the then prior of Penmon and two monks had been found guilty of keeping concubines. Moving the market from Llan-faes to Beaumaris had severely dented the friary's revenues. Penmon's net income of £40 in 1535 made it the poorest Augustinian house in Wales. Being for some time past the stewards of Penmon's monastic estates, the Bulkeley family were ideally placed to snatch some of the confiscated property that came on the market. Itching for favours, Sir Richard Bulkeley I pleaded with Thomas Cromwell in 1537 to 'have it to farm ... for it lieth hard at my nose'. Though he failed with his request, his grandson eventually purchased the lands and buildings of the dissolved priory in 1566. Penmon was preserved for parish worship, and the shell of the monastic buildings still remain today. In the case of Llan-faes, Bulkeley, now wise with experience, had greased Cromwell's palm with £100 in 1539 to secure the lease of the friary. The building was completely demolished in 1539–40, with most of the stone carted off to repair the town wall and quay at Beaumaris.

At dissolution, the collegiate church at Holyhead – transformed following a period of reconstruction between 1480 and 1520 – was valued at £48. While the provost and twelve canons were pensioned off, the church of Saint Cybi continued as an ordinary parish church; its revenues would later be bequeathed to Jesus College, Oxford.

Religion had always been at the centre of most human activity, yet the Reformation changes of Henry VIII's reign caused no popular unrest in Anglesey. The closure of the monasteries did not lead to a public outcry; few appear to have mourned their passing, least of all the unscrupulous gentry who had profited from the sale of church property. Ordinary people failed to grasp the full implication of these developments because they hardly impinged on their daily lives. In truth, religious devotion was superficial, reflecting the lack of spiritual leadership given by the church. Undue emphasis was put on ancient saints and pilgrimages to sacred wells; Dafydd Trefor (d.1528), the poet-priest of Llaneugrad, clearly believed in the miraculous powers of Saint Dwynwen: *Awn dan nawdd Dwynwen i ne* (Go we under Dwynwen's protection to heaven). The suppression of the more popular aspects of religion would have more impact. Though the much-frequented shrine at Llanddwyn was officially abolished in 1538, Dwynwen's cult lived on in folk memory.

The break with Rome had also raised the spectre of an invasion from Catholic Europe, and, as in the past, Anglesey's vulnerability was highlighted. Increasingly, the government feared an attack via Ireland or Scotland and numerous reports emphasized the island's exposed position and weak defences. Appointed by Cromwell as one of the commissioners to watch the north Wales coast, Sir Richard Bulkeley I drew attention to the military deficiencies. Anglesey was 'open upon all countries', he stressed in a letter in 1539, 'it is but a day's sail from Scotland, Breton lies open on it ... the Spaniards know every haven and creek, and Ireland and other countries lie open upon it'. As for the castle and walled town of Beaumaris, an invading army could overrun both within an hour. In fact, the castle appears to have been deserted since 1518, when the garrison was withdrawn. Bulkeley's shire loyalty became evident. He mustered a force of 1,228 men in Anglesey and personally defrayed the cost of equipping those at Beaumaris with bows and sheaves of arrows. Similar fears were again expressed in 1545 when news came that a fleet of eighty French ships had sailed past the Isle of Man. Beacons were prepared lest they attempted a landing in Anglesey on their return journey from Scotland, but the danger passed without incident.

New policies in the short reign of Edward VI saw the birth of an advanced Protestant church to replace Catholicism. The appearance of the English Prayer Book in 1549 meant that no part of the service would be in Latin (it was accompanied by a Welsh commentary). Doctrinal changes in a language alien to the ordinary people were now being imposed. These, and the extinction of many cherished features of traditional worship, touched off considerable resentment. As a staunch champion of the Catholic faith, the poet Siôn Brwynog, who lived in the parish of Llanddeusant, voiced popular unease in his poem 'Y Ddwy Ffydd' (The Two Faiths). Nothing could disguise the contempt he felt towards extreme Protestantism. Devoid of altars, images, ornaments, vestments, candles and incense, the churches were left 'like barns' in 'icy coldness'. Bewailing the absence of the mass and confession, he satirized those clergy who rushed into marriage, and their pathetic efforts to hold English services with little understanding of the new Prayer Book. Yet, it was the lot of the people to conform in silence, even though the shock of the change could only have produced a fragile religious bond.

Mary's accession in 1553, leading to the re-establishment of Catholicism, put certain individuals to the test. It meant some nimble action on the part of Sir Richard Bulkeley II, who supposedly had her proclaimed 'traitress' at Beaumaris on the one day (he first backed Lady Jane Grey) and a 'lawful queen' on the next. His worldly concerns were to be dispelled: there was to be no restoration of former monastic property. Siôn Brwynog's joyous welcome for the return of the 'old masses' would seem to offer a more genuine representation of popular attitudes. The only upheaval in Anglesey was the removal of a few married clergy. Catholic reform received encouragement with the appointment of William Glyn as Bishop of Bangor in 1555. A Cambridge-educated theologian, who originated from Heneglwys, he was greeted by Siôn Brwynog as a 'pillar of faith'. Scarcely did another reformer, Gruffydd Robert, who became archdeacon of Anglesey in 1558, have time to make an impression before Mary's death a few months after William Glyn in that same year.

Rather than accept the Elizabethan religious settlement, a number of prominent Catholics went into exile on the continent. The outstanding figure among them was Owen Lewis. Born in Llangadwaladr and educated at Oxford, he became an influential figure in Rome and Milan and was consecrated bishop of Cassano. While exiles worked to bring about a Catholic conversion the prevailing mood in Wales was that of compromise. How much real enthusiasm existed for the Protestant state church cannot be accurately gauged, nor how many true Catholics still remained. Plainly, people had not turned their backs fully on the Old Faith. It was reported that one funeral at Beaumaris in 1570 savoured strongly of papist practices. Sir Richard Bulkeley II had remained a Catholic; more than that, his daughter had married the scion of Penrhyn Creuddyn (Caernarfonshire), one of the foremost recusant families in north Wales. After Bulkeley's death, this religious allegiance became somewhat diluted despite the presumptuous claim of a Catholic activist in 1574 that 'all the Bulkeleys are Catholics'. A year later, Pope Gregory XIII was being presented with a memorandum written by an exiled Welsh theologian that proposed a Catholic invasion of England with Anglesey as the initial back-door entry. This ambitious plan proceeded no further.

It was only to be expected that Catholic loyalties should linger among a conservative-minded people in the more remote areas. Even Sir Richard Bulkeley III, according to an accusation made by local foes in 1588, did not attend church or receive Anglican communion for a period of sixteen years. It might have been indifference rather than recusancy in his case, but there were other indications of underlying Catholic sympathies as circumstances surrounding the arrest and fate of William Davies, a missionary priest, attested. Along with four students bound for a Spanish seminary he had been detained at Holyhead in 1592 in the face of considerable hostility. Local people refused to co-operate with the authorities and no local man would act as executioner. When Davies was condemned to hang at Beaumaris in July 1593 a butcher from Chester had to be employed for the task. By this time, Sir Richard Bulkeley represented government authority. William Davies was the only priest to be martyred in Wales during the reign of Elizabeth. As intended, his show trial and execution served as a warning to Catholics. No further persecutions were necessary in Anglesey; most thought it wiser to outwardly conform. After all, Thomas Bulkeley, whilst rector of Llanddeusant between 1543 and 1579, had adapted himself to every religious change since the reign of Henry VIII.

Wherever their religious sympathies gravitated, the imperatives of war proved the determining factor for those who finally abandoned Catholicism. By the 1580s the threat of a Spanish invasion cast a shadow over the island. In 1581 Anglesey men were granted exemption from military service so that they could concentrate on home defence. As war approached, Spanish naval captains were said to have maps and descriptions featuring the isle of Anglesey. In such 'dangerous times' the local militia was mustered and drilled in the use of firearms – under the command of the firmly loyal Sir Richard Bulkeley. Even the defeat of the mighty Spanish armada in 1588 did not signal the end of hostilities. In preparation for the armada of 1597 the Spaniards had the report of a pilot, based on an earlier reconnoitre of the Irish Sea, which pinpointed the approaches to Beaumaris as a suitable place for anchorage. Besides this, he spoke optimistically of support on the island since 'they speak a language apart, there are many Catholics, and they are very friendly to Ireland'. Large numbers of Anglesey men would be in Ireland during the 1590s, not as allies, but to crush Catholic rebellion and fight Spanish invasion forces. At least fifty soldiers levied in Anglesey fought at the victorious battle of Kinsale in 1601.

Elizabethan churchmen were already initiating improvements that would ensure the success of the Reformation. Beginning with Rowland Meyrick, second son of Meurig ap Llywelyn of Bodorgan, in the 1560s, the bishops of Bangor gave doughty spiritual leadership at a time of great difficulties. The general poverty of the diocese, clerical absenteeism, the lack of preachers, persistent recusancy and the widespread ignorance of the peasantry were some of the problems confronting them up to the time of Henry Rowlands, archdeacon of Anglesey in 1588, and bishop a decade later. By the end of the Tudor period the New Faith had very slowly begun to win the affections of the people with the provision of a Prayer Book, Bible and other religious tracts in the Welsh language. Penrhosllugwy parish registers from 1578 to 1679 provide a very rare example of registers written in Welsh rather than Latin. Education remained a priority. And as more graduates, instilled with Protestantism, were ordained, clerical quality gradually improved. Between 1560 and 1637 twenty of the university-trained clergy in the diocese originated from Anglesey. To improve the standard of preaching and pastoral work, Bishop Rowlands also fostered grammar school education. Among the foundations to benefit from his generosity was the free grammar school at Beaumaris founded in 1603 by David Hughes, a native of Llantrisant who had made his wealth in Norfolk. Farms he bought in Anglesey provided an endowment. The school offered classical education through the medium of English and Latin; scholarships then enabled deserving pupils to proceed to Oxford.

Allegiance to the crown and the Anglican Church had drawn central government and county closer together, cemented by the abiding loyalty of the gentry. Families of native stock vied with newcomers to benefit from the Tudor Settlement. English law had facilitated the consolidation and growth of large landed estates. New opportunities for the control of local administration and justice provided the main spur for integration, as did the dominant role open to them in politics and religion. To safeguard their interests, the gentry class sought to preserve peace, order and stability. Sir Fôn (the county of Anglesey) not only became the main unit of administration but the territorial boundary of community life, evoking a sense of belonging, pride and social obligation. Though of moderate means in comparison with the distinctly affluent Bulkeleys, the families of Bodeon, Bodewryd, Bodowyr, Bodorgan, Plas Coch, Porthaml and Prysaeddfed similarly aimed to extend their influence in county affairs in the office of sheriff, justice of the peace, deputy lieutenant, or as member of parliament. However modest their country-house, lineage and ancestry gave them authority and respect. Those squires who rose to leadership were lauded by local bards as *blaenor Môn* (the leader of Anglesey) or *llywiawdwr Môn* (the governor of Anglesey). Accordingly, the *plasty* (mansion) began to replace the castle as the focus of political power, a tangible symbol of gentry rule that would remain unchallenged until the second half of the nineteenth century. Poets, too, promoted their close attachment to the island. Robin Ddu o Fôn and Lewys Môn were among a number who coupled their name with Anglesey, a trend that found fashionable expression again in later times.

A privileged education, prudent marriage ties, and further acquisitions of land (even if it involved costly litigation) were eagerly coveted. Wealthy gentry families employed private tutors or else sent their sons to the grammar schools at Beaumaris, Bangor or over the border in England. Anglesey, relative to its population size, was to be particularly well represented at the main centres of higher learning: in the period 1504–1642 there were 162 students at Oxford, 34 at Cambridge and 43 at the Inns of Court. Hugh Hughes of Plas Coch, who studied at Lincoln's Inn, became the Queen's Attorney in north Wales in 1596. A marriage alliance with a Northamptonshire lady and more lands in Anglesey brought valuable legal connections and riches, enabling him to reconstruct the imposing family mansion first built in 1569. Another lawyer, Sir Hugh Owen of Bodeon, married the heiress of the large Orielton estate in Pembrokeshire. Land was wealth, and the scramble for land often brought rival landowners to court. The process of estate building pitted the Meyricks of Bodorgan against the Owens of Bodeon in a protracted legal dispute concerning land at Aberffraw at the turn of the century, tinged with physical violence perpetrated by Owen ap Hugh of Bodeon – a JP! Some were less fortunate than others. Serious financial difficulties forced the Griffith family of Plas Newydd to sell its estate to Sir Henry Bagnall of Newry, Ireland, in 1602.

Members of the Bagnall family had been engaged in one of Anglesey's few industrial undertakings, namely the coal-mining ventures at Ysgeifiog, Hirdrefaig and Berw. From these limited operations a small cargo of coal left Beaumaris for Ayr in Scotland in 1595. Early the next century the coal pits at Berw encountered serious flooding. The continuing demand for Anglesey millstones turned the quarries between Benllech and Penmon into a lucrative local enterprise. *Moresg* (marram grass), cultivated to stabilize the sand dunes, provided raw material for basketry, ropes and rush mat making at Newborough, a local craft industry that survived into the twentieth century. The copper deposits of Parys Mountain were investigated in the late 1570s but the cost of commercial exploitation was too prohibitive. Nothing could challenge the dominant role of agriculture in the local economy.

Anglesey's growing population is estimated to have been 9,770 in 1563. Thrice married, and with thirty-six children, William ap Howel, 'the Patriarch of Tregaean', would make a sterling personal contribution: when he died in 1581 aged 105, his 'senses perfect to the last', the number of descendants approached 300. Beaumaris, with 555 inhabitants, remained the principal urban centre, noted for its prosperity. There were nine shops in the town and, laudably, care was being taken to keep the streets clean. Trade at the port thrived, much to the benefit of its largely English merchant community. Cargoes of iron, domestic hardware and wool-cards (for the purpose of home-weaving) were shipped mainly from Chester, its chief commercial link during the Elizabethan age. Wine came direct from Gascony; Beaumaris even had merchants operating in Spain. The main exports included farm produce, millstones and Caernarfonshire slates. Trans-Atlantic trade saw a Beaumaris ship, the *Victory*, sail to Newfoundland and Portugal in 1582–3, bringing back salt, soap and barley malt. Piracy posed a perennial problem for the authorities. Yet there were times when Beaumaris was being used as a base for robbing Irish and French ships. Not that the town's merchants proved immune to illegal trading: even Sir Richard Bulkeley III, the vice-admiral of north Wales, and his brothers were given to selling pirated goods.

Beaumaris ferry had kept to the traditional route. Travellers from Conwy would first make a four-mile journey across Traeth Lafan to catch the larger boat now in service. With its low sides it was able to take on horses in shallow water. Despite the presence of guideposts the trek across the tidal sands in fog and stormy weather remained hazardous. Yet there is no record of a serious mishap involving the ferry. Beaumaris still figured as an important stopping place on the post route linking London and Dublin, a service first commenced in 1561, although it was Holyhead that developed as the packet port for Ireland. Of the six crossing points across the Menai Straits the ferry operating at Porthaethwy assumed premier status. Favoured by its narrow waters and relatively sheltered position, it was described in the sixteenth century as the *porth ... yn llethu'r lleill* (doorway...surpassing all others). Passengers took to an *ysgraff*, a small round craft that carried no more than three horses.

The social structure was firmly based on the gentry–tenant farmer–hired labourer nexus, alongside a substantial number of small farmers owning freehold land. While the principal county families have their mansions, pedigrees and dynastic histories, very little is known of the inarticulate peasantry. Definitions of poverty are difficult to establish, but it is true to say that the majority were preordained to survive at subsistence level; a hard working life lived in dismal hovels. It was customary for the female poor of Anglesey to beg for cheese, milk and butter, hence the label *gwragedd cawsa* (cheese gatherers). Food shortages made conditions infinitely worse; even the famed breadbasket of north Wales had to import corn at times of harvest failure, as in 1602–3. Stock rearing and the cattle trade with England continued to grow in importance. From the early fifteenth century there is mention of the passage of animals across the Menai Straits at Porthaethwy. By the 1540s two Anglesey *porthmyn* (drovers), Rhys ap Cynfrig and Rhys ap Llywelyn, had grown rich exporting cattle to Staffordshire markets. Buyers from as far as Kent were dealing at the cattle fairs held at Llannerch-y-medd and Newborough.

Altogether, the Tudor Settlement had been undeniably beneficial to Wales. Progress and economic development, justice, peace and stability all contributed to its successful acceptance, most auspiciously in the case of the landowning gentry. Age-old problems would continue to cause concern for those at the bottom of the social scale. Rising prices, unemployment, poverty, disease and vagrancy periodically plagued the countryside, leading to crime – especially theft and violence. But unlike Caernarfonshire there are no contemporary records surviving for the Court of Quarter Sessions in Anglesey. Taking the number of cases before the London Court of Star Chamber during Elizabeth's reign, Anglesey stands out as the least lawless of Welsh counties. Again, according to the antiquary George Owen, Anglesey people were 'quiet and civil'. When trouble occurred, it was not only the lower orders that occasionally flouted authority. Whereas Lewys Môn sang the praises of the gentry who preserved law and order in the local community, reference has been made to those unscrupulous individuals who transgressed when it suited their purpose. Despite the cult of gentility there were still violent encounters, and as most men carried a weapon bloodshed was not uncommon. When two Anglesey squires, from Bodowyr and Porthaml, locked horns on the streets of Caernarfon in 1554, each was accompanied by a band of retainers armed to the teeth with swords, daggers and shields.

Though the Acts of Union had decreed that English would be the sole official language, this failed to dim the cultural dimension. A poetic resurgence in the last quarter of the sixteenth century was largely sustained by the patronage of the leading noble families. Meticulous research has revealed the vitality of a well-supported bardic tradition in and around the parish of Bodedern, presided over by William Lewis of Prysaeddfed until his death in 1604. Anglesey's contribution to Welsh literature continued: Lewys Menai and Huw Cornwy were two bards to graduate at the Caerwys eisteddfod of 1567, when official standards were set; Sir Richard Bulkeley II was sufficiently Welsh to be appointed one of the commissioners. Far-reaching social changes, however, meant that it became a tradition in crisis, despite the appeals for professional poets to modernize their craft by incorporating all branches of Renaissance learning. One distinguished scholar who laid stress on this was Siôn Dafydd Rhys, a native of Llanfaethlu who had graduated as a Doctor of Medicine at the University of Siena. The linguistic interests he nurtured whilst in Italy were put into effect with the publication in 1592 of a grammar of the Welsh language in Latin. But to little avail; the old bardic order was in terminal decline. Robert ap Ifan, a literary nobleman from Brynsiencyn, thought it deplorable that even thieves were better off because they had more money. Standards were on the wane and the growing divide between poets and the gentry class would, by the middle of the following century, ultimately deprive them of traditional patronage.

III

The Stuart Age

With James I acclaimed king of 'Great Britain', the assimilation of the leading Welsh gentry into English social and political life was to be finally completed during the Stuart Age. All aspects of social conduct were imitated in fine detail, the ability to speak English being the chief prerequisite. Increasing care was taken to improve the breeding of the womenfolk. Robert Bulkeley of Dronwy, Llanfachreth, a distant relation of the Baron Hill family, sent his daughter to Chester in the early 1640s for her schooling. The anglicization of Welsh names became widespread; bizarrely, the Tudors of Penmynydd gloried in what they regarded as the more august moniker of Theodore. For those ambitious islanders in the upper ranks the avenues of opportunity became progressively accessible; no matter what condition the road, the route to London led to wealth and fame. Not so the lower classes. Their world was their shire; few were in a position to leave Anglesey, and less would have knowledge of outside events. Indigenous growth accounted for the increase in population to 16,456 by 1670; unlike the border counties the inflow of English settlers was negligible. Even so, the trend for English gentlemen at Beaumaris to acquire Welsh wives contributed to the gradual process of Anglicization. The marriage of John Sparrow, Red Hill, to the last heiress of Bodychen finally extinguished the traditional Welshness of that noble house; there would no longer be a welcome for the bards.

During a period of parliamentary apprenticeship Welsh MPs began to involve themselves in the business of the House of Commons. The interests of Anglesey were voiced by the ubiquitous Bulkeleys, who made their debut in 1571 when Sir Richard Bulkeley II sat on the committee reporting on navigation. Sir Richard Bulkeley III proved to be the ultimate committee member, dutifully serving on more than fifty committees in James I's first parliament and a further five in 1614, although frail and in his eighties. The family withdrew from the borough seat for a time, leaving allies among the lesser Caernarfonshire squires to hold the political fort. Differences between the king and parliament soon broadened into constitutional quarrels. In contrast to the apolitical Bulkeleys, William Jones, Castellmarch, MP for Beaumaris in 1614, was openly critical of the power of the crown, especially in regard to financial impositions. His lawyer son, Charles Jones, who also represented the borough, helped draft the impeachment charges against Buckingham, the king's reviled favourite. In Charles I's reign he was involved in preparing the Petition of Right that condemned taxes collected without parliament's permission.

Royal attempts to exact levies and subsidies made limited headway in poverty-stricken Anglesey. Contemporaries spoke frequently of 'our poore countie'. There were only three great landowners of note and the Bulkeleys stood out by a mile. At the time of his death in 1621, Sir Richard Bulkeley III had an annual rental income of £4,300, the estate on Anglesey alone being valued at £2,500. Baron Hill, his new stately mansion built overlooking Beaumaris, symbolized the family's commanding status. Otherwise, only Plas Newydd and Bodeon could claim rentals exceeding £1,000. The remaining squires had to make do on modest sums; even the Theodores of Penmynydd were reduced to £230. Neither could much be expected of a fragile economy dependent on good harvests, cattle rearing and the export of dairy produce. A serious agricultural slump in 1622–3 sent rentals tumbling. Purveyance, the right of the king to purchase cattle at below the market price, caused particular resentment in Anglesey. When Charles I imposed the Ship Money tax, Anglesey's annual allocation of £448 in 1635–7, indicative of its poverty, was amongst the lowest in Wales. Yet the county responded more readily in this case, despite the problems of collection during the 'dead' winter period when the stagnant cattle trade restricted the flow of ready cash. For the sea, apart from providing a livelihood, was the island's first line of defence. Reluctant he may have been, but Robert Bulkeley of Dronwy paid his quota of 10 shillings towards 'ye King's ship' in October 1635.

Proximity to Ireland – but eight hours' sail given a fair wind – again proved too close for comfort. From Irish coastal bases the scourge of piracy reappeared. Two ships laden with goods worth £2,000 were intercepted off Anglesey in 1629; shortly after, a 'Turkish' ship (probably a Barbary Coast pirate) robbed a Holyhead packet boat. When the armed patrol vessel *Ninth Whelp* came into service during the 1630s shipping in the Irish Sea received some welcome protection. Religious anxieties compounded local nervousness. Regardless of their own tenuous attachment to the Church of England, islanders retained an obsessive fear of Catholic invasion involving Ireland and Spain. Demonstrably there was a need to shore up defences. Since 1609 Beaumaris castle had been 'utterlie decayed'. Though exempt from external military service, the local militia neglected their training. As put by the bishop of Bangor, a hundred men 'would overrun the Isle of Anglesey'. Even the merest rumour created panic – notably in the summer of 1625 when the 'Romishe recusant' Hugh Owen paid a flying visit. Only a few years earlier he had left his ancestral home at Gwenynog, Llanfflewin, to serve the Catholic Earl of Worcester. But with few Catholics to speak of, reports of a sinister papist conspiracy proved false. No more than fifteen Anglesey recusants were recorded in 1640, including William Brwynog, a direct descendant of the Catholic poet Siôn Brwynog.

But to what extent was the Church of England better placed? Hatred of Rome was a powerful stimulus to Protestant beliefs. On the other hand, crown interference in administrative matters contributed to the spiritual apathy that unquestionably existed. A visitation report in 1623 exposed some of the manifest shortcomings. Preaching was sadly neglected in several Anglesey parishes; no sermon had been heard at Penmon for some six years. The curate of Llanddeusant, a habitué of the local tavern, was often 'brawling and quarrelling' with his parishioners. He could not have felt out of place. Robert Bulkeley often tottered home to Dronwy after drinking 'a great deale'. Moral standards were generally low. If an anonymous account of the state of Anglesey in the early seventeenth century is to be believed, there were 300 alehouses on the island, turning people of all classes slave to the 'beastly vice of drunkenness'. Social occasions such as a *neithior* (wedding feast) would be a time for merriment with dancing and singing to traditional harp music. No matter his 'wanton minstrel' days, Robert ap Huw of Llanddeusant, grandson of Siôn Brwynog, eventually graduated as *pencerdd telyn* and became an accomplished harpist who played in the court of James I. An assortment of other popular recreations was on offer to break the monotonous hardships of everyday life; horse-racing, cock-fighting, football, tennis, dice and card games. Puritanism, with its moral absolutes, had yet to appear in Anglesey.

For all the criticism of the king's ministers and particular policies, Welsh MPs had stopped short of any outright challenge to the monarchy. Royalist sentiments nurtured in Tudor times remained strong. Not until the final levy of Ship Money in 1639 did Anglesey partially default – by a measly £11 4s – on the demand for £448. In political terms, the county displayed electoral apathy. When the House of Commons reconvened in 1640, after eleven years of personal rule by Charles I, its parliamentary representatives were drawn from the Caernarfonshire squirearchy regardless of their views. Charles Jones resumed his critical stance; John Bodvel, MP for the county, sided with the militant Protestants in opposition to the court. The savage Catholic rebellion in Ireland the following year caused terror in Anglesey, renewing fears of an invasion. As the crisis finally turned parliament against the king, events moved swiftly to the declaration of war. At the crunch, both John Griffith, who succeeded Charles Jones as MP for Beaumaris, and John Bodvel rallied to the royalist side. Even before the royal standard was raised in August 1642 the gentry of Anglesey, together with their counterparts in north Wales, declared their allegiance to the crown. Griffith left the Commons to join Charles I at Oxford; Bodvel followed later.

While the royalist gentry dictated events in Anglesey, parliamentary support was non-existent. Thomas Bulkeley of Baron Hill took the lead. As commissioner of array, supported by other leading squires, he began recruiting forces for the king. Ordinary islanders were dragged into the conflict whatever grasp they had of the constitutional issues at stake. Three regiments would be raised: one cavalry and two infantry, under Colonel Thomas Bulkeley, his son Colonel Richard Bulkeley, and Colonel Hugh Owen, Bodeon. But with Anglesey far from the sound of battle, only on English soil could they experience military action. Aged sixteen, Richard Bulkeley fought in the early campaign to defend Chester, the key to north Wales. Back home in Beaumaris the family pursued its own micro-civil war. A simmering feud between the Bulkeley and Cheadle families boiled over in 1643 when the upstart Sir Thomas Cheadle, as deputy constable of the castle and captain of the local militia, schemed to gain control of the town. (He had already married the widow of Sir Richard Bulkeley IV; later both were acquitted of conspiring to murder him by mixing poison with his tobacco). When that failed, Cheadle began to repair and fortify the old Norman castle at Aberlleiniog with *materiel* stolen from Beaumaris castle.

As the point of entry for royalist reinforcements and military equipment from Ireland, the port of Beaumaris assumed a vital importance from the outset. The castle's lamentable defences had to be strengthened in readiness. Prodded by Archbishop John Williams of Conwy, the King's principal organizer in north Wales, Thomas Bulkeley would ultimately spend £3,000 on repairs, aside from his other contributions. By the end of 1643 the cost of feeding the soldiers and ships' crews was placing a heavy burden on the island's creaking economy. For those gentry who were being continuously badgered to dip into their private purse, or provide mounds of salted beef, generosity had its bounds. Particularly after the disruption of the cattle trade, which prevented them from dealing at the London Smithfield market, the strain became intolerable. Soon the leading north Wales squires were petitioning the king, requesting a safe passage for their herds. Despite such difficulties, the financial demands never ceased. Anglesey's Ship Money assessments were nothing to what was demanded of the island now. At least Thomas Bulkeley's services were rewarded when he was created a viscount early in 1644. Further satisfaction came with the incarceration of Sir Thomas Cheadle – a defector to the parliamentary side – in the dungeon of Beaumaris castle.

Fears of a parliamentary offensive in the summer of 1644 added to the urgency in Gwynedd. Able-bodied men were mustered on Beaumaris Green as the gentry struggled to meet the island's monthly contributions to defence costs. The appointment of unpopular outsiders did little to raise morale: Sir John Mennes, the governor of north Wales stationed at

Beaumaris, bickered endlessly with the Anglesey gentry. Worse followed. Defeat at the battle of Naseby in June 1645 proved the final disaster for the royalist cause. Among the many Welsh prisoners was one David Parry, a low ranking officer from Anglesey. But more dramatic news overshadowed the fate of local combatants. Revelations that Charles I planned to seek help from Catholic forces in Ireland meant that Beaumaris would be the most likely landing spot. At one time it was thought that the king himself would make the town his winter headquarters. By now the Anglesey gentry were in a desperate mood. It was not so much petty squabbling that weakened the side from within, as the plotting early in 1646 to ditch the king and make terms with Thomas Mytton, the parliamentary commander, who had been authorized to offer £2,000 as a sweetener. Even Viscount Bulkeley was suspected of making peace overtures, but not his arrogant, swashbuckling son.

In any case, parliamentary troops under Mytton were soon being deployed in bringing north Wales to heel. One by one the Edwardian castles that served as royalist strongholds gave in. Whilst laying siege to Caernarfon, Mytton invited the Bulkeleys and other leading figures to surrender Beaumaris castle so as to avert 'the many miseries of a bloudy warre'. Support for the king had reached breaking point. Tired of hostilities, the depletion of their food stocks, and the interference with shipping, most of the beleaguered islanders were ready to compromise. A split in the ranks of the gentry delayed the cease-fire; Richard Bulkeley, who commanded the garrison at Beaumaris, was still in no mood to yield. The presence of two parliamentary warships, the *Rebecca* and the *Rupert*, anchored in the Menai Straits proved persuasive, and on 14 June 1646 Anglesey submitted to Mytton. As the first civil war ended, the gentry counted the cost of defeat. Parliament fixed Bulkeley's fine at £5,000, Cheadle's at £3,000; even more devastating was the sequestration of John Bodvel's estates, that included Caerfryn, Llaneugrad. Instead of contributing to royalist coffers, payments were henceforth handed to parliamentary tax collectors; all of which added to the undercurrent of discontent. Only one squire of note openly supported the victors: Richard Owen Theodore of Penmynydd, who helped raise money for the upkeep of parliamentary troops.

The second civil war in Wales in 1648 was virtually over before the malcontent elements on Anglesey showed their hand. Urged on this time by Lord Byron, stalwart royalists became involved in a planned counter-offensive that stirred north Wales. Heading the Anglesey insurrection were the indomitable Bulkeleys. Owen of Bodeon, Meyrick, Bodvel and other grandees also appended their signatures to a high-flown manifesto declaring for the king (dated 14 July) which was penned by Viscount Bulkeley's chaplain and Robert Morgan, the rector of Llanddyfnan. Contingents from many other counties joined in. To oppose them, parliament dispatched 1,500 cavalry and infantry under Mytton. Major Richard Cheadle, Sir Thomas Cheadle's son, arranged for an armada of fifty to sixty small boats to ferry them to Cadnant. On 1 October, below Red Hill on the outskirts of Beaumaris, the last battle on Anglesey soil was fought. In reality a chaotic, one-sided skirmish, it took less than three hours for the well-disciplined professional troops to crush a larger but mainly rag-tag force. Both sides lost between twenty and forty soldiers, but nearly 400 royalists were taken prisoner. As Richard Bulkeley took refuge in the castle, the officer commanded to guard the church fled leaving his men locked inside. Mytton entered Beaumaris without resistance. Given its condition, the castle could not withstand a siege, and so on the following day the second surrender of Anglesey was signed.

Fortunately, the island had again been spared the trauma and devastation of a prolonged struggle, if not the financial cost. As part of the articles of submission the inhabitants agreed to pay immediately £7,000 towards defraying the wages of the parliamentary troops mobilized for the expedition. Added to which was the fine of £9,000 in 1649. Reflecting the seriousness of Anglesey's 'delinquency', this quota far exceeded the penalty imposed on other north Wales counties. As prime instigators the Baron Hill family, who forked out £1,000, paid the heaviest price. Knowledge that Major Richard Cheadle had received £2,000 out of the fine for his services must have poured salt into unhealed wounds. Colonel Richard Bulkeley, meanwhile, fled to mainland Europe where he spent a few months in exile. Shortly after returning the Bulkeley-Cheadle vendetta ended in a violent showdown. A chance encounter on Traeth Lafan in February 1650 escalated into the duel that saw Richard Bulkeley run through by a rapier; deemed to be a murderer, Richard Cheadle was subsequently hanged at Conwy.

As conquered territory, Anglesey was placed under military rule. For a while Colonel John Jones (who signed Charles I's death warrant) served as constable of Beaumaris castle. It was garrisoned until the late 1650s and then partially dismantled, probably deliberately to prevent any further military use. Mytton remained in charge of the county, running a humane regime as the principal gentry withdrew to the fringes. By contrast to the rest of north Wales the one-time royalists here were less pliable. Such was the depth of their loyalty to the crown that only a handful of sympathetic small fry from the lower social ranks could be found to serve parliamentary interests on the Anglesey County Committee set up in May 1649 to govern the island. It was later brought up to strength with additional army personnel from outside. In due course, members of the minor gentry found a place in local administration, followed by the old established families (signatories of the 1648 manifesto) who finally thought it expedient to reassert their authority on home ground. When Robert Bulkeley, the future second viscount, re-entered public life as both sheriff and county committee member, it must have seemed like the return of old times. Parliamentary representation, however, would be mainly the privilege of Caernarfonshire men for the remainder of the interregnum.

Into this new political environment came the religious enthusiasts, Puritans determined to shed light in 'dark corners' and 'purify' the church of Catholic ways. Reports on the state of religion at the beginning of the century had signalled the island's spiritual impoverishment. Untouched by pre-war Puritanism, it remained the blackest of dark places. Yet one of the most zealous Puritan apostles, Vavasor Powell, had good reason to remember his brief visit to Anglesey in 1648; as 'military preacher' on horseback he suffered a slight wound during the battle of Red Hill. Only five Puritan ministers, of dubious quality, were at work in the county at the end of the decade. Oliver Cromwell's victory in the civil war presented fresh opportunities, and under the Act for the Better Propagation and Preaching of the Gospel in Wales (1650) seventy-one Commissioners were appointed to lead the crusade. Their task was to examine and weed out unsatisfactory clergy. A body of twenty-five Approvers then selected suitable 'godly' men to take their place, funded by appropriated church revenues. Just two Commissioners were connected with Anglesey: Captain Hugh Courtney, deputy to Mytton at Beaumaris, and Major Thomas Swift, in charge of postal communications at Holyhead. Being military men they had to involve themselves not only with Puritan indoctrination, but also guard against a second royalist insurrection in Anglesey.

Meeting at Beaumaris in September 1650, a panel of Commissioners purposefully set to work, and as a result eleven Anglesey clergymen were ejected from their livings, mainly for pluralism. Others continued on condition that they served only one parish. Remarkably, among them was Robert Morgan of Llanddyfnan, a king's man, who had helped to draw up the royalist manifesto of 1648 (and who survived to become the bishop of Bangor). In many cases, poverty or the ability to preach secured their survival. Replacing ejected ministers with new blood was another matter. Llaneugrad remained unoccupied for eight years. As it proved impossible to fill the churches left vacant, itinerant preachers were employed. William Fowler, a rare example, received £25 for officiating at Beaumaris for eighteen weeks in 1650–1. Being a parliamentary garrison, the town had the makings of a useful Puritan springboard. Yet an ill-assorted collection of lay preachers that included illiterates and a 'nonsensical blacksmith' named Benjamin were hardly likely to garner converts. They certainly failed to convince a sceptical gentry class, let alone a monoglot populace unmoved by English sermons.

Education was an additional concern for the Commissioners. Alongside preaching, attention focused on the provision of schooling with a strong Puritan bias in order to remove 'ignorance and prophaneness'. Open to all classes they offered a free education mainly through the medium of English. Of the sixty-three schools established in Wales, only one was sited in Anglesey – at Amlwch, where the schoolmaster received a salary of £20 a year. The parish had evidently become a pocket of Puritanism. Beaumaris grammar school continued to function as before, though doubtlessly under close Puritan supervision.

After three years, the 1650 Act lapsed and a London-based body of Triers replaced the Commissioners. Abandoning the system of itinerant preachers they licensed permanently settled ministers that had been issued with a testimonial. Between 1654 and 1659 seventeen approved ministers were sanctioned for evangelical work in Anglesey. But an outstanding candidate such as Hugh Humphreys, a 'good and frequent preacher' at Amlwch, was an exception. Most were obscure opportunists or nonentities who could not be relied upon to uphold Puritan standards. The upshot was that countless churches were again left without ministers. Lacking sufficient manpower, the crusade to puritanize the land ended in conspicuous failure. Other dissenting sects fared worse. The Quaker leader, George Fox, on a missionary tour of Wales in 1657, visited Beaumaris with John ap John (who may have served there previously as a military chaplain). They were to receive an 'unchristian' reception; John ap John suffered a short imprisonment and Fox faced a similar fate should he venture into the streets to preach. After such hostility it was little wonder that the Quakers failed to win converts. Neither did the Baptists or Independents have any adherents in the county.

Better by far was the outcome of other challenges that arose during Cromwell's Protectorate. In 1655 an abortive royalist rising implicated two Anglesey men. Understandably, the Bulkeleys and most leading gentry families held aloof from the ambitious plot to seize a number of north Wales castles, including Beaumaris, in the name of the exiled Charles II. Captain Nicholas Bagnall of Plas Newydd and his cousin Nicholas Bayly, the chief local conspirators, could count themselves fortunate to escape with a pardon given by Cromwell himself. Attention also had to be given to coastal defence during the war with the Dutch. More patrol vessels were built and a convoy system introduced to safeguard shipping and trade in the Irish Sea.

Occasionally, pirates slipped through the protective naval cordon; two ships were plundered near Holyhead in 1656 and Major Thomas Swift was obliged to pay £50 to redeem the vessels. Right up to the end of the Protectorate the army, too, maintained a state of alertness, stocking up ammunition at Beaumaris and Holyhead. Later, troop-ships ferried the forces of William III to subjugate the Catholics in Ireland. Piracy would soon be eliminated, but French privateers harassed ships off the Anglesey coast well into the next century.

Once the Church of England regained its ascendancy following the welcome restoration of the monarchy in 1660, Puritan clergymen were sacked from their livings. These included four Puritan ministers installed by the Triers in Anglesey. Lukewarm 'trimmers' who had played along with Puritanism expediently turned conformists very quickly. Vestiges of Puritanism, sure enough, could be detected among the military; soldiers in the Holyhead garrison were reported to have 'profaned God's house'. Overall, few counties proved as loyal to the crown and the Established Church as Anglesey. A small step towards religious toleration came with the Declaration of Indulgence (1672), when dissenting ministers were granted licenses to preach in private meeting houses. Not a single licence was applied for in Anglesey. Further confirmation of out- and-out rejection came with the (admittedly crude) Religious Census of 1676. The whole island was overwhelmingly Anglican. Only five Puritan dissenters were noted: two in both Llaneugrad and Penmynydd and one at Llanffinan; but significantly, none at Beaumaris or Amlwch. Barely did they outnumber the lone Catholics at Llanbeulan and Llanddona. All the evidence therefore is that Puritanism had failed utterly in Anglesey, making impossible any great religious change for some time yet.

Restoration in the case of Anglesey meant that the county's first family was reinstated high on its political pedestal. Various fines had made a substantial dent in the Bulkeley finances but at least their great estate remained intact to regenerate wealth. Having weathered the republican storm, various members of the Baron Hill clan or their nominees would monopolize both the county and borough seat until the end of the century. Whereas party labels – Tory and Whig – generally counted for little, they were by then arguably the most powerful family in Wales. Famously Tory and Jacobite (sympathetic to James II and his dynasty), the Bulkeleys also valued parliamentary representation in that it boosted family prestige and gave control over patronage. One of their nominees had already enhanced Wales's standing at Westminster. The careerist lawyer, Sir William Williams, son of a Llantrisant clergyman, was speaker of the House of Commons prior to being elected Tory MP for Beaumaris in 1689. Jealousy and resentment soon resulted in challenges to Bulkeley predominance. Though initially in the Bulkeley camp, Owen Hughes, an ambitious self-made attorney, successfully headed an anti-Baron Hill faction. As mayor of Newborough he reasserted the ancient town's electoral claims, organizing a block vote of burgesses to win the borough seat without a contest and to sit as Whig MP for three years between 1698 and 1701. Besides showing political nous, Hughes's Midas touch in various property deals earned him the sobriquet 'Yr Arian Mawr' (Moneybags).

A further threat to the Bulkeley hegemony came early in the eighteenth century, again from the Whig element on the western side of the island.

Through inheritance, marriage and purchase the Bodorgan landed estate grew commensurately with the political ambitions of the Meyrick family. Owen Meyrick was the same age as Richard Bulkeley, the fourth viscount; both were to accumulate public offices, and their intensely personal rivalry dominated Anglesey politics for two decades. Widely regarded as a haughty, unpleasant bully, Bulkeley's notoriously Jacobite views further antagonized his Whig opponents. At the county election of 1705 Meyrick dropped out of the running when a preliminary canvass of votes showed Bulkeley in the lead. Open voting bound tenants to their landlord, and encouraged the 'bribery' of independent forty-shilling freeholders. Rival candidates would pay for the transport, lodgings and meals of supporters at the shire town of Beaumaris – the total electorate was little more than 350 – for the duration of the poll. With a partisan sheriff as returning officer in 1708, Meyrick felt he had the edge. Nonetheless, in this first contested election in the constituency Bulkeley carried the day by 167 votes to 152. Despite a memorial to parliament accusing Viscount Bulkeley of a host of sins, including the manslaughter of a local ferryman when worse for wear, he increased his majority to over 100 at the 1710 election. A Bulkeley nominee also successfully withstood the Whig attack in the borough, headed by Sir Arthur Owen of Orielton, owner of the Bodeon estate. Ominously, the House of Commons ruled that Newborough burgesses had no right to vote.

By the end of the seventeenth century wider divisions within Anglesey society meant distinctly separate classes. Pronounced economic, political and cultural differences distinguished the great county families from the lesser squires, tenant farmers, freeholders and landless labourers. The Bulkeleys, typically, had far more in common with Englishmen of similar status across the border. Sir Richard Bulkeley III, 'always a great stock of ready money lying in his chest', had an array of business and maritime interests and was a shareholder in the Virginia Company of London. Robert, son of the first viscount, married the daughter of a rich London merchant. To augment the income from their estates the gentry had to be business-minded, or else risk their social standing. Maritime trade with Liverpool, Chester and Dublin flourished as the demand for agricultural produce and fish increased. Anglesey ships still carried Caernarfonshire slate; the pre-1690 vessel wrecked at Pwllfanog contained a cargo of 48,000 slates. Traditional imports included salt, coal and household goods. Though Beaumaris possessed a natural harbour its trade and commerce were in temporary decline. The postal service and passenger traffic raised Holyhead's status so that by 1670 its population of 870 surpassed that of Beaumaris with 710. Sometimes the port of Holyhead contained three or four sailing packets ready for the Irish Sea crossing.

Financial limitations were no bar to the social ambitions of the lesser squires, who made willing sacrifices to secure the advantages of education. If Oxford, Cambridge or the English public schools were beyond reach, they could always send their sons to the grammar school at either Beaumaris or Bangor, or one of the local private academies kept by graduate clergymen in Anglesey. He may not have studied at university, but John Griffith, the royalist squire-poet of Plas Llanddyfnan, proved equally fluent in Welsh, English and Latin. Advancement, invariably, was defined as success in connection with the church, the professions or the business world. Some local boys who made good endeavoured to benefit their native community with benevolent deeds by which they would be remembered. Lewis Owen of Twickenham, his family roots in Penmynydd, left land for the annual maintenance of two pupils at Beaumaris grammar school. Others bequeathed money towards apprenticing poor children. Owen Lloyd of Penrhosllugwy and London stipulated in his will (1665) that at least one boy should serve his apprenticeship in London. Such opportunities were rare. Low literacy levels existed in most parishes; the only educated commoner in Llanfihangel Tre'r-beirdd in the 1680s was Siôn Edward, a cooper, and it was he who taught local youths to read.

Agriculture, of course, continued to be the principal occupation. Scattered strips and open fields were still prevalent in the early seventeenth century, with only a gradual movement towards enclosures. Cattle rearing began to eclipse the growing of corn. Contemporary wills often contain a significant inventory of cows; Owen Holland of Berw left a stock of cattle worth £164 10s in 1656, over one-third of the value of his personal estate. For the majority of inhabitants, activities during the farming year dictated the pace and quality of life, not forgetting the contribution of skilled craftsmen – blacksmiths, carpenters, coopers, tanners, cobblers, tailors – who serviced the rural economy. Those at the lowest end of society had barely sufficient to survive. What chiefly characterized the *gwerin* (common people) was the chronic poverty and low expectation of life. Yet, extraordinary cases of longevity have been recorded. Hugh ap John of Penrhosllugwy reached ninety a few months before an epidemic struck the parish during 1623–4, leading to a sudden upsurge in the death rate when fifty-nine perished. There also existed a substantial underclass. As the most tragic reflection of this, one account (*c.*1620) spoke of 'heaps and troops' of 'beggars, rogues, vagabonds and idlers' who menacingly roamed the island. Half of the beggars were 'thieves and stealers' who filched food and clothing. Hardship forced the destitute into crime. Marrie Owen had ventured far from her parish of Llanfair-yng-Nghornwy to steal a hat at Caernarfon in 1638.

On top of a multitude of local government duties, justices of the peace struggled to uphold law and order by imposing punishments. The

Anglesey Quarter Sessions dealt with the less serious crimes, and from 1614 they were held in the court-house built at Beaumaris. Under the Elizabethan Poor Law, JPs also administered poor relief. One way of tackling the problem of vagrancy was to provide work at a House of Correction, but the establishment apparently opened in the county in 1631 failed to outlast the civil war. Early displays of social conscience ensured that some of Anglesey's poor benefited from charitable action. In addition to the grammar school, David Hughes endowed the alms-houses erected outside Beaumaris in 1613. Four years later, Lewis Rogers of Penmynydd bequeathed £1,000 so that alms-houses could be erected in the parish for ten poor men aged over fifty – though two women were later admitted to nurse the sick. Both charities enforced strict disciplinary rules; those guilty of drunkenness, swearing or failure to attend the parish church on Sunday received a fine, and persistent offenders were expelled. Similar acts of philanthropy saw paupers in various parishes being supplied with clothing and small doles of money or food. In 1670 William Wynne provided for six loaves to be distributed to the poor of Llangoed each Sunday. As a special reminder of his kind-heartedness six white coats bearing the initials W W were presented to indigent parishioners on Christmas day.

A revived church conducting services in the Welsh language strengthened popular support for Anglicanism. Dr Michael Roberts of Llanffinan, the controversial Principal of Jesus College, Oxford, had earlier edited *y Beibl Bach*, the popular version of the Welsh Bible in 1630. Increasing concern for the spiritual welfare of the illiterate *gwerin* during the post-Restoration period found philanthropic expression with the provision of Bibles and successive education initiatives by voluntary organizations. Anglicans and moderate Puritans who combined to form the Welsh Trust in 1674 distributed free copies of the Bible and other devotional works, and opened charity schools. By the following year Anglesey had one such school at Beaumaris, where forty-eight of the poorest children learnt to read and write under the supervision of the rector and churchwarden. Beaumaris grammar school continued to provide a strictly classical education for boys; a catalogue of its library books lists volumes on grammar and rhetoric, Latin, Greek and Hebrew dictionaries, and a range of classical authors. When the Welsh Trust published another report in 1678 there was no mention of a school on Anglesey. From the outset education had been conducted entirely in English, a failure that the solely Anglican body, the Society for the Promotion of Christian Knowledge (SPCK), founded in 1699, would address. Dr John Jones of Plas Gwyn, Pentraeth, Dean of Bangor and chief promoter of the SPCK in north Wales, had already established schools in a private capacity and was familiar with the basic problems confronting 'ye poorer sort'.

IV

The Eighteenth Century

For all the substance and style associated with the gentry during their 'golden age', the eighteenth century was also a time when the long neglected *gwerin* received considered attention. Very much forgotten in history, this growing class would benefit especially from the interlocking educational and religious movements. Natural growth had brought the population of Anglesey to roughly 22,800 in 1700, increasing to 26,900 by 1750. Most were still engaged in agriculture, either as small tenant farmers or rural labourers. In the course of the second half of the century industrialization made a striking impact in the northeast of the island. Activities associated with the Parys Mountain copper mines radically changed the occupation structure and social fabric around Amlwch. By the 1780s the industrial workforce far exceeded the number in the locality who toiled on the land. This one factor largely accounted for the increase of 25.7 per cent in the population between 1750 and 1801, when the first official census recorded 33,806. Next to Flintshire, Anglesey had become the most densely peopled county in Wales. The vast majority remained monoglot Welsh speakers, with the small market centres of Llannerch-y-medd, Aberffraw and Newborough as thoroughly Welsh as the 'pretty little village' of Llangefni. Only in the relatively larger towns of Beaumaris, Holyhead and Amlwch were there significant pockets of English influence.

Everywhere the poverty was acute. Most people lived a wretched existence perilously close to subsistence level. Very little separated the small farmers from the unskilled craftsmen and ordinary labourers. In mid-century the average daily wage for craftsmen was one shilling; labourers were paid less than half that amount. By the 1790s agricultural workers in Anglesey received eleven pence a day, one of the lowest rates in Wales; except for those in the neighbourhood of Parys Mountain where competitive industrial wages boosted levels to as much as sixteen pence. But there was a higher price to pay when noxious mining operations polluted acres of local farmland, turning them into barren desert. Women in employment normally produced domestic articles; in 1736 Ann Parry knitted stockings at the established daily rate of one penny. They, too, would find better wages in the copper industry. Houses were crudely built, their unhygienic condition open to disease. Fragile structures often succumbed to the elements; at one time a family of squatters apparently sought shelter within Prysaeddfed burial chamber! For food, the poor of Anglesey existed chiefly on a diet of barley bread, porridge and stews, occasionally supplemented by dairy produce and herrings. Unlike the previous century there were no great hordes of beggars to arouse fear. Instances of voluntary charity, organized by the church or parish, relieved hardship and suffering within the community – for instance, the public collection in 1738 'for a man of Rhosbeirio that lost all he had by fire'. Poor rates were first levied in Anglesey from about 1760. By the end of the century an average of £1,000 a year was spent on poor relief in the parish of Amlwch. To discourage claimants, paupers had to display a large letter P blazoned on their clothing.

Even in untroubled years begging from door to door was commonplace. As Dean John Jones lamented, destitute children found it difficult to attend school regularly because they had to 'go ever and anon to beg for victuals'. This problem was compounded at harvest time when they were withdrawn to work in the fields. A dedicated churchman, full of compassion, Dean Jones propagated SPCK enterprise in education and publishing. Between 1714 and 1719 he personally set up schools at Llangeinwen, Beaumaris, Llanfihangel Ysgeifiog, Pentraeth, Rhoscolyn and Llandegfan. Poor children were instructed to read the Bible through the medium of Welsh, as well as the rudiments of writing and arithmetic. On his death in 1727 specific bequests enabled five Anglesey schools to continue, money also being provided for books and clothing. The building erected at Llanfihangel Ysgeifiog continues to bear the name *ysgoldy* (schoolroom). Altogether, ten endowed charity schools were to be founded by the middle of the century, with Sir Arthur Owen (Aberffraw, 1735) and Dr Edward Wynne (Holyhead, 1748) as the most eminent benefactors. Under Church of England control, they however only created places for a restricted number of poor children – totalling no more than eighty – in a dozen or so parishes. Adopting English as the medium of instruction in some schools would also prove self-defeating.

On behalf of the SPCK, Dean Jones also worked assiduously to provide religious tracts and a new edition of the Welsh Bible. After his death a small group of local Anglican clergy, principally Thomas Ellis, Holyhead, and James Vincent, Beaumaris, replicated his concern for the welfare of poor parishioners. They arranged for the payment, shipment and distribution of further editions of the Bible and devotional literature. Parcels sent from London came by waggon via Chester or by ship to Holyhead, Beaumaris or Caernarfon. Their arrival evidently caused great excitement locally; it was said that 'the poor almost scratched Mr Ellis' eyes out' to obtain a free copy of the Bible. Between 1754 and 1758 a total of 820 Welsh Bibles and 614 New Testaments were distributed in Anglesey. Education provided the main impetus. No more SPCK schools would be established, but the circulating schools movement had already created a new generation of readers.

Griffith Jones, Llanddowror, had purposely adapted his educational vision for the salvation of souls to the prevailing conditions in Wales. From the 1730s an expanding network of circulating schools achieved unprecedented literacy levels by holding sessions for three to four months in the less busy agricultural period or during the evenings. Both children and adults were taught to read the Bible and catechism in Welsh by itinerant teachers in farmhouses or more usually the parish church under the supervision of the local clergyman. Once the schools had established a foothold in Anglesey in 1746 they soon dotted the island. Within a year there were eleven schools attended by 522 scholars. Initial doubts evaporated, and from that time hundreds were being instructed annually, many learning to read perfectly within three months. Eager to spread the benefits of education among the poor, the clergy repeatedly requested that the session be extended to another quarter. Those who personally examined scholars in the catechism on Sundays warmly acknowledged the extraordinary success of the schools. In letters to the *Welch Piety*, the annual report of the movement, time and again they remarked on the transformation in the attitude of their parishioners. Thomas Ellis testified to the 'great advancement of Christian knowledge' in the parish of Holyhead, where previously children grew up 'in a manner wild for want of schooling'.

In 1761, the year of Griffith Jones's death, Anglesey had thirty schools and 1,190 scholars. After a barren interlude the movement soon flourished again under Madam Bridget Bevan. Itinerant teachers, including two schoolmistresses, were undertaking their duties in the county. Robert Jones had 106 scholars under his tuition by day at Llangeinwen in April 1771, and 77 at night. According to the last extant report (1777) there were eighteen schools attended by 1,088 scholars. But two years later, when Madam Bevan herself died, the movement collapsed. There is no denying that the circulating schools had a narrow educational design – only reading was taught – yet the magnitude of what they achieved in numerical, social and religious terms has to be appreciated. Over a period of some thirty years between 1746 and 1777 in Anglesey alone 435 schools (or sessions) were held, covering almost all parishes, and attended by over 20,000 scholars, though the number attending more than one session led to duplication. Nothing previously could compare in scale. What is more, a literate *gwerin*, displaying a 'great veneration for Religion and Godliness', was far more likely to respond to the 'enthusiasm' of evangelical preachers. The ground had been well prepared for the Methodist religious revival.

Nonconformist writers eager to magnify their triumphs have often discoloured the religious condition of the people prior to the Methodist revival. Blame for immorality, social degradation, ignorance and superstition was laid firmly at the door of the Established Church. As the most extreme example, *Methodistiaeth Môn* (1888) concluded that the church had become more of a 'synagogue to Satan'. Whatever the true scale of social failings, it is impossible to accept that spiritual guidance had sunk this low. Hard as life was for the common people, certain occasions continued to be enjoyed to the full, and accounts of traditional customs show little change. From time immemorial, family celebrations, *gwylmabsantau* (saints' days) and other festivals combined boisterous entertainment and communal ale drinking, usually home-brewed. Football matches between neighbouring parishes became fiercely fought battles – 'more like dogs fighting for a bone' – lasting up to four hours. Cock-fighting, offering silver spoons as prizes, generated some keen side betting. *Anterliwtiau* (interludes) containing lewd satire found an appreciative audience. All were to be castigated by the Methodists as moral vices that the Established Church had too readily tolerated. Yet the time of the worst excesses was past; at any rate, no longer could anyone claim to gulp down a 'large Beddgelert pint' (equivalent to four pints) in one breath!

Anglesey had remained thoroughly loyal to the Established Church since the rejection of Puritanism and dissent. An official return in 1704–5 noted the presence of only one 'Papist' on the island. Religious life was subsequently dependent upon the character and influence of Anglican clergymen. Almost all of the clergy in the county by mid-century were Anglesey men, generally learned and devout, who lived in the parish. By all accounts, many took great care to raise the spiritual condition of parishioners by discharging their duties faithfully. Those clergymen closely associated with the outstanding success of the circulating schools movement accomplished some of the most important pastoral work. A 'great congregation' often attended services held by the Revd Richard Bulkeley at Llanfechell. Under a conscientious clergyman the parish church continued to be the hub of community life and villagers could be encouraged to show moderation or reform their ways. Having put an end to superstitious wakes at Holyhead, Thomas Ellis did his utmost to get ordinary people to listen to 'Holy Scripture instead of dirty interludes'. Before long he was able to draw a congregation of 500 to the Easter communion.

Other features of church life did have an adverse effect, and very often only the negative aspects are remembered. The failures of successive alien bishops in the diocese of Bangor brought a decline in standards. Though church services were usually conducted in the Welsh language, linguistic sensibilities could be flouted. Appointing a monoglot Englishman like Dr Thomas Bowles to be rector of Trefdraeth and

Llangwyfan in 1766, when only five of the 500 parishioners could follow an English service, understandably caused great controversy. When the matter came before the principal ecclesiastical court, Bowles, in keeping with his unsavoury character, presented fabricated evidence, but though admonished for his behaviour he was not deprived of the living. All this added to the sourness of Goronwy Owen's earlier failure to secure a permanent church appointment in Anglesey. Seldom has such a literary talent been spurned to the loss of his native county. Then again, instances of pluralism and non-residence were tolerated, while the poor quality of the curates who stood in could be ascribed to their miserable remuneration. Crucially, what evidence we have strongly suggests a widespread failure to preach sermons, or when they were delivered, easily understood sermons that would appeal directly to ordinary people. Even the diligent rector of Llanfechell was sometimes guilty of 'very incoherent unintelligible bombast'.

Preaching: intense, impassioned and challenging would be the key to Methodist success. Contrasted to what appeared as a bland outdated institution, the Methodist movement offered something new. Though officially within the Established Church, Methodist preachers placed strong emphasis on individual repentance. Thus the joy of spiritual salvation from sin was laden with personal emotion. Converts subsequently gathered together in the *seiat* (society), which, along with a separate organizational structure based on the monthly meeting and association, gave Methodism its own distinctive character. Dissenting minorities were already separate; in what had been previously barren territory, the Quakers registered meeting places at Holyhead, Llangefni and Beaumaris as early as 1733. Well before the arrival of the circulating schools, Methodist and Independent emissaries from south Wales began open-air preaching in Anglesey. While the very beginnings are difficult to trace, it appears that Richard William Dafydd, a native of Cardiganshire, was the first Methodist exhorter to visit the island around 1740, when he preached in the parish of Llanfechell. Two years later, two Independent pioneers were beginning their mission: William Prichard, who moved from Caernarfonshire to Penmynydd, and Jenkin Morgan of Glamorgan, one of Griffith Jones's schoolmasters.

Faced with enmity and persecution they made only desultory progress. Many of the early exhorters would suffer at the hands of armed hostile crowds. Jenkin Morgan, who worked closely with the Methodists for a time, caused a stir with his preaching and was viciously assaulted by a riotous mob at Penmynydd. But this did not deter William Prichard from having Minffordd cottage in the same parish licensed as a meeting house for 'Protestant Dissenters to worship' in 1743. According to the Revd Thomas Ellis's own account, the Methodists were making headway in the centre of the island. Reporting on the rapid increase in activity by 1745, William Morris depicted their zeal as 'religiously mad'. Before long, major Methodist leaders such as Peter Williams, Daniel Rowland and William Williams made missionary tours. On the second of his five short visits, in October 1748, Howel Harris claimed to have preached to a crowd of 2,000 on Pen-y-groes common outside Llangefni. Only the English Methodist, John Wesley, bemoaned the linguistic barrier; when he preached in Anglesey his sermons had to be translated into Welsh. Through evangelization in private houses, streets, and open fields converts were won by the dozen. Drawn, at first, mainly from the ranks of the farmers, smallholders and craftsmen, they provided leadership based on the local society.

On his last journey to the island in 1751 Howel Harris felt he was 'travelling in a conquered country'. Such optimism could not be substantiated. For much of the century Methodist penetration into Anglesey was patchy, piecemeal and local in character. There were only eight societies in existence by the time the first Methodist chapel was built at Llangristiolus in 1764. Yet their exact status had already presented difficulties for Anglican clergymen. Methodists maintained an autonomous stance within the Established Church, while remaining apart from the dissenting sects. And because the circulating schools had been closely identified with Methodism, most clergy were at first reluctant to involve themselves. Thomas Ellis saw them as 'nests of schism'. Once such fears were allayed, they went on to give wholehearted support; most likely the circulating schools offered a bulwark against dissent. In teaching the catechism to the children of the poor and their parents Anglican clergymen hoped to encourage attendance at the parish church.

The battle for the religious allegiance of the *gwerin* was long fought out. Indeed, persuading ordinary people to amend their worldly ways presented a far greater challenge. Methodist exhorters such as Robert Jones, Rhos-lan, continued to infiltrate the circulating schools, although his stay at Brynsiencyn in 1770 was cut short by the local clergyman. Shortly after the demise of the movement, Church visitation returns reported the presence of a new wave of itinerant evangelists, variously described as 'strangers', 'vagrants' or 'field preachers' from south Wales. They would supplement local exhorters like Richard Jones, Newborough, who served the Methodist cause for over forty years prior to his death in 1788. Inexorably, both the Methodists and principal dissenting sects were at last making significant progress. Among a handful of Independent chapels Rhos-meirch (erected 1748–9) stood supreme; drawing adherents from a wide area it claimed a membership of 800 by 1772. Baptist missionaries to Anglesey in 1776 preached to large congregations, and despite the limited number of baptisms, they were able to gather sufficient followers to build their first chapel, Ebeneser (Cildwrn) on the outskirts of Llangefni, in 1781.

Visitation returns in 1788 recorded how the Methodists, Independents and Baptists were rapidly gaining ground. At Llanfwrog, it was ruefully acknowledged that the Methodist preacher had 'many followers' from the Established Church. A number of clergymen complained that parents no longer sent their children to be catechized. The end of the circulating schools movement in 1779 meant there were few Anglican schools to win new converts. The initiative, crucially, passed to the Methodists. Adopting the Sunday schools as early as 1786 – first held, it is claimed, by the local blacksmith at Llanfwrog – they were able to cater for the religious education of both young and old. In 1798 Thomas Charles reported the presence of twenty Sunday schools and 1,200 scholars in Anglesey, with 'new ones rising every week'. Methodist society members could now be numbered in hundreds, organized and regulated by the monthly meetings. Land was being acquired, and money raised by the societies, to erect more chapels; £47 was borrowed for the building of the chapels at Caergeiliog and Newborough; so that by the end of the century there were at least twenty-four Methodist chapels in Anglesey. Concerned Anglican clergy noted the scale of their success as numbers increased 'annually' and even 'daily to an increased pitch'. At Llanfair Pwllgwyngyll and Llandysilio they had become 'the prevailing sect'. Methodists were clearly poised to gain the ascendancy once the final break with the Established Church came in 1811.

The spiritual fervour of the age added to the demand for Bibles and Welsh religious books. Various local printing ventures were contemplated. As early as 1732 Lewis Morris had proposed setting up a printing press at Llannerch-y-medd along with a free school, public library and bookshop where Bibles and prayer-books could be sold. This ambitious project failed to enthuse public support and was soon abandoned. John Rowland had better luck with his press at Bodedern, where between 1759 and 1761 a volume of hymns and two theological works were produced. About the same time, John Robert Lewis, a Methodist exhorter from Caernarfonshire, settled at Holyhead. Watchmaker, mathematician, astrologer, bookbinder, his talents were many-faceted; and as an author of some renown he published five collections of hymns as well as the first scriptural dictionary in Welsh. With farmers, tradesmen and craftsmen willing to subscribe in increasing numbers, more and more books were published. As literacy spread among the lower classes there was a growing reading public not only for religious tracts but also cheap popular publications, most notably the annual almanacs. John Robert Lewis is best remembered for launching the famous *Almanac Caergybi* (Holyhead Almanac) in 1761, and which continued in publication for almost two centuries until 1954.

Not even an enhanced religious awareness could overcome human flaws and basic needs. Circumstances forced individuals into crime. Despite instances of public charity, poor relief, and the presence of local constables, little could be done to prevent petty larceny, the most common offence, as the Anglesey Quarter Sessions records, available from 1768, show. Thefts of food, money, clothing and household utensils were recorded, and miscreants, men and women, usually punished by public flogging or branding. In 1784 one hapless felon was whipped at both Beaumaris and Amlwch markets. The House of Correction opened at Holyhead in 1741 – said to be no better than a pigsty – seems to have been intended chiefly for Irish 'vagabonds', whereas imprisonment in the county jail at Beaumaris (built a decade later) proved expensive. Transportation to the colonies offered a convenient solution. Found guilty of stealing a cloak and apron in 1773, Margaret Thomas of Llanbedrgoch was dispatched to America for seven years. Two prostitutes were publicly humiliated at Beaumaris in 1788 when placed on a ducking stool and immersed in the sea. Sheep stealing remained a capital offence as John Williams, a labourer, found to his cost. A murky reputation surrounded the treacherous Crigyll rocks near Rhosneigr where wrecked vessels were plundered by the infamous 'lladron creigiau Crigyll' (the robbers of Crigyll rocks). Purportedly lured by 'false lights', the sloop *Charming Jenny* became stranded after a violent storm in September 1773. Farm carts were used to make off with its cargo and the body of the captain's wife barbarously robbed of seventy guineas and a gold watch. Three local looters later appeared before the Shrewsbury assizes, one going to the gallows.

Smuggling had acquired a thicker gloss of legitimacy than stealing cargo from wrecks that lay providentially alongshore. High duties imposed on both luxuries (wine, brandy, tobacco) and everyday necessities (candles, tea, soap) fuelled a lucrative black market. With a 125-mile coastline to guard, the authorities on Anglesey had little effective control over illicit activities endorsed by the public. The coves near Amlwch and Moelfre were ideal places to land smuggled goods. Outwardly respectable figures such as the diarist William Bulkeley of Brynddu thought nothing of buying direct from the smugglers despite the fact that he was a Commissioner of Excise! In one of many such diary entries he celebrated a particular bargain on 21 September 1742: 'Paid a Flintshire smuggler that was come to Cemaes from the Isle of Man 25s for 5 gallons of French Brandy which I think is right good'. Collusion of this kind made a difficult task much harder for officials. Expressing his frustrations as a customs officer at Holyhead, William Morris resented how the island had become 'a den of runners, the gentry turned smugglers'. Again, in 1773 the vessel *Fox* was able to land contraband goods with impunity.

Travellers to Anglesey often commented on its 'barren' and 'ill-cultivated' aspect. Yet agriculture, though generally backward in that it incorporated long-standing features, had excellent potential. Most tenant farms were very small, and whereas no other county in north Wales was better suited for growing crops the emphasis still lay on pastoral farming – the rearing of cattle, sheep and pigs. Native black cattle were bred for dairying or sale at the fairs held in Aberffraw, Newborough and Porthaethwy. By the 1790s the thriving export trade reached an annual total estimated at almost 10,000 head. Large herds were forced to swim the Menai Straits at low water to follow well-defined drovers' routes. One noteworthy dealer, Thomas Lewis of Tre Feibion Meurig, amassed a fortune of £1,400 by the time of his death in 1736. But drovers could not always be taken on trust. Returning from Smithfield in 1765 John Owen of Llansadwrn falsely claimed to have been waylaid in Bedfordshire and robbed of £250. The *pandy* (fulling mill), some twenty-three in number, attested to a small-scale domestic woollen industry that struggled to keep up with local demand. Both Llangefni and Llannerch-y-medd were centres of activity. A coarse blue-coloured cloth became the speciality of Anglesey weavers, with a craftsman being paid 8 shillings in 1757 for weaving 34 yards of woollen cloth and 11 yards of flannel.

Fairs, local weekly markets and travelling pedlars supplied the essential foodstuffs, clothing and household goods. Well-to-do families could purchase luxury items directly from England. As expected, retail trade on the island was concentrated in the main towns, primarily Beaumaris, but small village stores were also established in country areas. Those propitiously located nearest the gentry mansions built up a lucrative business: the proprietor of the 'bazaar' at Llangadwaladr supplied flannel, candles, tea, sugar, tobacco, paper and ink to the Meyricks of Bodorgan. Full-time shopkeepers were few and far between; not until the nineteenth century did Anglesey's shopocracy find its place in the commercial sun.

Only a small proportion of the land was put under the plough, barley being the dominant bread grain along with a little wheat and oats. Windmills dotted the island, most of them built between 1730 and 1760. Melin Llynnon, Llanddeusant (reopened in working order in 1984) dated from 1775–6. Dependent on the vagaries of the weather, Anglesey normally produced enough corn for export. In 1770, 90,000 bushels left the island. Conversely, ruined harvests caused scarcity, leading to malnutrition and disease. Periodic outbreaks of influenza, typhus and smallpox always took a heavy toll. Following a particularly cold winter, the harvest of 1740 was one of the poorest in living memory, resulting in countless deaths. Inequality in the face of epidemics led one Anglesey clergyman to comment bluntly that it was 'the common sort that drop off'. But in 1742 even the well-respected apothecary, Dr Richard Evans of

Llannerch-y-medd, fell victim. Much to the alarm of the authorities, food shortages precipitated discontent among the lower classes and very little could be done to avert mounting social unrest. Hungry people acted collectively at times of famine to prevent the export of corn, or to plunder ships and storehouses. A posse had to be assembled to deal with a well-armed mob that stopped a shipload of corn from leaving the port of Beaumaris in 1728. A few years later the warehouses at Red Wharf Bay were robbed. Imports from England often saved the day, but in 1757–8 the situation was little short of a crisis. Food riots erupted again. A hungry crowd, 150 strong, marched from Beaumaris and Llannerch-y-medd in January 1757 stealing butter and cheese from a trader's house at Rhydbont on their way to Holyhead. An attempt to loot the corn storehouse in the town was thwarted only by armed militia. Similar violent disorder occurred throughout the following winter as several shiploads of corn, butter and cheese were ransacked by desperate, starving mobs.

Several enlightened landowners had already given the county a reputation for agrarian improvement. From as early as the 1640s some agriculturalists had successfully experimented with fertilizer using shell-sand. It enriched the land particularly around Red Wharf Bay and was followed by the use of lime in the 1660s. The antiquary Henry Rowlands, Plas Gwyn, Llanedwen, the vicar of Llanidan, in his book *Idea Agriculturae*, noted these developments. Written in 1704 but not published until 1764, it was essentially a record of local agricultural conditions and early experimentation. Another eminent Anglesey clergyman, Dr Edward Wynne, Bodewryd, had meantime introduced progressive husbandry on his 2,500-acre estate. As a practical farmer he pioneered the new methods he observed on border farms when chancellor of the diocese of Hereford. By adopting the six-year rotation, and applying a liberal use of sand as manure, Wynne was able to produce excellent field crops each year. He grew the first turnips on the island in 1714, long before Lord 'Turnip' Townshend popularized their use as animal winter feed in England. Wynne kept a large stock, including working oxen. No expense was spared in erecting or replacing farm outbuildings, raising new walls or digging ditches.

Despite the example shown by 'improving landlords', the new methods aroused only a limited interest. Most squires stuck obstinately to the old ways, placing a higher premium on rebuilding their mansions. Kay's *General View of the Agriculture of Anglesey* in 1794 observed that crop rotation was not widely used, neither had there been many attempts to grow turnips. Other contemporary writers criticized the unprofitable system in place with much of the land remaining uncultivated. All the same, a few enthusiastic gentry were again setting good standards. Agricultural reformers such as Owen Putland Meyrick of Bodorgan and Paul Panton of Plas Gwyn, Pentraeth, played a prominent role in the so-called Anglesey Druidical Society (founded in 1772) that encouraged farming improvements. Prizes were awarded for the growing of crops, hedging, ditching and draining. In 1795 five guineas was offered to the farmer who planted the greatest area with potatoes. Because the quantity grown in Anglesey was insufficient to meet local needs, they had to be imported from Ireland. Given the conservative attitude that prevailed, bolstered by custom, most of the agricultural advances gained only a slow acceptance. Progress often went hand in hand with the enclosure of land. Apart from the initial reclamation work at Cors Ddyga (Malltraeth Marsh), begun in 1788, widespread enclosures of common land did not take place until the following century.

Industrialization affected Anglesey very early when additional demand was created for two of its extractive commodities: coal and copper. Previous operations at Llanfihangel Ysgeifiog and Parys Mountain received a new lease of life. Those spirited gentry fortunate to own the land were not slow to venture their capital or seek outside business partners in the pursuit of more wealth. Though the Bayly family of Plas Newydd figured as prime movers in both enterprises, only the copper industry would respond fully to the profitable market. Once more, there was surface coal mining in the Pentre Berw area from the 1730s. Later, Sir Nicholas Bayly explored the possibility of combining local coal and clay to produce bricks. By 1753 his attention focussed on the new pit sunk at Penrhyn-mawr. Wary of the dangers from flooding, the miners raised objections to working there, only to be contemptuously branded by Bayly as 'the vermin who work underground'. When production eventually commenced in 1766, 75 tons of coal were raised during the month of April alone. Miners were housed locally and paid both in wages and in kind. Intermittent mining continued for the remainder of the century, but the thinness of the seams meant output was negligible and of no use to the island's copper industry. An official at Amlwch smelting works in 1817 dismissively described Anglesey coal as being 'half dirt and very wet'.

Renewed mining activity on Parys Mountain signalled Sir Nicholas Bayly's intention to exploit its potential mineral resources. Demand for copper was increasing, more especially as protective sheathing for the wooden hulls of naval warships. Expectations rose following work in 1761–2 by Alexander Fraser, a Scottish prospector in Bayly's employ, but were soon dashed by the hazard of floods. A business link with Roe and Co., Macclesfield, appeared hardly more successful until 1768, when miners guided by Jonathan Roose, a company foreman from Derbyshire, struck a rich vein of copper. Following this find Bayly became embroiled in a boundary dispute with Edward Hughes, another proprietor of land on Parys Mountain. Litigation brought Thomas Williams of Llanidan on the scene. First, as a resourceful lawyer, he unscrambled the complex rival claims, allowing the copper to be mined separately by two companies on opposite sides of the mountain. Then, he involved himself on the business side. The Parys Mine Company (1778) was run by Edward Hughes, Thomas Williams and John Dawes, a London banker. To replace Roe and Co. in 1785, Henry Bayly – Sir Nicholas Bayly's heir, who took the name of Paget before being created Earl of Uxbridge – set up the Mona Mine Company in partnership with Thomas Williams.

Popularly known in Anglesey as 'Twm Chwarae Teg' (Tom Fair Play), Williams emerged as a hard-nosed entrepreneur who provided unity of management and visionary enterprise. He participated in every aspect of mining, smelting and manufacture to gain overall control of the whole British copper industry. The resources of the Parys Mountain copper mines had allowed him to undercut prices and break the hold of Cornish mine-owners. In his day he won recognition as a leading businessman, the undisputed 'Copper King' who dictated trade dealings between 1787 and 1792, and whose companies were capitalized at £800,000. He not only dominated the naval copper market in Europe, advancing British maritime supremacy in the process, but developed world-wide trading links that also embraced the African slave market. At his death in 1802 his own personal fortune was said to be over half a million pounds. Though he can be counted among the great pioneering giants of the early industrial revolution, the name of Thomas Williams of Anglesey, sadly, has failed to attract the same historical lustre as that of Boulton, Wedgwood and Watt.

Copper extraction provided a grand spectacle for visiting painters, writers and scientists. While the Mona Mine Company sank shafts over 300 feet deep, the Parys Mine Company worked a vast open-cast area. Artists captured its dramatic scale and terrifying dangers: how miners were being suspended precariously from protruding platforms into a deep chasm to cut the ore. A workforce of approximately 1,500 was employed at the time of peak production in the 1780s and early 90s, when Parys Mountain accounted for over a third of the copper produced in Britain. Working an average twelve-hour day, wages ranged from 10 to 14 pence for labourers to 15 to 18 pence for skilled miners, masons and carpenters. Women (known as 'copper ladies') and children received 7 to 10 pence for breaking the ore into small pieces. To meet the large wage bill, the mining companies issued their own copper penny and halfpenny tokens as coinage – which remained legal tender until 1817. Miners had to purchase gunpowder, candles, ropes and tools from the company store, but the proprietors at least provided medical care and gave generous donations towards the alleviation of poverty. Farmers were contracted to cart the ore to local smelting houses (good quality coal had to be imported) and then to Amlwch Port for transportation to Lancashire and south Wales where further smelting was undertaken. This trade grew steadily so that between 1786 and 1789 over seventy ships operated, owned by the Amlwch Shipping Company as well as local people. Harbour facilities were subsequently improved to cater for larger vessels.

Greed, exploitation, despair and faith found expression. Mona Mine Company profits rose annually, reaching £16,905 by 1793. Such riches enabled the Bayly (later Paget) family to remodel their Plas Newydd mansion in castellated Gothic splendour at an outlay of at least £17,000. Amlwch, meantime, was transformed from an insignificant hamlet into a 'boom town' with a population approaching 5,000 – one of the largest urban centres in Wales. Working-class families were housed in small, poorly constructed, close-packed, insanitary hovels that contributed to the high infant mortality index. There were no fewer than 842 infant deaths during the last two decades of the century. Misery and degradation existed on a scale not previously experienced in Anglesey. For good reason, the local curate praised the circulating schools as the means 'to dispel the great darkness that overspreads this part of the world'. Methodism also made significant inroads. A chapel was founded in 1777 and soon most miners were reported to be Methodists. Because of the bishop's obstructive attitude the building of a new parish church had to be delayed until 1800, hence the local clergyman found his exertions 'totally inadequate towards checking the increase in Methodism'. One visitor remarked on Amlwch's unusually law-abiding atmosphere, which he attributed to Methodist influence. Yet the fashionably named Miners Arms was but one among sixty other alehouses in the town supplied by local breweries. Fear of crime and disorder was never absent; in 1788 it became necessary to form a society for the 'prosecution of felons'. Hell-fire preachers who railed against the wicked had little need to harp on the torments of everlasting damnation; Parys Mountain itself evoked a sulphurous vision of the inferno.

Poor communications continued to limit the island's accessibility. From building materials to Bibles, all goods had to be transported by sea. Fishing and coastal trade thrived, making it essential that local vessels and their crews were protected from Royal Navy press-gangs. As the centre of this trade, Beaumaris by the 1780s boasted more ships than all the other Welsh ports. Ferries still provided a regular link to the mainland. More and more travellers, however, preferred to bypass Beaumaris and take the direct route from Bangor. Concern about the dangers of Traeth Lafan prompted the postal authorities to demote Beaumaris in 1718 in favour of Bangor and the ferry crossing at Porthaethwy. Larger boats capable of transporting carriages were in service by the second half of the century. Abermenai ferry connected Anglesey to the market town of Caernarfon, but competition from both the Tal-y-foel and Moel-y-don ferries heralded a steady decline, that ended in closure during the 1830s. Like all sea crossings, danger lurked in the treacherous waters of the Menai Straits. Mainly as a result of single disasters over 250 people were to drown between 1664 and 1820. When seventy-nine perished with the sinking of the Abermenai ferry in 1664 many believed this to be divine retribution as the boat had been constructed of timber stolen from Llanddwyn church! In almost all cases the chief cause was reckless overloading on market or fair days, the majority of victims being Anglesey country folk. Islanders baptized Hugh Williams might have less to fear than most; legend has it that three men bearing this name emerged as the sole survivors of the catastrophes of 1664, 1785 and 1820.

If the Romans had failed to build a road in Anglesey, neither did succeeding generations. Only during the sixteenth century would each parish become responsible for the maintenance of roads and bridges. This requirement was widely neglected and failure usually resulted in financial penalties; in 1780 the inhabitants of the township of Llawr y Llan in Amlwch parish were fined a hefty £200. Considering its strategic importance, even the post road was no better than a dirt track suitable only for pedestrians and horsemen. With no signposts or milestones, wayfarers were often obliged to hire a reliable guide. From 1718 the post road ran directly from Porthaethwy to Penmynydd, and through Ceint, Bodffordd and Bodedern to Holyhead. By mid-century milestones were placed for the convenience of the light horse-drawn carriages now in vogue. Gwyndy, Llandrygan, built in 1758, became an important coaching inn acclaimed for its hospitality. It was here that the leading gentry, Bayly, Bulkeley and Panton, met in January 1760 to petition parliament for a turnpike-road. Trustees authorized to take over responsibility recouped their expenditure by charging tolls. Sanctioned by the Anglesey Turnpike Act of 1765, the 26-mile post road was generally widened and improved and toll-gates erected at Braint, Llangefni, Llanynghenedl and Holyhead. In October 1785 the first daily mail coach from London via Chester commenced service. Holyhead claimed three good inns for passengers thankful to reach the port after their 48-hour journey. Despite the increase in shipping no improvements were made to the harbour. The town's prospects however encouraged a growth in population that reached 2,000 by the close of the century.

These developments placed Anglesey well and truly on the map. Cartographers from the time of Lluyd (1573), Mercator (1595) and Speed (1610) had already produced atlases depicting the island, the latter adding a town plan of Beaumaris. As the first road atlas, Ogilby's *Britannia* in 1675 featured the London to Holyhead post route. Smaller atlases were published in the eighteenth century specifically for the traveller. By now an ever-growing stream of Irish gentry, government officials, gentlemen tourists, traders, drovers, religious evangelists, botanists, artists, pedlars and vagrants would journey across the Menai Straits. Writers, who made a tour through Anglesey, Defoe and Pennant among them, displayed an eye for detail. Not all the descriptions were flattering; some found the island 'dreary' and 'unpleasing'. Joseph Hucks in 1794 thought it 'one continued picture of desolation'. Discounting the fascination with Parys Mountain, the Anglesey landscape also failed to impress the artist. It could not match the natural beauty of Snowdonia, neither did the views of Beaumaris castle compare with the castle at Caernarfon. When Turner visited Beaumaris in 1798 he made no record in his sketch-books, hence the topographical errors in the watercolour of Beaumaris castle he painted as late as 1835. All this, in turn, led to the gradual introduction of new ways and a weakening of community insularity. In parishes around Parys Mountain it was quickly eroded by swarms of immigrant miners, including a number of English workers.

Travellers on the Menai ferries continued to court danger while suffering delays, overcrowding and insolent ferrymen. One terrified passenger spoke of the 'horrors of an open boat'. Though the 'ancient rate' had doubled to one penny per person and two pence for a horseman, the touring gentry in carriages frequently complained of being overcharged to the amount of one shilling. By the early 1780s the feasibility of constructing a bridge across the Menai Straits was seriously mooted. Numerous meetings were held, and a committee of Anglesey gentry and clergy formed to consider the alternative schemes submitted by John Golborne and Joseph Nickalls, two leading engineers of the day. These were an embankment with openings spanned by a drawbridge; a stone bridge; or a timber bridge supported by wooden piles. Objections on the grounds of cost, impracticality, and the adverse effect on navigation came mainly from the Caernarfonshire side. The project had to be abandoned in 1786 when Nicholas Bayly's bill proposing a timber bridge met stiff opposition in the House of Commons. Over 4,000 ships were said to ply the Menai Straits annually and the prosperity of Caernarfon could be jeopardized.

Be it in the interests of Anglesey or Caernarfonshire, it was the landed gentry class that dictated parliamentary politics. MPs were born in mansions, inheriting family ambitions and manipulative traits. Leading squires played an increasingly convoluted political version of musical chairs in both county and borough constituencies while allowing in the occasional outsider. This oligarchic grip mainly involved the families of Baron Hill, Bodorgan, Bodeon, Prysaeddfed and Plas Newydd, supported by loyal tenantry and venal freeholders. The threat of eviction was ever-present: Morris Prichard,

Pentre-eiriannell, father of the Morris brothers, almost lost his farm in 1741 as a reprisal for voting against the wishes of his landlord. Anglesey's total electorate was little more than 800, and popular opinion played no part in the political process. Candidates were Whig or Tory in name only. Parliamentary representation continued to be the means of asserting family or personal supremacy within the shire, and with so much at stake there were inevitably ceaseless broils at the upper echelons of society as rival squires jostled for power. Only the richest would survive. Consequently the number of contested elections gradually diminished, ending with just two gentry families taking monopolistic control of the county and borough seats.

Piqued by the accession of the Protestant king George I, the fourth viscount Bulkeley stood down as Tory MP at the 1715 election. He might have long concealed his Catholic sympathies but cherished Jacobite sentiments could not, at that moment, be abandoned. Instead, he conceded the Anglesey constituency to his old adversary Owen Meyrick as part of as alleged deal whereby the latter pledged to vacate the seat when called upon. Bulkeley soon rued his tactical error. Official positions in north Wales went to the new wielders of power aligned to the Bodorgan family. Worse, Meyrick refused to budge at the next election, and went about reviving Newborough's ancient rights. Old scores were reopened. Meyrick could count on allies such as the Owen family of Bodeon but not Edward Bayly, the new name at Plas Newydd; although a Whig like Meyrick he maintained studied neutrality. Bulkeley therefore recruited the assistance of Sir Watkin Williams Wynn, the powerful Tory MP for Denbighshire. Yet fellow members of his Jacobite club, the Cycle of the White Rose, never visited Anglesey in support, and in the event Bulkeley was forced to dig deep financially to reclaim the seat to the family name in an acrimonious contest in 1722. Jacobitism kept a slender toehold in Anglesey, but the Jacobite club that met briefly at Llannerch-y-medd between 1736 and 1738 was sustained by sentiment not conviction.

By again rejecting the votes of the burgesses of Newborough, a Bulkeley nominee also held the borough seat in 1722. This did not go unchallenged, but their claims failed to impress the House of Commons. Nor were they more successful following the next election in 1727. As a result Newborough was effectively disenfranchised three years later, leaving Beaumaris as a safe pocket borough controlled by the Baron Hill family until the Reform Act of 1832. If not family members or relatives, then allies or nominees would be given the Bulkeley stamp of approval by way of the municipal corporation of twenty-four voters. Following the death of the sixth viscount the family faced a long minority, so in 1754 the seat was put up for auction – prompting a Merioneth Tory squire to fork out £1,500 for the privilege of representing Beaumaris.

It was not so cut and dried in the county. The fourth viscount Bulkeley's death in 1724 had led to an earlier period of minority that entailed drafting a stop-gap candidate to represent Baron Hill interests. Once bitten, the family was wise enough not to trust an Anglesey family again; this time they opted for Hugh Williams, a 'foreigner' from Chester and a Whig to boot. At least he got the better of the Meyrick nominee in the 1725 by-election, repeating the feat at the general election of 1727. Party allegiances were again discarded when the Bulkeleys joined the Meyrick family to back Sir Nicholas Bayly of Plas Newydd, a Whig, in 1734. By the same token, family alliances of this kind could be blithely cast aside whenever it served a particular self-interest. For the 1741 election an anti-Baron Hill coalition emerged. The Tory John Owen of Prysaeddfed was able to win the seat with Bodorgan support, on condition that he, in turn, supported Owen Meyrick's son at a later date. When he reneged on the agreement in 1747, giving the Meyricks a taste of their own medicine, Sir Nicholas Bayly made a come-back. Disgraced by scandal – he had seduced a young girl half his age – Bayly would eventually give way to Owen Meyrick the younger, MP from 1761 until his death in 1770.

Because the Bodorgan heir, Owen Putland Meyrick, was a minor, and so, too, was the seventh Viscount Bulkeley, Sir Nicholas Bayly won the 1770 by-election by default. When he became of age, Bulkeley recovered the seat unopposed in 1774, and was re-elected in 1780, thereby restoring Baron Hill authority. But Henry Bayly (Paget) had other ideas. Wealth from the Parys Mountain copper mines had substantially added to Plas Newydd fortunes, and the family was keen to consolidate its political influence in both Anglesey and Caernarfonshire. This put them in direct opposition to Baron Hill, who desperately negotiated another Bulkeley–Meyrick alliance. As both Viscount Bulkeley and Henry Bayly were promoted to the peerage, Baron Hill persuaded Owen Putland Meyrick to stand against Nicholas Bayly, the younger brother of the Earl of Uxbridge. The election of 1784 was a particularly bitter and costly affair. Plas Newydd was willing to spend its way to victory to the tune of £8,373, the largest amount paid out to secure a single candidate in eighteenth-century Wales. Judging by the bills submitted by local hoteliers for accommodation, food, spirits, ale and tobacco, the voters who gathered for the two week poll-come-binge at Beaumaris had the time of their life, though it was only after Plas Newydd persuaded the Bodeon family to switch sides that Nicholas Bayly scraped through by a mere seven votes, 370–363.

The expense of contested elections concentrated minds on the need for a mutual political understanding between Baron Hill and Plas Newydd. Overreaching ambition already proved ruinous to one of the lesser squires; a part of the Prysaeddfed estate had to be sold to defray John Owen's election expenses. Separate spheres of influence were formally carved out, allowing the Bulkeleys to hold Beaumaris and Caernarfonshire in return for Paget control in Anglesey and Caernarfon boroughs. This convenient arrangement permitted a succession of Pagets to be elected unopposed in the county constituency between 1790 and 1832. At Westminster, the now Whig-Liberal Anglesey MPs turned out to be an undistinguished and unambitious lot, who voted but seldom spoke on the rare occasions they attended the House of Commons. There was no middle-class challenge to gentry family interests, no public voice to heed, no movement for parliamentary reform as in other north Wales counties. And yet, in the wake of the French Revolution we have the first minute stirrings of political radicalism. Concerned Anglican gentry and clergymen reported that itinerant Methodist preachers were peddling Thomas Paine's 'rights of man' doctrines at Brynsiencyn and Amlwch in 1792. A certain John Phillips of Llangefni, a small farmer, came before the Court of Great Sessions in 1800 for having publicly proclaimed himself 'a Jacobin and a Republican' at Llannerch-y-medd, a town where only a few years earlier seditious pamphlets had been distributed. The circulation of new political thoughts, such as it was, further indicated Anglesey's diminishing remoteness.

Profound changes in education, religion and economic life together shook the old social order to its roots as Anglesey became more open to outside influences. Literacy allowed ordinary people to make a conscious decision in religion; no longer did the Established Church command total allegiance. Copper mining at Parys Mountain tied the county economically to other parts of Britain, and as industry competed with agriculture, capitalist investment led to the making of a distinct proletariat class. Among the middle class, the farmers remained the most numerous, yet there were few large holdings to produce great wealth. A growing number of professional men figured prominently in their community – clergymen, government officials, lawyers, schoolmasters and doctors (though Anglesey had no doctor of note for some time after the death of Dr Richard Evans; those trained in medicine rarely returned to their native island). Many rose from humble backgrounds: Hugh Price, a Beaumaris lawyer, was the son of a Trewalchmai pedlar. An income of between £80 and £120 a year, as enjoyed by customs officials and some clergymen, ensured a comfortable life. The headmaster of Beaumaris grammar school would have to manage on £40. If only in education, ambitious middle class families were seen to emulate the squirearchy. An English private schooling was the first step on the ladder of opportunity and the process of social elevation; William Morris sent his son to Liverpool, while his daughter attended a private boarding establishment at Beaumaris. The 'free' grammar school at Beaumaris now attracted more and more fee-paying middle-class pupils to the detriment of poor children. Ultimate success enabled them to hobnob with the landed gentry. In leasing Plas Llanidan and its estate, Thomas Williams made clear his social pretensions.

Nothing had lessened the status of the old landed families. They still ruled the county. Incomes from the rent-rolls of their enormous estates subsidized a luxurious lifestyle beyond the imagination of ordinary *Monwyson* (Anglesey people). A well-chosen bride brought a valuable infusion of cash: like father, like son, both Owen Meyrick II and Owen Putland Meyrick married rich English heiresses. Many of the older mansion houses were extended or reconstructed in neo-classic style. By the time the new Baron Hill was completed in 1779 at a cost of over £10,800, work had begun on the £5,000 project of rebuilding Bodorgan Hall. House interiors incorporated all that was best; landscaped gardens and parklands added to the ambience. Venison, pheasant, oysters and pickled puffins were but a part of their lavishly supplied gastronomic tables. In tune with fashion there was the 'grand tour'; during 1784–6 the seventh viscount Bulkeley visited France, Italy and Switzerland. For further recreation they could attend official dinners and hunt balls at Beaumaris, visit the spas at Bath or Cheltenham, or cross over to Ireland. As Anglesey's unofficial metropolis, the gentry were more likely to visit the theatre or purchase goods in Dublin than in London. It was here that Anglesey people often sought medical treatment or presswork (prior to 1818 *Almanac Caergybi* was printed in Dublin). Yet it should not be forgotten that the gentry class remained deeply absorbed in all aspects of public life; there were frequent contacts between people of different social rank. Though the leading families had become thoroughly Anglicized, a few enlightened squires continued to foster native culture. Like his father and namesake, Paul Panton patronized Welsh poets even if he understood little of the language. Owen Meyrick I of Bodorgan was a benefactor of the Morris brothers and Dr Edward Wynne is said to have helped Goronwy Owen in his early days. Among the many subscribers to an anthology of poetry entitled *Blodeugerdd Cymry* (1759) were the Bulkeleys of Baron Hill.

Anglesey made a singular contribution to the renaissance of the eighteenth century, bringing with it a new confidence and pride in Welsh literature. Not that the ancient traditions had disappeared completely from the island. Among the *gwerin* a lively bardic awakening was led by Siôn Tomos Owen, a Bodedern weaver, who composed the century's first eulogy to Anglesey (*c.*1728–9), and who conducted a 'bardic war' with mainland rivals to defend the island's honoured status as *Môn, mam Cymru*. Unbelievers in Caernarfonshire were directed to climb Snowdon to view her fertile acres. A dozen poets attended a Llannerch-y-medd tavern eisteddfod in 1734. An appreciation of Anglesey's ancient past also manifested itself within the ranks of the lesser squires and middle class. In his greatest work, *Mona Antiqua Restaurata* (Dublin, 1723), the Revd Henry Rowlands concentrated on the island's ancient archaeological history, and in so doing pioneered an interest in Celtic antiquities. By overelaborating Anglesey's Druidic past his investigations became more a romantic flight of fantasy when he asserted that the *cromlechi* and standing stones were originally religious monuments set up by the Druids. Naively enthusiastic, Rowlands, nevertheless, contributed to the growing national awareness that surfaced more completely in connection with the remarkable literary advance in mid-century synonymous with 'Morrisiaid Môn' (the Morrises of Anglesey).

Born in the parish of Llanfihangel Tre'r-beirdd, the four Morris brothers grew up in Pentre-eiriannell, Penrhosllugwy. They received little formal education, but would inherit a love of Welsh poetry from their father, Morris Prichard. All were naturally gifted; few Anglesey men have surpassed the encyclopaedic talents of the eldest brother Lewis, 'Llewelyn Ddu o Fôn' (d.1765). A scholarly poet, antiquary, philologist, musician, mineralogist, craftsman, he was commissioned by the Admiralty to undertake a hydrographical survey of the coast of Wales before settling in Cardiganshire. Early in life, Richard (d.1779) left for London eventually to become chief clerk in the Navy Office. He immersed himself in London Welsh life and was a founder of the Cymmrodorion Society. The youngest, John, went to sea, only to die of sickness aboard a warship in the Caribbean in 1740. Neither Lewis nor Richard would return to Anglesey. Yet they kept in constant touch with William (d.1763), who remained a customs official at Holyhead. The letters they exchanged, and well over a thousand have survived, were more an erudite conversation in print, garnished with gossipy insights into various aspects of life in mid-eighteenth century Anglesey. Between them, the brothers took an active intellectual interest in a wide range of subjects, above all the language, literature and antiquities of Wales.

As patrons of poets and scholars, the Morris brothers drew around them a circle of talented men steeped in Welsh culture. Old manuscripts were diligently collected and copied, allowing medieval poetry, literature and history to be studied. Early on, Lewis Morris hoped to publish a selection of material. In 1735 he set up a private press in his then home at Holyhead but insufficient support meant he was only able to produce the first issue of the literary periodical *Tlysau yr Hen Oesoedd*. Later, the Morrises encouraged the publication of *Diddanwch Teuluaidd* (1763), a collection of poems that included the work of several Anglesey bards including Lewis Morris himself. Quite evidently, a ready market was being created among the like-minded literati emerging from both the middle class and educated *gwerin*. Following Rowlands's *Mona Antiqua Restaurata*, county histories found popularity in print. Happier as a scholar than schoolteacher, John Thomas, a master at Beaumaris grammar school, wrote *A History of the Island of Anglesey* (published posthumously in 1775). Another of the Morris circle, the poet and manuscript collector, Hugh Hughes, 'Y Bardd Coch o Fôn', remained in Anglesey, while Robert Hughes, 'Robin Ddu yr Ail o Fôn', became a librarian for the Cymmrodorion Society in London. As a bard, he modelled himself on one of the greatest of all Anglesey poets: Goronwy Owen, 'Goronwy Ddu o Fôn'.

Both talent and misfortune would collide in Goronwy Owen's personal life with tragic results. Despite his humble origins in the parish of Llanfair Mathafarn Eithaf, he received a thorough classical grounding at Friars school, Bangor, followed by a short period at Jesus College, Oxford. His father and grandfather were cultured country poets. Supported by his mentors, the Morris brothers, Goronwy Owen's dream was to write a great epic poem comparable to what Milton had achieved in English. He studied the craft of the court poets of the princes as well as classical Latin poetry and contemporary English work. Whether he came close to realizing his ambition with 'Cywydd y Farn Fawr' (The Great Judgement) is a matter for those qualified to comment; Lewis Morris thought it the 'best thing I ever read in Welsh'. As an ordained clergyman, Owen served as a curate in his native parish for only three weeks in 1746 before being compelled to leave. It was his fate never to return to Anglesey. Poverty, debt, alcoholism and family bereavement clouded his iconic exile, first in England, then in Virginia, America, where he died in 1769 aged only forty-six. Nostalgic release had come in the poems that eulogize his beloved island: the most celebrated speak feelingly of *Môn a'i thirionwch* (Anglesey and her gentle beauty); *Fôn dirion dir* (Anglesey pleasant land); *Môn araul* (serene Anglesey); *Goludog ac ail Eden … neu Baradwys hen* (a rich land, a second Eden … or ancient Paradise). Other poems express his personal lament for Anglesey, an inerasable longing that continues to resonate with the exile over the ages:

> *Pell wyf o wlad fy nhadau,*
> *Och sôn! ac o Fôn gu fau*
> (I am far from the land of my fathers
> Woe is the telling of it, and from my own dear Anglesey).

Bryn Celli Ddu Neolithic burial chamber.

Beaumaris Castle with the former Beaumaris Grammar School
in the background.

Parys Mountain open-cast copper mine. At its peak in the late eighteenth century, the world's largest copper mine.

Baron Hill, Beaumaris. A line engraving from 1779.

Telford's Suspension Bridge spanning the Menai Straits.

Brynsiencyn Calvinistic Methodist chapel (1883).

Gravestone with bust of John Owen Jones (Ap Ffarmwr) in the Dwyran
Calvinistic Methodist chapel cemetery.

The new Llangefni County Secondary School, which opened in 1900.

Comic postcard from Llanfair Pwllgwyngyll (1905).

Gaerwen war memorial (1922).
Over 1,000 islanders were killed during the First World War.

Nomination Day during the 1945 General Election. Candidates
Lady Megan Lloyd George and Cledwyn Hughes are both seen standing.

Anglesey Aluminium, Holyhead, for decades the island's largest employer.

V

The Nineteenth Century

Most aspects of life in Anglesey underwent great transformation during the course of the nineteenth century. Among the crucial elements of change were the improvements that would revolutionize communications. Bridges, roads, railways, better postal services and telegraph system all contributed to the removal of any residual sense of geographical isolation and to closer ties with the outside world. On 30 January 1826 the Menai Suspension Bridge was opened to establish a permanent mainland connection. Not since the military pontoon structure of 1282–3 had the Menai Straits been bridged. The last time that ordinary people were able to walk back and forth was during the Mesolithic period. What had been feasibility studies for engineers in the 1780s finally saw the light of day, stimulated by political demands. Since the 1800 Act of Union the government faced increasing pressure to arrange rapid communication with Ireland. Financed by state capital, Thomas Telford's engineering genius soon found expression in north Wales. He reconstructed the 'Great Irish Road' from Shrewsbury through Snowdonia to Holyhead and planned the crossing of the Menai Straits. It took seven years to erect the £120,000 bridge; at one time between 300 and 400 men worked at the Penmon quarries and Porthaethwy site. Imposing stone pier towers and arches were first raised; then two 550 ft long carriageways attached by vertical rods to sixteen iron suspension chains spanned the narrow channel. Over 100 ft above the water line it allowed sufficient headroom for shipping. Hailed as a wonder of the age, no visual image of Anglesey would ever be complete without the grandeur of Telford's masterpiece.

Meantime, work had proceeded on a new and more direct 21-mile post road further west across the island, connected to Ynys Gybi (Holy Island) by the Stanley embankment. Completed in 1823, the highway was placed under the authority of a single turnpike trust and five new toll-houses built – at Holyhead, Caergeiliog, Gwalchmai, Nant and Llanfair Pwllgwyngyll. A new coaching house, the Mona Inn at Cerrigceinwen, replaced Gwyndy. Another turnpike trust was created in 1829 to maintain the coastal road from Beaumaris to Porthaethwy financed by Baron Hill largesse in 1804–5. Well-trodden, narrow, winding lanes would otherwise pass for a road system. Harbour facilities at Holyhead had already been improved to cope with the increasing traffic; the Admiralty pier was completed in 1821 along with a new customs house and harbour office. By the 1830s overall improvements to the 'Great Irish Road' shortened the London to Holyhead coach journey from 48 to 27 hours. A good hour was saved traversing Anglesey. Though the new steamships speeded up the Irish Sea crossing from Holyhead, the Liverpool to Dublin service soon proved to be more economical. Consequently, the number of passengers crossing the Menai Straits diminished dramatically: the figure of 9,020 in 1831 was less than half the record achieved in 1824 when 18,970 used the now defunct Porthaethwy ferry. Apart from the obvious advantages to the movement of livestock, the bridge made little difference to Anglesey's economic prospects. As annual takings fell, the golden era of coaching was soon to be eclipsed by the railway age.

Railway development presented the opportunity for a fast regular route for the Irish mail service, and leading Anglesey gentry lost no time in singing the praises of Holyhead. Once it had been officially selected as the terminus port in preference to Porth Dinllaen on the Llŷn peninsula, Robert Stephenson engineered the line across the north Wales coast for the Chester and Holyhead Railway Company. This project ushered a brief period of prosperity. Local farmers received higher prices for their produce and for the horses needed in the construction work. From 1845 large gangs of navvies were hired, augmented by unemployed copper miners and local farm hands drawn by better pay. Over half the railway labourers came from the island. Housed in temporary wooden huts, they mixed with elements noted for their wild ways. For very good reason, the company employed two scripture readers from the Town Missionary Society in Anglesey. They could not deter the ethnic hostility brewing between Welsh and Irish navvies or the bouts of industrial unrest; workers on the Holyhead section downed tools for a week in 1846 in pursuit of a wage increase. Three months following the completion of the line to Bangor, the section of track from Llanfair Pwllgwyngyll to Holyhead opened to regular traffic on 1 August 1848. Six mainline stations were built during 1848–9, with Rhosneigr a late addition in 1907.

An earlier scheme for horses to draw railway carriages across Telford's bridge was shelved once it became clear that the only viable option would be a new rail crossing over the Menai Straits. Work soon commenced on the massive Britannia Tubular Bridge. Over 1,000 men would be employed, fifteen of whom died in accidents during construction. Riveted wrought-iron rectangular tubes were prefabricated onshore, floated out on pontoons, and hoisted into place by hydraulic presses to rest on three masonry support towers and two end abutments. The two parallel tubes, each composed of four sections, were 1,511 ft in overall length. Built between 1846 and 1850, the £620,000 structure incorporated the most advanced technology of the day and became Stephenson's greatest engineering monument in Wales. On 5 March 1850 the first train passed through the first completed tube; thirteen days later the line was opened for passengers on the London to Holyhead train. Soon it became possible to make the journey in less than ten hours; by 1908 the Irish mail express would cut the time to five and a quarter hours. Financial difficulties had forced the Chester and Holyhead Railway Company to sell out to the London and North Western Railway Company (LNWR) by 1859. A single-track branch line from Gaerwen to Amlwch, completed by the Anglesey Railway Company in 1867, was also subsequently amalgamated with the LNWR. An additional link from Pentre Berw (Holland Arms) through Pentraeth failed to reach the resort of Benllech; instead it terminated at the desolate Red Wharf Bay station, opened in 1909.

A proposed railway line via Newborough to the ferry crossing at Tal-y-foel came to nothing, though the ferry and also the boat at Moel-y-don continued to operate. The latter provided a direct link for Anglesey workers employed at the Dinorwig slate quarries. While secluded Newborough further declined – low enough to be smeared as 'the most miserable spot in Anglesey' – the towns and villages on the main road and rail arteries expanded rapidly in response to the new opportunities. Holyhead benefited directly. A gigantic breakwater was constructed to guarantee an extended area of sheltered anchorage for shipping at the port. In the process an estimated seven million tons of rock would be blasted from Holyhead Mountain and transported to the site. Commenced in 1845, the project gave employment to hundreds of men over a twenty-eight year period. Rising from 3,869 (1841) to 8,863 (1851), Holyhead's population increased by 130 per cent within a decade. An unprecedented influx of workers to both railway and maritime sectors led to overcrowding in the town, and streets of new housing had to be quickly erected for the labouring class – tiny terraced houses devoid of piped water and sanitation. Once again, relations between Welsh and Irish navvies became openly antagonistic; in 1851 the murder of a Welsh worker precipitated a riot. Home also to a substantial middle class, the town prospered with countless new shops, a market hall, and more hotels to cater for the increasing passenger traffic. Another indication of progress came in 1856 when parts of the town were illuminated by gaslight.

Population in the other main towns had peaked earlier in 1831: Amlwch with 6,285, Beaumaris with 2,497. Elsewhere progress was on a more modest scale. Porthaethwy (rechristened Menai Bridge in some quarters) and Llangefni, the up-and-coming market town, would both increase in importance with less than 2,000 inhabitants. Economic progress and employment opportunities in the first half of the century were mirrored in the total population figure. Following this period of robust demographic growth the 1851 census counted 57,327 people in Anglesey. Holyhead continued to thrive and its population reached 11,077 by 1901. But with the passing of the boom years, a high incidence of unemployment began a process of migration from the island. The exodus from Amlwch between 1871 and 1891 brought the population down to 4,443. Many families settled in Liverpool, along with the majority of the 5,000 or so Anglesey-born people enumerated in Lancashire in 1891. From 1871 the rate of natural increase kept population levels in Anglesey itself at a plateau of around 50,000 until the 1930s.

The rail network facilitated movement. As well as increasing passenger traffic, freight trains carried Irish cargo, local livestock, agricultural produce and coal to the steamers at Holyhead. Copper from Parys Mountain could now be transported at a cheaper rate. Conversely, imported goods hastened the decline of local handicraft industries and, in due course, the disappearance of many rural craftsmen. Bootmaking at Llannerch-y-medd, which in 1833 employed 250 cobblers mainly to supply the copper miners, suffered when cheaper factory produced boots from Northampton became available. Turnpike roads could not compete with the railways although it was 1895 before Anglesey's roads were freed from toll. Rail travel also led to the beginnings of popular tourism. Increasing numbers of visitors were brought within reach of the seaside resorts of Benllech, Cemais and Rhosneigr. Places that had remained unchanged for centuries found unaccustomed popularity as the holiday industry gained ground, characterized by high-class hotels, boarding houses and quaint picture postcards. The 58-letter artificial 'Welsh jaw-breaker' at Llanfair Pwllgwyngyll was nothing more than a subtle marketing ploy concocted by a local tailor in 1869 to draw tourists. Scores of humorous postcards cashed in on the long name. An early plan to connect Beaumaris by rail, with a line running from Llanfair Pwllgwyngyll to the centre of the Green, failed to materialize. Holidaymakers could still take pleasure steamers to the fashionable 'watering places' of Beaumaris and Menai Bridge crossing Beaumaris bay, acclaimed by George Borrow to be 'superior' in scenic beauty to that of Naples.

Continuity in maritime traditions gave seafaring and shipping an increasing relevance; the sea came to dominate the life of Anglesey as never before. As a nursery for seamen there was a greater call for navigational instruction. Largely neglected in the elementary schools, select private academies at Holyhead and Amlwch prepared pupils for a maritime career. Over some forty years (1814–53) William Francis gained a reputation as a teacher of mathematics, navigation and nautical studies at Amlwch. Each new ship added to the profusion of master mariners in local ports. That, and the propensity for the middle class to invest in ship-owning ventures. Displaying a spirit of communal capitalism, a variety of Anglesey people held shares in local vessels: sea captains, merchants, shopkeepers, farmers, wealthy spinsters and even flush ministers of religion like John Elias. Until the railways offered a serious challenge, coastal trade, particularly to Chester and Liverpool, continued to flourish. In home waters the sloop *Darling* of Beaumaris regularly transported building stone from Red Wharf to Holyhead for the construction of the breakwater. With 236 registered vessels in 1836 Beaumaris continued to be the principal port for another decade when it was swiftly overtaken by the growing commercial importance of Holyhead. Off the northeast coast the rich herring ground sustained a local fishing industry that accounted, in part, for the importance of the sea in the lives of villagers at Moelfre. For Anglesey as a whole it had become second to agriculture as a source of employment. By 1861 there were more than 600 seamen serving on merchant ships, let alone the assortment of marine-related occupations at the ports.

Coastal trade and fishing accounted initially for the small-scale shipbuilding activity around the Anglesey coast. Most of the ninety-five vessels recorded for the period 1766–1840 were built (or rebuilt) at Amlwch, Beaumaris and Holyhead, although little havens such as Moel-y-don and Pwllfanog also turned out small sloops. Gradually, construction gravitated to Amlwch, where shipbuilding became a major industry and where its shipwrights and workmen earned a reputation for high quality workmanship. Much of the shipbuilding and repair work at Amlwch Port was developed by the Treweek family to take advantage of the lucrative copper shipments. One of their first vessels, the 65-ton sloop *Marquis of Anglesey*, launched in 1826, remained in this trade for almost forty years. In all, they controlled a substantial shipping business that involved sixty-seven vessels (1825–55), and among the many ship-masters in their employ was Captain William Thomas of Amlwch. Already the part-owner of a vessel, he astutely set up a separate shipbuilding venture in 1858 that built the *Mary Catherine*, the first iron schooner in north Wales. During the 1870s his ship-owning and shipbuilding concerns expanded rapidly. A revitalized copper industry, artificial fertilizer from Hills' chemical works, and involvement in the Cumberland iron ore trade, meant more business for shipping at Amlwch. Treweek's yard and dry dock were taken over in 1872 and from this time on the shipbuilding firm of William Thomas and Sons maintained the great tradition to produce schooners, steamships and a paddle-steamer. Between 1849 and 1908, when Amlwch Port faced serious decline, the family had owned or built over seventy-two ships.

What the Thomases achieved as ship-owners, the Davieses would surpass. Once again, individual Anglesey men were showing exceptional entrepreneurial flair. Rhisiart Dafydd (Richard Davies snr), the founder of the dynasty, began with a general store at Llangefni. Showing a keen eye for business he opened a branch at Red Wharf, and in 1828 leased a warehouse and timberyard at Menai Bridge where the ship-owning company would be concentrated two decades later. Under his two surviving sons, Robert and Richard jnr, carrier ships transported slates, countless emigrants and Canadian timber across the Atlantic. Starting, appropriately, with *Anglesey* in 1875, seven new iron vessels named after Welsh counties indicated growing business confidence as they engaged in long haul trade to the Pacific, India and Far East. Their last two vessels, the *Afon Alaw* and *Afon Cefni*, both over 2,000 tons and built at Glasgow, commemorated Anglesey rivers. In total, sixty-nine ships had been part of the Davies fleet at some time between 1843 and 1905. Both brothers, however, chose to live on the Caernarfonshire side of the Menai Straits, in mansions that were a demonstration of wealth and elevated status: Robert at Bodlondeb, Richard at Treborth. Death revealed the measure of their riches. In 1896 Richard Davies left a personal fortune of £294,446; nine years later his reclusive brother's estate was valued at £446,383. A life-long supporter of temperance, Robert had earlier dispensed with a further £500,000 in charitable donations to various causes, but not the wine and spirits collection that gathered dust in his cellars. These were immense fortunes made on the backs and bodies of their sailors, men who sweated for shillings and meagre rations, or who drowned in one of the fifteen ships lost at sea.

Over the centuries innumerable ships had been wrecked off the treacherous Anglesey coast in storms or dense fog, leading to the loss of hundreds of lives. At least sixty vessels came to grief in the three years 1825–7. The name of one ill-fated passenger ship is long remembered. Caught by a force 12 hurricane on the last leg of her voyage from Australia to Liverpool, the steam clipper *Royal Charter* was shattered on rocks near Moelfre on 26 October 1859 and about 450 people drowned. Charles Dickens later visited the scene of the disaster and paid tribute to the Revd S. R. Hughes, rector of Llanallgo, who wrote no less than 1,075 letters to comfort bereaved families. Almost all of the consigned bullion of £322,440 was recovered, but dark tales abounded of villagers who grew rich pilfering gold sovereigns and valuables from corpses washed up on shore. True or not, Anglesey people were by now better known for saving lives than plundering wrecks. As more and more ships came to be manned by islanders the psychology of the Crigyll robbers lost all sympathy. New lighthouses had long been operational at Ynys y Moelrhoniaid (Skerries), Ynys Lawd (South Stack), Trwyn y Balog (Point Lynas), Amlwch, Penmon and Llanddwyn to safeguard shipping. Following the initiative taken by the Revd James Williams, rector of Llanddeusant, and his wife Frances, the first lifeboat was stationed at Cemlyn in 1828, a few weeks prior to setting up the Anglesey Association for the Preservation of Life from Shipwreck – the first of its kind in north

Wales. Not long after, there were lifeboat stations at Holyhead, Rhoscolyn, Penmon, Llanddwyn and Moelfre, and Anglesey was cited as one of the most active counties in this respect. By 1857, when the association became a branch of the Royal National Lifeboat Institution, over 400 lives had been rescued by local crews, a tradition of selfless courage that has lived on.

Attachment to the land remained an equally strong trait. Self-made entrepreneurs often had deep roots in rural Anglesey. Like Captain William Thomas, the Davies family descended from smallholder stock, and all would channel a portion of their cash pile into real estate. Thomas owned extensive holdings of land in the county, while Richard and Robert Davies acquired over 4,700 acres between them. It may have been a safe capitalist investment, but as with their fine mansions land was symbolic of social advancement. In many ways they became the equal of the long-established gentry families. Whatever their comparative financial positions, it would have been difficult to match the prodigious acreage accumulated by the 'great landowners' over the centuries. By the late 1870s that distinction went to Meyrick of Bodorgan with 16,918 acres, Williams-Bulkeley of Baron Hill (16,516 acres), the Marquess of Anglesey at Plas Newydd (9,620 acres) and Lord Boston of Porthaml (9,507 acres). Agrarian reformers advocating 'the land for the people' would find two-thirds of the farmed area of Anglesey concentrated in the hands of seventeen landed proprietors. The increased aloofness of the gentry class was symbolized most powerfully by the high stone walls erected around their property. Accentuating the social difference, Sir John Williams had Rhianfa, Llandegfan, modelled on the style of a small French chateau.

Almost half the male population of Anglesey in 1851 were engaged in agriculture. Farming remained the chief industry and the preponderance of small family-run farms was indicative of the productiveness of the land. By far the largest grouping were the approximately 3,000 mainly tenant farmers with under 50 acres. Indeed, the average size of Anglesey holdings was 40 acres. Anything over 100 acres would be considered a substantial unit. In 1885 there were 389 farms between 100 and 300 acres and only twenty of between 300 and 1,000 acres. Interestingly, 41 per cent of farms exceeding 100 acres had retained close historic association with the settlement pattern established during the early Middle Ages. Over 90 per cent of the largest consolidated farms occupied medieval township or hamlet settlement sites as instanced by Bodednyfed, Gwredog, Hirdrefaig, Lledwigan and Tresgawen.

Landowners made large profits during the Napoleonic wars; the rental of the Bodorgan estate rose by 72 per cent. Farmers also did well, but when this period of prosperity ended in 1816 they faced three decades of agricultural depression. Tenant farmers found it extremely difficult to pay rents. That said, a new progressive spirit, which would see considerable improvement in farming, was given impetus by the Anglesey Agricultural Society founded in 1808 (and revived in like form both in 1858 and 1872). It did much to educate farmers in more scientific ways and encourage the adoption of the latest farm implements. Annual agricultural shows were held at Llangefni with exhibitions and competitions. Two leading lights set the pattern for advanced methods. The Revd James Williams was the first in the county to use an iron plough, and he later contributed notes to a pioneering treatise on the breeding of livestock. Sir Richard Williams-Bulkeley organized ploughing matches to popularize the more efficient Scotch plough. Agricultural education always merited a keen interest. In 1897 the first college farm in Britain was established at Lledwigan outside Llangefni operated by the university college, Bangor.

Enclosure of common and open land generally proved beneficial. Following parliamentary legislation almost 7,000 acres of common land had been enclosed and cultivated by 1815, with several more enclosures at later dates. Such consolidation improved farm production, but favoured the large landowners in that their estates increased in size, raising land values. Sometimes this was done at the expense of the rural poor; at Newborough and Llangeinwen they were no longer able to graze their animals on the common. Not all enclosure schemes proved a success. Despite raising an embankment (Cob Malltraeth) by 1812, the 3,000 acres of reclaimed land at Malltraeth Marsh suffered from poor drainage.

Agricultural production had increased over the years with oats and barley as the major corn crops. To complement the artificial fertilizer produced by Hills' chemical works at Amlwch, ships from the Davies fleet imported South American guano. Steam-powered threshing machines indicated a drift towards mechanization on the larger farms. There were still over a hundred corn-mills in 1851, the tallest being the four-storey windmill at Amlwch Port. When cheap foreign grain made corn growing unprofitable, Anglesey farmers soon turned their attention to the rearing of livestock. From about 1870 the acreage devoted to agricultural crops declined while the annual returns of horses, cattle, sheep and pigs showed a phenomenal increase. Local fairs and markets flourished; Llangefni emerged as the main market-place for livestock, supplanting Llannerch-y-medd. Railways gave farmers easier access to outside markets. Over 35,000 sheep and 9,850 cattle were transported from the station at Llanfair Pwllgwyngyll in just a single year (1862). Buyers extolled the qualities of the Anglesey breed of cattle. Leading agriculturalists also won recognition. Owen Thomas excelled as a farmer: Neuadd, Llanbadrig, won a special prize in 1881 for the best stocked farm, and in 1883 his one and a half ton bullock, Jumbo, won second prize at the Smithfield show – the first time that an Anglesey farmer had ventured to exhibit in London. Prime agricultural land was increasing in price as ownership began to pass from the traditional county families to tenants, businessmen and others who competed for holdings put up for sale at public auctions. Tenants who had shouldered the cost of improvements and paid an increased rent were often obliged to pay twice over when purchasing their farms. As a result of this trend a third of the agricultural land in Anglesey had changed hands by the 1890s.

Labour came cheap, the workforce docile. Whereas the pool of male agricultural and general workers diminished from 4,423 (1851) to 3,222 (1891), conditions hardly changed. At the twice-annual hiring fair, farm-workers and servant girls humiliatingly stood at the roadside to sell their labour to the highest bidder. Men frequently put in fifteen hours (more at harvest time) for little more than 12 shillings a week. They were housed in insanitary stable lofts or else lived in small cottages described as 'miserable hovels'. On the larger farms up to a dozen labourers would be employed alongside a number of domestic servant maids. Few women undertook outdoor farm work by 1891. In general, labourers and servants appear as a class apart, relegated to an inferior social position that did not allow them to tread the parlour of their employers. By all accounts, many farmers enjoyed a comfortable lifestyle. Agricultural depression or not, more 'small fortunes' had been made on the land in Anglesey by the 1890s than any other part of Wales. Typically middle class they harboured social ambitions. Private tutors and governesses were engaged for their children prior to dispatching them off to private boarding schools to pick up English. Owen Williams, tenant of the small 55-acre farm at Gaerwen Uchaf, Llanfihangel Ysgeifiog, had his daughter educated at 'Mrs Williams's establishment for young ladies' at Chester.

After the prosperous years of the 1850s and 60s another, more serious, crisis developed in the last quarter of the century. Corn and livestock prices fell sharply, adding to the economic distress caused by high rents, rates and church tithes. Despite the generally friendly relations between Anglesey landlords and their tenants, farmers' representatives by 1888 were disappointed that their calls for permanent rent reductions went unheeded. Anglesey was a heavily tithed county and aggrieved Nonconformist farmers made a formidable interest group. Local protest meetings had been held in 1886–7 to demand a tithe reduction of up to 20 per cent. Anti-tithe sentiments were especially virulent in the parish of Llaneilian, fanned by radical leaders such as Lewis Hughes. It engendered great hostility against the clergy, and as the movement acquired a political tinge demands grew for the disestablishment of the Anglican Church. Though the situation did not deteriorate to the degree that the 'tithe war' gripped some other Welsh counties, attempts to distrain those guilty of non-payment caused localized disturbances. Bailiffs acting on behalf of the Ecclesiastical Commissioners visited the parishes of Heneglwys,

Llangefni and Amlwch in 1888 escorted by a large force of police and an infantry company of the Cheshire Regiment. Soldiers responded to riotous disorder at Amlwch by fixing bayonets. In the end all that was secured was £5 3s 10d out of over £100 due. Agitation rumbled on into 1890, when an anti-tithe association was formed at Llangefni, but petered out the following year when liability changed from tenant to landowner. Though the Marquess of Anglesey paid the whole tithe without increasing the rent, others passed on the extra sums to their tenants. This led the Anglesey Farmers' Society, set up in 1892, to seek rent reductions.

One man who had sympathized with the plight of the farmers was John Owen Jones, a native of Trefdraeth, better known by his journalistic pseudonym 'Ap Ffarmwr' (son of a farmer). But he soon realized that the travails of agriculture were not confined to one class, and in a series of impassioned newspaper articles entitled 'Gweision Ffarmwrs' (Farm Labourers) in 1889 he exposed the tyranny and exploitation at the base of rural society. Labourers suffered far worse conditions at the hands of the farmers, whom he described as the 'meanest, stingiest, most cowardly beings under the sun'. Yet few Nonconformist ministers or radical leaders spoke out. His articles uncovered the true feelings of an embittered workforce. No sooner did the series end than letters from ordinary workers appeared in the press. Their grievances were also aired at numerous meetings, held in village schoolrooms and smithies, allowing a local leadership to emerge. Self-educated members of the *gwerin*, men like George Jones and Hugh Williams, displayed extraordinary personal qualities. From the outset the formation of a trade union was mooted, but a reduction in the working hours remained the first priority. The historic conference held at Llangefni on Easter Monday 1890 to discuss their claims was without parallel in Wales. A reported crowd of several thousand escorted Ap Ffarmwr through the streets of the town in an unprecedented show of collective strength. Anxious to defuse the situation, the farmers shrewdly agreed to reduce the working day to twelve hours, though Ap Ffarmwr noted that those who held out longest against the concessions were chapel deacons. His ultimate aim was the establishment of an independent trade union, but the Anglesey Agricultural Labourers' Union, set up in June, died at birth. With most farm-labourers content with their gain, only five localities had shown a degree of interest.

Once the proud seat of the princes of Gwynedd, Aberffraw had long been reduced to an isolated rural backwater dominated by the landowning Meyrick family of Bodorgan and a few wealthy farmers. Yet the village emerged as a hotbed of working-class dissent. One leading figure, John Hughes, a cultured farm-labourer, had experience of militant coalfield unionism in south Wales. As the only Methodist minister actively to support Ap Ffarmwr's movement on the island, the Revd John Thomas had perhaps nurtured a sympathy for the underdog when serving as a missionary to India. Again, in 1891 and 1893, Ap Ffarmwr tried to foster interest in a trade union organization, but to no avail. Nor was any attempt made to seek higher wages or improved sleeping accommodation. Labourers patently lacked the spirit of class solidarity shown by the farmers. Disheartened by failure, Ap Ffarmwr left Gwynedd. Three years after his untimely death in Nottingham, loyal followers in Anglesey unveiled a monument bearing a bust of Ap Ffarmwr above his grave at Dwyran in 1902. Advocating land nationalization, he could be seen as a socialist pioneer. But, above all, the name of Ap Ffarmwr became synonymous with rural trade unionism in Wales, and over the years he acquired the legendary status of a peasant hero.

Copper miners had reverted to agriculture when Parys Mountain was in decline. By 1808 the workforce fell to 122. When Thomas Williams's family relinquished their interest, the Earl of Uxbridge secured control of the new Mona Mine Company in 1811 in partnership with the owners of Swansea copper-works. In the same year the appointment of James Treweek as mine agent introduced a Cornish element into the industry. During his stewardship of forty years Treweek directed every aspect of the mining operations involving both the Mona and Parys mine. He adopted new mining techniques and with the sinking of deeper shafts production at the Mona mine rose steadily to reach over 9,000 tons of ore per annum in 1819–26. It was only a partial recovery. Difficult market conditions in the long term forced cuts in production, profits fell, and there were further redundancies. Between 1830 and 1851 the number employed by the Mona Mine Company plunged from 400 to 84. Despite an attempt to develop Amlwch as a centre for smelting, dependent on ore sourced from outside, cheaper copper imports from America accelerated the downturn in the second half of the century. It spelled the end of Parys Mountain's greatness. Another short-lived revival came in the 1870s when various new companies attempted to work the mines. But by the early 1880s the deep mine workings and smelters were largely abandoned, to bequeath a toxic legacy. Amlwch's fortunes declined; the wealth from copper had gained few material benefits for the town.

Working conditions and rates of payment had shown little improvement. Accidents often resulted in death and serious injury. Only a minority, usually miners' widows and invalids, received financial assistance. Men of up to eighty years of age who spent a lifetime at the mines had no prospect of a pension. Though the mining companies paid for hospital treatment, general medical care was initially unsatisfactory: of the three doctors in practice during the 1830s, one lacked surgical skill and the other two were seldom sober. Most times the unfavourable bargaining system merely guaranteed a subsistence wage of 12–14 pence a day. Bargains set gangs of workers against each other, undermining labour solidarity. Truck shops operated against the workmen's interests, while Treweek's blatant policy of appointing Cornishmen to positions of authority at the Mona mine – unlike the Parys mine, which promoted Welshmen – caused further antagonism. A wily management style enabled Treweek to ward off serious labour unrest until the 1840s, when workers gathered sufficient strength to act collectively. If the 1846 strike failed to secure higher wages, industrial action in 1860 and 1863 successfully overturned an unpopular payment structure and shameless Cornish bias in bargain-setting. Welshmen fought hard to preserve their traditional monopoly of labour against outsiders. In truth, very little could be achieved without an effective trade union body. Strikers at the smelting plants were better organized but no more successful in forcing wage increases. When violence was threatened, as in 1860, the owners called in the police to restore order.

An ailing copper industry exacerbated social problems and human suffering at Amlwch. Discontented elements could not always be kept in check. A poor harvest aroused fears of food shortages. Coupled with low wages and unemployment this triggered the corn riots of 1817 – by far the most serious disturbances in Anglesey early this century. Like the incident at Pwllfanog in 1801, a shipment of grain was prevented from leaving Amlwch Port. When mine-owners and their agents failed to raise sufficient funds to alleviate the distress, an armed mob took to the streets. Among the 200 or so were local tradespeople, women and children. Aside from the first days of trouble, the working miners, though sympathetic, stood aside. Magistrates sought military assistance and troops transferred from Ireland eventually restored order. For much of this period little had been done to improve conditions for the working class. Children roamed the streets barefoot and in rags. The presence of many beggars and vagrants underlined how 'extreme poverty' persisted into mid-century. Several schemes were implemented to relieve unemployment and starvation, including work on local road and harbour improvements. Opportunities for self-improvement existed at the Literary and Scientific Institution. When appealing for funds to erect a hall (opened in 1845), its library of 400 volumes was said to be of great advantage to young men 'humble in station'. Beaumaris had a library as early as 1823.

Various joint ventures attempted to exploit Anglesey's limited coal reserves, made easier following the drainage of Malltraeth Marsh. Whereas the grander schemes foundered, the Anglesey Coal Company, run by small farmers, produced a few hundred tons annually between 1815 and 1828 to supply the local market. Until poor quality coal became cheaply available, the common people continued to use peat and turf as domestic fuel. Later pits in the area between Penrhyn-mawr and Ceint made little progress; nor did the new, deeper mines around Tai'r Gors, forcing the Anglesey Colliery Company Ltd into liquidation in 1865. Collieries at Morfa Mawr, that produced 800 tons a month, also declined in the 1860s, to be followed by those across the river Cefni in the parishes of Llangristiolus and Trefdraeth. In sum, insufficient investment, geological difficulties, flooding, and cheaper coal brought by rail, all contributed to the rapid demise of the industry. Roughly 140 workers had connection with coal mining in mid-century, but by 1877 the number dropped to 17. More were employed at the old-established quarries near Penmon and Benllech. A total of 321 quarrymen were enumerated in the 1851 census. Beaumaris castle presented a 500-year guarantee of quality for the building stone now used in the construction of the two bridges over the Menai Straits and the improvement of port facilities at Holyhead.

Private banks aided commercial development. Branches of the Anglesey Savings Bank, founded in 1818, sprang up in the main centres, to be followed by the North and South Wales Bank and others. A considerable number of middle-class traders, merchants and shopkeepers made a good living in the material environment of the towns. John Lewis, draper, of Holyhead, and Roger Evans, grocer and flour merchant at Menai Bridge, who employed 18 men in 1861, were typically well-heeled businessmen. Sectional interests underpinned the United Society of Amlwch Traders formed in 1876. Then there were the professional people: solicitors (Samuel Dew figured prominently), doctors, bank managers, architects, and auctioneers. Keenly class-conscious, many built large houses, kept domestic servants, and snobbishly aspired to give their children a privileged English-based education. It was the 'respectable' parents who invited Dr F. Weymouth to Holyhead and John Hughes to Bodedern to set up élitist 'collegiate schools' that prepared pupils for public examinations. By far the greatest number of 'quality' establishments, and the list is long, were the boarding and day schools for young ladies. Mr and Mrs Hobday of Birmingham opened a school at Amlwch in 1877 at the request of the 'leading families' anxious that their daughters should receive an English education. Others chose to send their children to private boarding schools in England, now made more accessible by rail. All this was in keeping with the new cultural values prevalent in Victorian Wales. Ostentatious titles – London House, Oxford House, The Emporium and Bon Marche – appeared above even the smallest shops. When signing official correspondence, Morris Jones, shopkeeper at Llanfair Pwllgwyngyll, thought 'Maurice' had a better ring; his son, John Morris-Jones, went for the double-barrelled format.

What linked significant sections of the middle class was Nonconformity; bound together they formed a highly cohesive power structure. Ministers and chapel deacons, drawn invariably from this social segment, became the almost undisputed leaders of society. Lord Stanley of Alderley, Plas Penrhos – a rare convert to Islam – thought the Welsh farmers were more afraid of the preachers than their landlords. Be that as it may, increasing economic strength, prestige and confidence gave the Nonconformist middle class a spirit of independence that enabled them to further their interests. An influential activist circle, whose names became all-to-familiar, were eager to control and direct communal action. Time and again, this assertive leadership group occupied the central stage in Anglesey. What they attempted, and achieved, filled columns in the weekly provincial press. (A county-based newspaper did not appear until 1881, when the *Holyhead Mail and Anglesey Herald* was printed at Holyhead.) Driven by resentment at Anglican privileges, they challenged the ascendancy of the Established Church. No longer subservient to the landed gentry, they spearheaded political change. As we shall see, the power of this new 'ruling élite' decisively influenced the course of religion, education and politics in the county. First, it is essential to trace the main avenues of religious dissent, for it was recognized that the 'chief caste feeling' at this time was 'the feeling of church and chapel'.

Further evangelization gave added dynamism to Nonconformity. Each denomination produced its outstanding preacher: Christmas Evans (Baptist), Jonathan Powell (Independent) and John Elias (Calvinistic Methodist) – all of whom had settled in Anglesey during the 1790s. Wesleyan Methodist missionaries in 1800 concentrated chiefly on English speakers in Beaumaris, Holyhead and Amlwch (strengthened by Cornish families in the copper industry). Within the local communities there was increasing sectarian polarization. Clergymen who filled in visitation returns in 1811 and 1814 often acknowledged that the majority of parishioners were dissenters of 'different denominations', with the Calvinistic Methodists, now officially separate from the Established Church, as the 'most numerous'. Another contemporary reckoned that 'little less than nine tenth' of Anglesey people were Nonconformists, and that chapels 'abound in every district'. Between 1798 and 1812 Jonathan Powell registered twenty-eight places of worship for the Independents. In 1822 a powerful religious revival throughout the island added hundreds to the ranks of the Calvinistic Methodists, followed by another in 1840 that benefited the Independents. Historically, the progress of Nonconformity during the century has been well mapped by various authors; added to which are the numerous individual chapel histories (written in many cases to mark their centenary) and biographies of prominent preachers. Together they bear testimony to the unstinting devotion of ministers, deacons and ordinary members.

Anglesey had become a Nonconformist stronghold. One jaundiced observer in mid-century noted how it was sprinkled with 'square, new, whitewashed and ugly' chapels. Unlike most parish churches they were usually situated conveniently within towns and villages. It had been a remarkable achievement; funding chapel building, ministers and preachers entailed self-sacrificing efforts. Though there was initial difficulty in acquiring land, political considerations mellowed the attitude of most Anglican landowners. The contract book of an Amlwch builder records prices of £195 and £270 for chapels erected in 1839–40. Many incurred considerable debt. Some eight years after its foundation, Tabernacl Independent chapel, Holyhead, struggled to liquidate a debt of £400 in 1831. Ministers were only paid modest sums. Christmas Evans had received an annual salary of £17 'for serving Anglesey'. Sixty years later, in 1852, John Hughes was given £20 a year for his ministry at Menai Bridge. Visiting preachers might be paid between one and three shillings for a Sunday, and supplied with *cwrw'r achos* (literally, chapel beer). Because of the poverty of their local congregations, virtually every minister established a private school or business to supplement his meagre stipend. William Griffith and William Roberts opened 'academies' at Holyhead before 1850, later to be followed by the sort of superior 'grammar school' that E. Cynffig Davies ran at Menai Bridge between 1875 and 1908. At Amlwch both William Roberts and John Pritchard combined the pulpit with a shop. Apart from his flourishing building and grocery interests at Llangefni, James Donne kept a keen eye on the stock market. John Elias happened to be doubly fortunate with his marriages into money; first with the owner of a profitable shop at Llanfechell, then the widow of Sir John Bulkeley, Prysaeddfed.

Each denomination published membership figures to denote progress. Given the intense nature of sectarian rivalry, their numerical strength mattered greatly – never more so than in the comparative position of church and chapel – though it was often highlighted by questionable statistics. Sunday schools were accorded special mention with good reason; for it could be argued that they sustained the growth of Nonconformity, more especially the Calvinistic Methodists. Biblical instruction was available to scholars of all ages, and literacy levels in the Welsh language rose substantially. Thomas Charles related how he met a twelve-year-old Anglesey girl who had memorized the entire book of Psalms. Soon after his arrival in Anglesey, John Elias promoted the Sunday schools; following a sermon at Llannerch-y-medd, membership there reached 600. All the while, Anglican clergy struggled against the prevailing tide. A survey in 1838 claimed ninety-four Sunday schools for the Calvinistic Methodists, with 10,381 scholars taught by 2,076 voluntary teachers. In the same year the total number of dissenting Sunday schools was put at 162; none could be found in connection with the Established

Church. A more objective assessment, perhaps, came later when the 1847 Education Report listed 122 Nonconformist Sunday schools, 70 of which belonged to the Calvinistic Methodists, against ten Church of England schools. To meet a growing demand, the Anglesey Auxiliary Bible Society came into being in 1813, and by 1840, 40,390 Bibles and New Testaments had been distributed in the county. Almost every family boasted a copy of the Scriptures.

The Religious Census of 1851 listed 140 Nonconformists chapels: the Calvinistic Methodists had 65, Independents 33, Baptists 22, Wesleyan Methodists 20. After the initial pre-1800 phase, chapel building (and rebuilding) reached its peak during the 1820s and 30s. Indicative of inter-denominational competition, a number of localities – Beaumaris, Bodedern, Holyhead, Llangefni, Pentraeth – had one or more chapel representing each sect. Eight chapels catered for the increasing population at Holyhead; both Hyfrydle (Calvinistic Methodist) and Bethel (Baptist) had been enlarged twice since the 1800s. Four Calvinistic Methodist chapels dominated the parish of Amlwch. Calculating attendance at the places of worship, on the other hand, is problematic. Numbers appear to have been purposely swollen. Clergymen complained that dissenters were induced to come out in force on Census Sunday to be enumerated, in the words of the rector of Llanfechell, with their 'own clan'. Counting the attendants at the morning, afternoon and evening services necessarily led to duplication. Unfortunately, moreover, the twenty-one parishes that formed part of the Poor Law Unions of Bangor and Caernarfon were included under Caernarfonshire. Discounting the thirty-four chapels in these parishes, the total number attending a place of worship in Anglesey showed an overwhelming Nonconformist majority of 85.7 per cent, with the Calvinistic Methodists comprising 50.6 per cent.

Mainly through stirring pulpit oratory, finely honed in the case of John Elias through visits to the theatre in London, ministers exerted tremendous personal authority. It was a measure of Elias's status that congregations of over 10,000 – a fifth of the island's population – would come to hear him preach outdoors, the same number that attended his funeral at Llan-faes in 1841. The evils of the age were condemned and strict discipline instilled. Christmas Evans scolded a Holyhead couple for allowing 'unsuitable' music and dance celebrations at their wedding. Elias halted threshing and fishing operations on Sundays. Degrading customs were suppressed during the 'moral revolution' that swept the county in the 1830s, though efforts to end the age-old Welsh practice of *caru ar y gwely* (courting on the bed) encountered stubborn opposition. Unmarried mothers would be expelled from their chapels. Following a lecture on temperance by Evan Davies, an Independent minister at Llannerch-y-medd, the first teetotal society in Wales was established at

Llanfechell in 1835. Backed by the principal dissenting leaders, Anglesey claimed forty-six teetotal societies three years later, representing a membership of 24,780. Nonconformist values had permeated deep into the social fabric, due in large part to the sway of the preachers. Not without reason was Elias dubbed the 'Anglesey pope', or that Christmas Evans took to calling himself the 'bishop of Anglesey'. Images by artisan painters perpetuated this personality cult. Engraved reproductions of the oil portrait of Elias by William Roos, Amlwch, were hung in countless Methodist chapels, later followed by photographs of similarly revered pulpit giants of succeeding generations.

Minority sects hardly made an impression. Calvinistic Methodist intransigence ensured that Mormonism was unwelcome. At Llannerch-y-medd in 1849 the Methodist minister forbade the town-crier from announcing a public sermon by Abel Evans, the Mormon missionary. Evans presided over fifty-five members in Anglesey at this point, but only in 1857 is there mention of a Mormon meeting-house – at Amlwch Port. After a lapse of two centuries, and in the face of deep-rooted hostility, Catholicism reappeared. An immigrant population of Irish labourers and merchants at Holyhead led to the opening of a Catholic church in 1855, part of which was allocated for a school.

Only a small minority attended the seventy-five parish churches. Manifestly, Anglicanism had failed to retain the allegiance of the people. Accounting for the 'indescribably disgraceful' condition of the Church of England in 1832, one commentator noted how lay impropriators had diverted revenues and how the lack of spiritual leadership at parish level was aggravated by pluralism and absenteeism. In addition to Llanbeulan, the Revd W. Roberts cared for another four parishes. No less than sixty-two parishes were in the hands of non-resident incumbents; the Revd S. Majendie selected to reside in Staffordshire, 150 miles away. The position hardly improved during the crucial period when dissent took hold. Many churches provided only one Sunday service, often in English. Few clergymen could match the Revds James Williams, Llanddeusant, and W. Wynn Williams, Llangeinwen, for their devotion to ordinary parishioners. Church building was neglected. For historic reasons, most of Anglesey's ancient churches lay in remote locations, but apart from some restoration work and the erection of the new church at Llangefni (1824) there would be little activity of note prior to the formation of the Diocesan Church Building Society in 1838. In Anglesey this positive phase began three years later with the new churches at Brynsiencyn and Bryngwran. Unfortunately for the Anglican cause, charity ran thin among sections of its moneyed adherents, to hamper progress. Poor financial resources meant that the Holyhead parish church struggled on a net income of £167. Very few of the 2,000 inhabitants of Llannerch-y-medd in

1850 attended the church due to the 'wretched state' of the building. And a 'lack of funds' explained why the new church at Llanfihangel Ysgeifiog remained unfinished for years.

It was mid-century before the programme of church building and extension work made headway. Population growth spurred the effort that resulted in the new church opened at Menai Bridge in 1858, on land donated by the Marquess of Anglesey. Between 1860 and 1886, thirty-four churches were either rebuilt or repaired at a total cost of £30,655; the Stanley family of Plas Penrhos setting a fine example by donating over £6,000 – mainly towards the church at Holyhead. Anglican morale was further raised by the work of diligent clergymen such as the Revds P. Constable Ellis, Thomas Meredydd and H. Grey Edwards. But, yet again, these were exceptional cases; others made headlines for the wrong reasons, chiefly drunkenness and immorality. Anglesey clerical scandals in 1875 almost 'broke the heart' of the bishop of Bangor. Despite all that was achieved in rectifying earlier deficiencies, the Established Church regained only a fraction of the ground lost to dissent. Anglican communicants at the turn of the century were put at 4,807.

Religious fervour maintained the Nonconformist momentum. During the powerful awakening of 1859, David Morgan, the Cardiganshire revivalist, toured the county, beginning in Newborough where 200 were converted. At Holyhead the converts numbered 1,149. Richard Owen, who heard Morgan preach at Llangristiolus, inspired spiritual revivals in 1876 and 1884–5. Hundreds of young people flocked to the chapels and prayer meetings. A new generation of mainly college educated ministers, better remunerated, came to the fore. As each denomination competed for members, chapel rebuilding or enlargement had proceeded without pause and at considerable cost. In 1861 the debt on Baptist chapels stood at almost £3,000. When Moriah, the ornate John Elias memorial chapel at Llangefni, was opened in 1898 at a cost of £5,467 a debt of £2,500 remained. Wealthy benefactors from the Nonconformist middle class were often at hand. In addition to footing the £1,500 renovation bill of the Welsh Methodist chapel at Menai Bridge, Robert Davies gave £6,000 to build an English chapel (it was here that the first 'English Cause' in north Wales started in 1867). By the 1890s, the Independents had 3,200 members; the Baptists a thousand less. As the main beneficiary of religious developments, the Calvinistic Methodists went from strength to strength. A succession of eloquent preachers had followed John Elias – principally the Revds William Roberts, Amlwch, Robert Hughes, Gaerwen, and John Williams, Brynsiencyn, one of the true masters of pulpit oratory. In 1890 they had 83 chapels, 69 ministers and preachers, 10,707 communicants and 20,671 adherents; 13,369 scholars attended the 107 Sunday schools. With tongue in cheek it was said that putting a roof over Anglesey would merely confirm its status as one huge Calvinistic Methodist temple.

Nonconformists might reign supreme in matters of religious observance, but it took some time for them to achieve predominance in education. Far from abdicating its role, the Anglican Church had utilized day schools provided by the National Society. Leading this effort in the diocese was the Revd J. H. Cotton, later Dean of Bangor. Under the control of the clergy, the National schools offered basic instruction to poor children from the lower classes but also insisted that they be instructed in the catechism of the Established Church. In an attempt to regain the initiative pupils were moreover compelled to attend Sunday service in the parish church irrespective of their parents' religious persuasion. Cotton founded the first National school in Anglesey at Llandyfrydog in 1815, helped by the financial support of local landed proprietors. The pattern was set. As donors of land and annual subscriptions the families of Baron Hill, Bodorgan, Plas Newydd, Plas Penrhos and Porthaml gave the movement an initial advantage, so that during the next three decades another twenty-one National schools were started. Beaumaris National school was erected in 1816 on land donated by the Bulkeleys, who also paid the teachers' salaries. Still standing in Steeple Lane, this school proved a better bargain than the 'unsightly' edifice at Amlwch (also surviving) opened in 1821 at a cost of £1,015. Despite the patronage of the Marquess of Anglesey and the Mona and Parys Mine Companies, a huge deficit meant that the schoolmaster was unpaid and the building remained unfinished for some time.

Added to these were the eighteenth-century endowed schools and the privately founded establishments, such as the Duchess of Kent's school at Llanedwen. All came under Church of England control. It was usually the individual clergymen who undertook responsibility for running the schools, most of which struggled to survive on miserably inadequate funds. The Revd James Williams personally gave £200 towards the cost of Llanddeusant National school. If it were not for the leading gentry the situation would have been far worse. Yet, Anglican landowners would be berated frequently for their parsimony. While they flinched at the unrelenting requests for donations, the expenditure hardly dented their sizable rent-rolls. Plas Newydd (estimated rental £9,132) aided fifteen schools at an annual outlay of £106, later drastically reduced. Baron Hill (estimated rental £16,000) spent no more than £80 on nine schools. Philanthropic gestures, however small, attracted social prestige and there were, of course, self-serving political advantages; come election time, voters would be reminded of their beneficence.

Given their avowed aim of winning back worshippers to the Anglican Communion, and stemming the tide of dissent, it was appropriate that most National schools, at first, be held in the parish churches. For some children, proselytization left a bitter taste. Compulsory attendance at church services was later recalled in language redolent of the Babylonian captivity. Others appear to have had few qualms about subjecting their children to Anglican indoctrination; even a deep-dyed dissenter like Rhisiart Dafydd sent his sons to Llangefni National school. As it turned out, the Anglican clergy not only failed to plant a National school in all parishes as hoped, but were also unable to secure the allegiance of the young on the day it mattered, as the great number of Nonconformist Sunday schools attest. When the master of Beaumaris National school insisted that they should attend church twice every Sunday, pupil numbers fell from 240 to 147.

Nonconformist acceptance of unsectarian education under the auspices of the British Society was slow in developing; chapel building and the removal of outstanding debts had greater priority. Only with the publication of Hugh Owen's famous 'Letter to the Welsh People' in 1843 did they respond in earnest. A Llangeinwen personal success story, in that he climbed high on the civil service ladder in London, Owen came to regard the educational advancement of his countrymen as a lifetime mission. Nonconformist connections enabled him to rally support, and it was on his word that the Revd John Phillips, a Calvinistic Methodist minister at Bryn-teg, became the British Society agent in north Wales. Hitherto, only the schools at Holyhead, Heneglwys and Llanfachreth had links with the society, but backed by other Nonconformist ministers Phillips was soon active in Anglesey. Like his counterpart, Dean Cotton, he displayed energy and dedication, and within three years of his appointment new British schools had been erected at Marian-glas, Llanrhuddlad and Cemais, with another four held in chapel buildings. Set against the preponderance of dissent, their progress in the county was slow. Other denominations were wary of the Calvinistic Methodists. Not surprisingly, the landed gentry shunned the British schools on purely sectarian grounds. Lord Boston thwarted parish efforts in Llanidan when he subsidized a church school at Brynsiencyn. Before 1860, Rhos-y-bol was the only non-church school on the Plas Newydd subscription list. James Treweek, the Wesleyan mine agent, had argued that an English education would benefit those hundreds of poor children facing future emigration to England in search of work. Otherwise, the British schools' movement was reliant on middle-class tenant farmers, traders and shopkeepers, who, in the economic climate of the time found it an onerous undertaking.

Debt haunted both sets of promoters. They found it difficult to maintain school buildings, pay adequate salaries or purchase books and other essential equipment. The 1847 Report into the state of education in Wales laid bare the depressing picture in Anglesey. Thirty-six parishes did not have a school at all. Llansadwrn church school was held in a loft above a coach-house and stables. Apart from the highly praised Sunday schools, only two out of the total sixty day schools could be regarded as efficient. Here the honours were even: the masters of both Beaumaris National school and Llanrhuddlad British school received commendation for their discipline, organization and systematic instruction. The fact that Anglesey had but six trained teachers largely accounted for the patently unsatisfactory standards. The master of Penrhosfeilw church school still worked as a labourer when the opportunity arose; he had no control over his pupils. Few could argue with the educational content of the report. What provoked sectarian outrage was the scathing attack on the religion and morals of the people by an Anglican commissioner and his assistants (Samuel Dew, the only Nonconformist, left after a few days). At Newborough, morals were said to be 'at a very low ebb'. More controversially, J. W. Trevor, rector of Llanbeulan, presented evidence entitled 'On the Prevalence of Bastardy in Anglesey, as a Consequence of Defective Education'. Whatever truths it contained, his destructive testimony added to the furore that 'Brad y Llyfrau Gleision' (the Treachery of the Blue Books) aroused in Wales. Significantly, perhaps, there was no great explosion of public outrage in Anglesey. This indifference prompted adverse comment and, belatedly, Nonconformists held a protest meeting at Amlwch in 1848. Despite the ignominy surrounding the illegitimacy charges, only in December 1852 did Anglicans and dissenters combine to form the Anglesey Society for the Improvement of Morals. Its reforming efforts were short-lived.

Undoubtedly, the education of young girls from the lower classes had been particularly neglected in Anglesey. Their lives were bound by narrow perceptions of femininity. Women slotted into the traditional domestic roles of wives and mothers, though the sixty-five female 'copper miners' enumerated in 1851 shattered any assumptions of their physical inferiority to men. Limited employment opportunities ensured that a very high proportion would enter domestic service as 'indoor servants'. The Penrhos Industrial School for Girls, instituted by W. O. Stanley and his wife at Holyhead in 1864, taught orphans and children of poor parents 'all useful household employment' prior to securing domestic appointments. By the time of the 1891 census the number of indoor servants had reached 2,306, so that almost 58 per cent of the female working population was employed in domestic service. Since the landed gentry preferred English speakers recruited from outside the island most found employment in middle-class households, notably on farms, where they endured gruelling work regimes. Ordinarily, maids worked from 5.30 a.m. until 9.00 p.m. Milliners, dressmakers and washerwomen also constituted significant female occupation groupings at this time. Hotels and guest-houses supplied work for a substantial number of washerwomen at Beaumaris. Working-class girls able to benefit from improved educational opportunities later in the century still suffered inequalities. Of the few professions open to women, teaching provided the main career option in Anglesey, and the number of schoolmistresses grew from twenty-eight in 1871 to ninety-six by 1891. Heroines were few. Literary achievements invariably accounted for the rare female name that intruded into the three volumes dedicated to *Enwogion Môn* (Famous People of Anglesey).

Events in 1847 aggravated the bad blood already existing between church and chapel. Rivalry, division, argument, controversy: these were the ingredients that caused conflict as Anglicans and Nonconformists went on to feud interminably over the control of education. Sectarianism dictated the agenda. Four Nonconformist ministers came together at Holyhead to push for a British school. The rector of Penmon viewed the local National school as a 'valuable medium through which to advance the cause of the church'. At Gaerwen, Menai Bridge and Llangefni the provision of schools was fiercely contested. In their determination to establish British schools, ministers and middle-class leaders galvanized popular support by holding meetings and drawing up petitions. The names of Richard Davies, Samuel Dew and the Revd James Donne appeared regularly. Sectarian rivalry at Llangefni during 1850–2 escalated into a venomous confrontation, and when 700 people met in the town hall to support the case for a British school the power of Nonconformity in Anglesey was plain to see. Similar discord surrounded parallel efforts elsewhere in the 1860s. In the race to establish schools the Established Church succeeded in maintaining a healthy lead due mainly to the exertions of local clergymen, many of whom found themselves out of pocket. This could be gauged in 1865–6, when there were fifty-one Church schools with 3,297 pupils (most of whom, disconcertingly, came from Nonconformist homes) and only thirteen British schools with 1,525 pupils. Nonconformists in general, and Calvinistic Methodists in particular, had failed to match Anglican achievements despite the land and money donated by Robert and Richard Davies. In the long run, neither could it be said that proselytization within classroom walls benefited the Established Church.

The 1870 Education Act set out to fill the gaps left by the two voluntary societies. School boards, elected triennially, were empowered to establish new schools aided by the local rate. Drawn by the favourable possibilities, two leading Methodist ministers, the Revds Daniel Rowlands and Simon Fraser, drummed up support in Anglesey. With contested elections, the rancour between church and chapel entered a new cycle. Dissenters gained control of all but one (Beaumaris) of the twelve boards set up in 1871; on seven, Calvinistic Methodists formed the majority. Most elections, however, went uncontested to avoid expenditure, with Anglicans granted minority representation. Boards could sanction unsectarian or secular education and secure educational appointments of their choice. From the first, hard-pressed managers welcomed the opportunity to hand over a struggling British school to the local board, and all save Tŷ Mawr school would be transferred. The National schools, on the other hand, fought to maintain their independent denominational status. Nine new schools were built and others enlarged. But in difficult circumstances nine Church Schools would eventually be 'surrendered' by 1902, leaving the remaining twenty to limp on with total projected repair costs upwards of £7,000. Initial enthusiasm for school boards, meantime, had given way to resistance and indifference. Parochial antipathy undermined official attempts to amalgamate the smaller parishes; villagers at Llanfaethlu and Llanfwrog treated their neighbours at Llanfachreth as if they were a 'hostile tribe'. School boards were monopolized by the usual bevy of solid middle-class citizens. Displaying shameless self-interest, rate-conscious farmers did everything to cut down expenditure on the education of working-class pupils whilst resorting to private tuition for their own children. In protest at this abuse of power, Ap Ffarmwr encouraged five labourers to stand for election at Aberffraw in 1890. Only two were returned. Very rarely did 'labour' candidates have a voice on any of the thirty-four school boards formed between 1871 and 1897.

The saga of Beaumaris grammar school could fill volumes. Aside from its increased attachment to the Established Church, successive headmasters had gradually transformed it into a select boarding academy for 'young gentlemen'. Providing a mainly classical curriculum on the lines of a Victorian public school, only the sons of wealthy English families were able to afford the high fees. Local middle-class parents, deploring the usurpation of David Hughes's charity, campaigned to have the school adapted to their requirements. Collaterally, radical dissenters attempted to wrest control from the Church of England trustees and eliminate its Anglican image. Years of unending acrimony followed. At one point Robert Davies offered £5,000 if the school was moved to a more central site on the island and placed in the hands of a popularly elected governing body. Finding a course that would please all parties proved impossible, though an attempt was made to attract more Anglesey boys in the 1870s. An 'Anglesey County Scholarship' scheme, and even the university college at Bangor, had been established before the Welsh Intermediate Education Act of 1889 imposed a system of undenominational secondary schools. Here was the ideal opportunity completely to reorganize secondary education. Control passed to a democratically based authority, the Joint Education Committee. A scheme to establish five 'intermediate' schools – at Beaumaris, Holyhead, Amlwch, Llangefni and Llangaffo – was however declared financially unsound, and after further wrangling only three schools were approved by the Education Department by 1894. Under a new County Governing Body, Beaumaris was joined, at first in temporary premises, by schools at Llangefni (1897) and Holyhead (1901). Open to both boys and girls of proven ability, the county schools retained tuition fees and the education content of the traditional grammar school. The élitist needs of pupils from predominantly middle-class families were catered for, at the expense of vocational subjects more suitable to local requirements.

Besides the formal curriculum content, many primary schoolteachers became preoccupied with the high levels of absenteeism and the medium of instruction. Desperate poverty meant parents were unable to buy suitable clothing for their children, let alone pay the school fees. In 1847, pupils within the 10–15 age group received an average schooling of sixteen months. Even during the late 1860s a forgotten tribe of 'ragged, dirty, capless and shoeless urchins' roamed the streets of Holyhead and Amlwch. Entries by exasperated teachers in school log-books continually blame poverty, sickness, parental apathy, seasonal agricultural work, religious festivals, fairs, and rural customs such as 'clapping' for eggs at Easter, as the chief causes for irregular attendance. Over the years twenty-eight new board schools were built in the county, yet the average attendance only improved gradually – from 55.6 per cent in 1877 to 71.8 per cent by 1900. It still meant that a quarter of Anglesey children were absent from school. Even the advent of compulsory education, free schooling and the appointment of attendance officers had made little difference. At the turn of the century 2,500 children were still regularly absent, 500 of them at Holyhead. In June 1901, Holyhead school board spent four hours discussing the 186 names on the truant list.

Whereas Welsh was the everyday language of the home, community and place of worship, parental choice deemed that English would be the medium of secular instruction. Understandably, knowledge of English enabled their children to 'get on' in the world. Less comprehensible is the unbending way that teachers set about this task. In their enthusiasm to infuse English, the speaking of Welsh was banned in most schools even though, at first, the teachers themselves understood or spoke little English. At Llandrygan in 1846 the commissioner had to employ an interpreter! Small wonder, then, that the pupils failed to grasp the rudiments of education. Yet, the advantages of bilingualism were rarely considered. Where Welsh was adopted as the medium of instruction children benefited; it explained why Llanddeusant National school proved to be the best school on the island in mid-century. Instead of emulating this policy, many head teachers followed the line taken at Dwyran National school in 1873 stating that: 'the Welsh language is strictly prohibited in school'. First mentioned in the 1830s, the punitive 'Welsh Not' (a piece of wood suspended around the neck of a pupil speaking Welsh) was in regular use at a number of Anglesey schools throughout most of the century. At Aberffraw it was meant to 'check' Welsh speaking in both classroom and playground, and remained in use until at least 1894. Log-books reveal the extremes teachers would go to prevent largely monoglot children from conversing in their native tongue; the most common punishment being the cane, lines or detention. For thirty seven years until his retirement in 1897, Robert Davies, headmaster of Llangefni National school, kept up a personal vendetta against the Welsh language only to see his 'little schemes' to suppress it end in failure. By then a more tolerant attitude appeared, with Welsh introduced as a 'specific' subject in some schools. Campaigners on behalf of the language gained only modest success. Welsh songs and Welsh poetry slowly found a place on the syllabus. A number of school boards began keeping their minute books in Welsh, though such a suggestion was quashed by the Revd D. Mathias at Llanfachreth on the grounds that the school was an 'English school', and that records should be kept in English.

No matter the rational argument for the place of Welsh in education, generations of schoolchildren had come to view their language as something inferior. English was the fuel of self-improvement. Welsh, secure and unthreatened, was amply cared for in the Sunday schools and numerous literary activities. In this language stronghold, 91.8 per cent of the people of Anglesey in 1901 could speak Welsh. As many as 48 per cent were monoglot Welsh-speakers. One contemporary traveller remarked that *dim Saesneg* (no English) served as the standard reply in most villages. Developments during the course of the century had increased the English element in the county, yet outsiders bearing non-Welsh surnames were soon assimilated into the community; they, or certainly their children, became fluent in Welsh. Progress had its price. In different ways outside influences brought a change in popular attitudes. Very few were given Welsh Christian names. Old traditions died out; not merely everyday things like items of dress and basic food dishes such as *picws mali* and *brwas bara ceirch*, but long-established cultural customs and communal activities: story-telling, folklore, merrymaking festivals and entertainments. Along with many dialect words, expressions and agricultural terms common to the *gwerin* of Anglesey, they would be irretrievably lost.

Anglesey's rich literary tradition dated back to the age of the princes, but in striking contrast to previous centuries no major poet emerged prior to John Morris-Jones, a mathematics graduate of Jesus College, Oxford, who began publishing his work in the 1890s. All the same, a vibrant popular culture expressed itself through the eisteddfod, local printing and publishing. The first recorded eisteddfod of the century was held at

Llangefni in 1816, but Anglesey poets took little part. Attracting gentry support, the Beaumaris eisteddfod of 1832 proved a grand affair; the young princess Victoria, visiting the island, presented the awards. Most of the prizewinners came from outside Anglesey, including Angharad Llwyd who won the premier essay competition, in English, with *A History of the Island of Mona*. The Aberffraw 'royal' eisteddfod of 1849 was again patronized by the upper classes, who were seated apart from the lower orders in the huge marquee. Such glamorous trappings had been absent from the Llannerch-y-medd eisteddfod of 1835; conducted in the Welsh language it rewarded mainly local poets. Initial Methodist opposition to the eisteddfod – on the grounds of 'the immorality and evil things that happen at such gatherings' – subsided and from the 1850s they too held competitive literary meetings. The ever-increasing popularity of the institution led to a succession of local eisteddfodau; Eisteddfod Môn (Anglesey Eisteddfod) was first held at Llannerch-y-medd in 1869. The unique Anglesey workers' eisteddfod at Llangefni in 1894, backed by Ap Ffarmwr, failed to catch on, though it gave a literary platform to future rural trade union activists.

Poets were popularly known by their bardic pen-names that left English outsiders bewildered. And the eisteddfodic accomplishments of 'Gwalchmai', 'Bardd Du Môn', 'Nicander', 'Gweirydd ap Rhys', 'Hwfa Môn' and 'Llew Llwyfo' earned them fame and status in society, whatever their personal flaws. Competitive topics in Anglesey eisteddfodau ranged widely – from 'the Menai Bridge' to the 'invasion of China', 'the creation' to 'commerce'. When fair play was perceived to be lacking, bardic spats could turn into major scandals as at Aberffraw in 1849 following a controversial adjudication for the chair competition won by Morris Williams, 'Nicander', a literary-minded clergyman. It may be that most of the poetic output was prolix and of little literary value, and that eisteddfodic glory became a sufficient achievement in itself (Rowland Williams, 'Hwfa Môn', would pose aristocratically in his archdruid robes). But at a time of limited educational opportunity the eisteddfod drew out latent talent and kindled considerable public interest in Welsh literature and history. *Enwogion Môn* (1877), commemorating Anglesey worthies, first appeared as an essay for the Holyhead eisteddfod of 1872 by Richard Parry, 'Gwalchmai'. Entirely self-educated, Robert John Pryse, 'Gweirydd ap Rhys', won prizes at the National Eisteddfod for his treatises on the history and literature of Wales, and he was subsequently able to make a living through his pen. His son John Robert Pryse, 'Golyddan', who studied medicine at Edinburgh University, also distinguished himself as a poet. Women rarely made an appearance in the literary world, but his daughter Catherine Prichard, 'Buddug', is remembered for the well-known song 'O na byddai'n haf o hyd'.

Nonconformist Sunday schools had created a vast readership among the *gwerin*, and the growing market for Welsh books kept local presses busy. Needless to say, there were scores of religious tracts and biographies of eminent preachers. By mid-century popular demand broadened to encompass increasingly secular tastes; not only books with an educational content aimed at the upwardly aspiring, but publications for the mass-market. Printing presses had been set up early in the century. At Llannerch-y-medd, Enoch Jones printed religious works before venturing with *Y Sylwedydd* (1831). Like *Eurgrawn Môn*, brought out at Holyhead in 1825–6 by Robert Roberts, it contained poetry, contemporary news and items of general information. Both periodicals folded because of insufficient support. The dissemination of popular knowledge was also the concern of Thomas Jones, Amlwch, a self-taught preacher and teacher, who wrote several Welsh books on religion, geography and arithmetic. In the wake of the critical 1847 Education Report came reference books and dictionaries for those wishing to learn English. Drawing on years of experience as a Newborough schoolmaster, Robert Williamson, 'Bardd Du Môn', produced *Hunan-Gyfarwyddyd i Gymro ddysgu darllen, ysgrifenu a deall yr Iaith Seisoneg* in 1849. Monoglot speakers could always turn to a Welsh ready reckoner, *Y Cyfrifydd Parod*, printed by William Aubrey at Llannerch-y-medd in 1853.

Early novels carried a distinct moral message in keeping with the times. Temperance in the case of *Llewelyn Parri: neu y Meddwyn Diwygiedig* (1855), written by Lewis William Lewis, 'Llew Llwyfo', before his own boozy descent into poverty and the workhouse. Social convention was refreshingly defied by the popular satirical magazine *Y Punch Cymraeg*. Launched by Lewis Jones at Holyhead in 1858 it became a thorn in the flesh of the middle-class, Nonconformist élite, exposing the sort of hypocrisy that allowed those who signed the pledge to take alcohol 'medicinally'. Three short-lived publications aimed at the ordinary reader – *Y Nofelydd* (1861), *Aelwyd y Cymro* (1865), *Y Gwyliedydd* (1870) – were produced at Llannerch-y-medd. But Amlwch overshadowed the self-proclaimed 'Athens of Anglesey', where the press of David Jones published a formidable list of books and pamphlets, encompassing religion, local history, poetry and ballads between 1864 and 1891. Written by mostly local authors for a local market, they were the staple diet of a cultured *gwerin*. Soon, divergent cultural attitudes within the education system induced a gradual shift in reading habits. Once the English language was mastered, more and more turned to English publications for information and news. The demand for Welsh books decreased with predictable results for the local press. Tellingly, there was little printing at Amlwch, Holyhead and Llannerch-y-medd after the turn of the century. Welsh-language newspapers and periodicals were not abandoned lightly;

the homely style of *Y Clorianydd*, first printed in 1891 at Llangefni, gave Anglesey people a successful Welsh weekly newspaper.

Politics at first continued to be the preserve of the landed gentry. Though the Bulkeley-Paget *entente* of 1790 led to a long period of uncontested elections in Anglesey, political turbulence engendered by events in France and the demands for Catholic Emancipation outraged a nervous ruling class. Anglesey gentry and clergymen joined their mainland counterparts in 1808 to form the Menai Pitt Club in defence of the crown and constitution. A good number held posts in the Anglesey Local Militia (1809–16); others expressed strong anti-Catholic and anti-Methodist views. Excepting O. J. A. Fuller Meyrick, the chief county families remained Whigs, in contrast to almost all the lesser gentry, who were Tories. But party labels still counted for little; MPs were returned on the basis of their social standing and personal qualities rather than political views. Henry Paget, MP for Anglesey 1820–32, first appeared as a die-hard Tory opposed to Catholic Emancipation (reflecting the virulent anti-Catholic sentiments evident in the county), but later supported the Reform Bill. On both occasions political opponents deferred to the eldest son of the first Marquess of Anglesey. Beaumaris boroughs continued to be controlled by the Bulkeleys; in 1807, true to style, they had even purchased the castle for £735. When Thomas James Bulkeley, the seventh viscount, died without issue in 1822 the unbroken family line ended after four centuries. Sir Robert Williams, the son of his half-brother, took over the seat in 1826, followed by his son Sir Richard Williams-Bulkeley (who had assumed the Bulkeley title). Only in 1832 were there significant changes to the political scene. Under the Reform Act, Amlwch, Holyhead and Llangefni would be added to the boroughs constituency, and as a result of a secret deal, the Bulkeleys and Pagets agreed to switch seats.

More far-reaching was the division that arose in gentry ranks between the liberal elements who favoured additional reform and the conservative faction opposed to further change. As a result, party affiliations gained weight. Sir Richard Williams-Bulkeley's reputation as a forthright Whig MP for the county irritated the leading Tories. Political considerations now meant more than social niceties to Meyrick, Lord Boston and W. Bulkeley Hughes of Plas Coch, but lacking sufficient support in the 1835 election, a possible Tory challenge fizzled out. Their opportunity came the following year when, as a result of a serious fire at Baron Hill, the depressed Williams-Bulkeley decided to vacate the seat and go abroad for a time. Very quickly, the Tory lesser gentry persuaded O. J. A. Fuller Meyrick to declare his candidature. When W. O. Stanley of Plas Penrhos emerged as the Liberal choice at the 1837 by-election, blessed by Baron Hill and Plas Newydd, the island was unexpectedly split into rival political groupings. Landlord influence became paramount, strengthened by the trend towards annual tenancies. Subservient electors dutifully trooped to the hustings, and with more tenant voters answerable to the great Whig landowners, Stanley secured victory by 693 votes to 586. All but seven of the Marquess of Anglesey's 144 tenant voters declared for Stanley (nine did not vote); 82 of the 94 Williams-Bulkeley tenants did likewise (with four not voting). Stanley, however, was merely a 'warming pan' who kept the seat snug until Williams-Bulkeley's comeback at the 1847 election.

Religion had featured prominently in the 1837 contest and in many ways this by-election was a crucial turning point in Nonconformist attitudes. At Holyhead, dissenting preachers campaigned publicly for Stanley as the defender of religious liberty. Nonconformists were reminded of the malevolent anti-Methodist pamphlets written in 1801–2 by the Revd T. E. Owen, rector of Llandyfrydog, which labelled them 'Jacobins' and 'rebels'. Since then, the autocratic John Elias had done everything to prevent the Calvinistic Methodist denomination from 'meddling' in politics. When George IV visited Plas Newydd in 1821 Elias helped to draw up a 'Loyal Address' in their name. But the younger, progressive wing was no longer willing to tolerate his reactionary views on Catholic Emancipation, the tithe and disestablishment – made worse when he personally voted for Meyrick. Overthrowing Elias's 'iron yoke', leading Calvinistic Methodists in Anglesey publicly congratulated Stanley on his success and pledged future support; among them were several ministers, Rhisiart Dafydd and his son Richard jnr. Another indication of the awakened political interest was the 141 per cent rise in the number of freeholders who registered to vote. Anglesey's electorate of 2,457 in 1841 surpassed that of Caernarfonshire, which had a far greater population. Although the Tories thought better of contesting the seat in succeeding elections, various contemporary issues contributed substantially to the radicalization of the Calvinistic Methodists during the 1840s and 50s, not least the mounting sectarian controversy in the sphere of education.

Once the interests of the emergent middle class fused with Nonconformist aspirations, parliamentary representation was sought from their own ranks. As early as 1852 Richard Davies had embarked on the political trail when he stood, unsuccessfully, as a Liberal dissenter in the Caernarfon boroughs. In the opinion of Sir Richard Williams-Bulkeley it was 'the introduction into Wales of a direct religious warfare'. Elsewhere the sway of reactionary Anglican Tory landowners came increasingly under threat – but not in Anglesey. Ostensibly Liberal in politics both Sir Richard Williams-Bulkeley and Lord Clarence Paget, MP for the boroughs, enjoyed a virtually unassailable position. Periodic nods of approval towards religious dissent and unsectarian education (he overturned the Anglican status of Beaumaris National school) masked Williams-

Bulkeley's abysmal parliamentary record and right-wing proclivities, and ensured that he remained unchallenged. When Paget stepped down at the 1857 election to let in W. O. Stanley, his progressive views and patronage at Holyhead made him a popular candidate who earned Nonconformist respect.

Religious dissent bred a fierce political awareness as the middle-class Nonconformist leadership steadily exerted its influence at local level. The Liberation Society – which sought the disestablishment of the Established Church – laid down a strong organizational base in Anglesey: by 1868 it had 6 branches and 105 subscribers comprising the familiar radical dissenters. Since the Reform Act of the previous year extended the vote to small farmers and shopkeepers, the very backbone of Nonconformity, the essential preconditions were in place prior to Williams-Bulkeley's long awaited retirement, and the end of a long political dynasty. Local activists, quick off the mark, drafted Richard Davies as Liberal candidate for the 1868 election, and went about harnessing Nonconformist support. At a grand meeting in Llangefni, 'packed with Calvins', Dew, Donne, John Lewis, Roger Evans and the usual cluster of farmers and ministers came to eulogize Anglesey's favourite son. Williams-Bulkeley also nodded his approval; while the chief landed proprietors gave assurance that their tenantry would be free to vote as they wished. With a superior organization and promising canvass returns the Davies camp exuded confidence. All this put paid to the half-hearted claims of Lord Clarence Paget, then abroad on naval duties. Richard Davies was allowed a walkover. While the 1868 election in the county failed to generate the same excitement as the celebrated triumph over Tory landlordism in some other Welsh constituencies, the return of the Methodist 'idol' was a moment for all Anglesey dissenters to savour. It signalled a fundamental shift away from the traditional rule of the landed gentry and the dominance of the *plasty*. In the boroughs, on the other hand, W. O. Stanley saw off the challenge of Morgan Lloyd, an ambitious Merioneth barrister, in only the second contest of the century.

Electoral success aggravated sectarian tensions. One of Nonconformity's worst enemies was D. Watkin Davies, rector of Llanfair Pwllgwyngyll. The following year, at the funeral of the Revd Henry Rees (Richard Davies's father-in-law and the most prominent Methodist preacher of his day) he refused to allow dissenting ministers to speak at the graveside in Llandysilio churchyard. Beyond that, a confident Nonconformist leadership group was able to exert greater power in the struggle for the control of school boards and Beaumaris grammar school. Contrary to expectations, however, Richard Davies had an unremarkable parliamentary career, dwarfed by the likes of Henry Richard. True, he expressed the radical opinions of his followers with his exemplary voting record, but the fact that he never once spoke in the Commons enabled Tory foes to brand him a 'silent member'. In time, even Liberal enthusiasts came to regret their lack of a 'hero' to defend in electoral battles. The first came in 1874. To the evident disappointment of his father, Captain R. L. M. Williams-Bulkeley, the heir of Baron Hill, provided a Tory challenge that was crushed by 1,636 votes to 793. Despite the secret ballot, Tory landlords made every effort to intimidate their tenants; two tenant farmers were said to have been evicted for openly supporting Davies. In the boroughs W. O. Stanley's retirement allowed the Methodist Morgan Lloyd to win a three-cornered fight. As a result, Anglesey became the first county in Wales to be represented by two Nonconformist Liberals. Lloyd sat unopposed until 1885, when the boroughs seat was disenfranchised and merged with the county constituency.

One significant outcome of the 1874 election was the establishment that year of formal party organizations. The Anglesey Conservative Association, with Lord Boston as president and O. J. A. Fuller Meyrick as vice-president, was followed by the Anglesey Liberal Association under Samuel Dew and John Morgan, owner of the woollen factory at Cadnant. Richard Davies continued to tramp through the division lobbies but as time progressed certain aspects of his lifestyle, business, and political outlook put him at odds with many of his followers. His social status at Treborth bordered on the aristocratic; he was a landlord and capitalist employer who grew rich at the expense of others. Such issues, on top of his timorous showing at Westminster, raised Conservative hopes in the 1880 election. Captain G. Pritchard-Rayner of Tresgawen, a popular figure in the county, gained 1,085 votes, cutting Davies's majority to 309 and shattering the notion that sectarianism denoted the lines of political demarcation in Anglesey. Things improved by 1885 when the electorate rose to 9,777 following the third Reform Act. The Anglesey Liberal Association was revamped. Davies had been appointed Lord Lieutenant of Anglesey, the first Welsh Nonconformist to gain the honour, and his record of benevolence remained unequalled. Despite the familiar personal attacks, he attracted 4,412 votes to 3,462 for Pritchard-Rayner. Boosted by the influx of radical support from Holyhead following the disappearance of the boroughs seat, the Liberals secured a more respectable majority of 950.

But the following year Davies's radical turn of mind veered towards a conservative direction on the question of Irish Home Rule. He failed to support Gladstone's government by abstaining in a crucial Commons vote. His consequent resignation and defection to the Liberal Unionist cause meant a break with the Anglesey Liberal Association. Davies's successor was the Cemais-born Methodist merchant, Thomas 'Palestina' Lewis (his trip to the Holy Land had become a well-worn lecture topic). It proved to be an unimaginative choice. In the 1886 election the Liberal majority again fell – to 307. Attracting 3,420 votes, Pritchard-Rayner's percentage share of 47.9 was the best recorded for the Conservatives in the county. When he declined to stand again, however, the Anglesey Conservatives were in disarray. Those Liberals opposed to Irish Home Rule who set up a Liberal Unionist Association in 1887 had good reason for optimism as they courted Richard Davies. The prospect of a comeback horrified Gladstonian Liberals. Davies, they said, was merely a self-interested Protestant landowner anxious to safeguard his Irish property (he and his brother held 1,682 acres in County Dublin). Though he declined to stand in the 1892 election, his personal endorsement of Morgan Lloyd, the Liberal Unionist candidate, backed by the Tories, further tarnished his reputation. In a separate political move, an abortive attempt was made to draft Owen Thomas in the interests of both farmers and workers. When the electioneering dust settled, Thomas Lewis trounced Lloyd by 1,718 votes to give the Liberals their highest ever majority.

Already there had been other indications of Liberal strength in the county. Beside the main Nonconformist issues of disestablishment, education and land came the programme of the Cymru Fydd movement that fused cultural and political nationalism. Though slow to gain appeal, the branch established at Llanfair Pwllgwyngyll in September 1887 was the first in Wales. Under the inspiration of John Morris-Jones members discussed a range of matters relating to the current national awakening. A sweeping victory in the first county council elections in 1889 saw thirty-three Liberals returned, against seven Conservatives and two independent members. No Anglican clergyman stood, and Sir Richard Henry Williams-Bulkeley appeared something of a token 'great landowner' amongst a phalanx of farmers. Both business and the professions were well represented. As many as twenty-seven were Calvinistic Methodists, and while their domination uneased the Baptists, the Tory press poured scorn on a 'Calvin council'. At the next round of elections in 1892 Liberal representation rose to thirty-five, many of the councillors being returned unopposed. No working-class candidate could hope to penetrate this overwhelmingly middle-class body for some time yet. When John Hughes stood in 'labour' colours at Aberffraw in 1895 he received only a derisory vote. As the new centre for local government administration, Llangefni replaced Beaumaris, the county town since 1549; the Shire Hall was built, appropriately, next to Moriah Methodist chapel. Long the symbol of landed gentry rule, Anglicized and out-of-the-way, Beaumaris had condemned itself.

As another politician lacking in charisma, rarely did Thomas Lewis make his presence known in the Commons. When ill health forced his resignation, the brilliant young barrister, Methodist, and Cymru Fydd supporter, Ellis Jones Griffith, was adopted as candidate. Fending off the Conservative challenge of J. Rice Roberts by 4,224 votes to 3,197 in the 1895 election, he joined the new generation of radical Welsh MPs at Westminster. But his parliamentary career did not live up to its early promise; he was slow to make an impression on the floor of the House. A close friend, baffled by this lack of political direction, saw him as 'the Anglesey sphinx'. Compared to his brightest contemporaries, Tom Ellis and David Lloyd George, Ellis Jones Griffith remained a second-rank leader who failed to attain high government office (only in 1912 was he appointed under-secretary to the Home Office). Consistently, then, the Liberal cause in Anglesey had to accept the flawed limitations of its parliamentary representatives in an age that revered inspiring political personalities. All the same, middle-class Nonconformists dominated local government at county and parish level, just as they controlled the school boards. While the authority of the great landlords diminished, Liberal activists secured a hegemony equal to that enjoyed by the Anglican Whig gentry earlier in the century. But it was power exercised with little regard to the interests of the working class; many social questions were conveniently marginalized.

Divisions based on sectarianism and party politics were as nothing compared to the social inequalities. The poor of Anglesey continued to endure economic hardship. Concern for their welfare inspired occasional humanitarian initiatives. Soup kitchens opened at Holyhead in 1855 fed up to 220 poor people. Before Christmas the poor in many parishes would receive gifts of coal and warm clothing. In November 1870 Lady Dinorben donated blankets, sheets and coats to over 450 of the poor at Amlwch and Pen-sarn. Not unexpectedly at other times, poverty and hunger accounted for the innumerable cases of petty larceny. Thefts of food, livestock, household items and clothing were commonplace. Clothes put out to dry quickly vanished; farmers could not reckon on holding to their poultry for more than six weeks. Thieves not only sneaked into people's houses when they attended a place of worship on Sunday, but also broke into churches to steal communion plate – as at Llanedwen in 1840. Shops proved to be favoured targets for children who pilfered from counters, or burglars like those who stole £37 in gold and silver from the cashbox of a Llannerch-y-medd grocer in 1871. Assault, malicious damage, begging and poaching were equally familiar offences reported in the press. Poaching for rabbits and pheasants, a very common crime in Anglesey, attracted not merely the archetypal hunger-driven labourer but a highly respected Anglican clergyman whose literary deeds earned him a place in *Enwogion Môn*. It said much about the character of the Revd Dr H. H. Davies, rector of Llangoed, that he was prepared to face five convictions of trespass and shooting partridges in 1859–60 in order to draw attention to the iniquitous

Game Laws. Blame for much of the crime could always be laid on 'outsiders'. A violent robbery by a wandering Irish tramp in 1873 precipitated the death of James King of Prysaeddfed, a former high sheriff. Irish labourers, hawkers, tinkers and the multitude of travelling beggars unquestionably presented a problem for the county authorities, but they also provided convenient scapegoats. Major crimes were rare in Anglesey and the occasional murder usually turned out to be a 'family affair'.

However impressive the Nonconformist ascendancy appeared at first sight, taken in proportion to the population there remained thousands untouched by religion. Neither could its moral authority insulate the island from vestiges of superstition or unsavoury activity. Belief in witchcraft was said to be prevalent at Llanddona; one designated 'witch', Siân Bwt, became more the object of curiosity in that she stood merely 44 inches tall. Even as late as the 1850s, Saint Seiriol's holy well at Penmon would be visited at dead of night and its 'sacred water' taken to cure sick people. Society always produced its opposites. Alongside those basking in godliness were the wrong-doers and outcasts whose values and code of behaviour remained completely different. Contrary to the image of Amlwch as a Methodist citadel, 'great numbers' never entered a place of worship. Illegitimacy rates, drunkenness and street fighting, especially in mid-century, caused great concern. Immediately following the 1859 religious revival the number of criminal cases in Anglesey showed a 57 per cent decrease. Yet, during the following decade there were hundreds of cases before the Petty and Quarter Sessions – often complicated by the inability of monoglot Welsh speakers to follow proceedings. Despite the work of various north Wales temperance associations in the 1870s, and the individual zeal of the Revd J. R. Hughes, Bryn-teg, prosecutions for drunkenness reached their peak in the same decade. Anglesey bristled with public houses and beer retailers, far outstripping the temperance hotels and coffee houses. Llannerch-y-medd had sixteen taverns in 1874; Amlwch boasted thirty-seven in 1885; while the list at Holyhead rose to fifty-eight by 1897. It was not only alcohol that provided solace. Almost every Anglesey man smoked or chewed the 'exceptionally strong' tobacco manufactured at Amlwch. Amid the *demi-mondes* of Holyhead, just as any port town, prostitutes attracted custom; many bore Irish surnames, though one Caddy Owen achieved notoriety as a brothel-keeper in the 1860s.

Entertainment and recreational activities found a place alongside Nonconformity, though certain pastimes might be frowned upon. A theatre at Amlwch in the 1830s staged English dramas performed by travelling companies. Local brass bands and choirs had their devotees, often competing at local eisteddfodau. Cricket and football clubs indicated a growing interest in organized sport. Cricket established itself in mid-century, encouraged by local gentry who ran a country-house eleven.

Baron Hill support opened the way to the formation of the Beaumaris Cricket Club in 1858. Within the next decade there were also clubs at Holyhead, Amlwch and Llangefni. Only during the eighties, when a Saturday half-day holiday became general, did this 'gentlemanly' sport attract working-class participation. In no time the Llangoed village team was defeating the established sides. Football attained a recognizably modern form in the 1870s. A shade less brutal, but no less intense than early eighteenth-century communal encounters, soccer's reputation for inciting brawling, rowdyism and drunkenness among its distinctly lower-class followers led one critic to bluntly dismiss the sport as an 'unchristian practice'. A short-lived, independent Anglesey League was set up during the 1895–6 season featuring teams from Amlwch, Beaumaris, Holyhead, Menai Bridge, Llandegfan and Llangefni. As the only Anglesey-born full international player, Robert Roberts of Beaumaris had already won his Welsh cap in the match against Ireland in 1890. Golf, lawn tennis and yachting (in 1885 the Beaumaris club converted into the Royal Anglesey Yacht Club) were for those several notches up on the social scale.

How far the message of Nonconformity influenced public attitudes to military matters is difficult to judge. Wars always generated interest. On the outbreak of hostilities with France in 1793 the militia was again summoned for duty. Recalling invasion fears of Tudor times, miners at Amlwch joined the Loyal Parys Mountain Volunteers in 1798. Anglesey men fought at Trafalgar and Waterloo. To commemorate the cavalry exploits of Henry William Paget, who famously lost a leg at Waterloo, work began in 1816 on the totemic column at Llanfair Pwllgwyngyll (created Marquess of Anglesey the previous year, his bronze statue was added in 1860). The Royal Anglesey Regiment of Militia had undertaken defensive duties in southern England prior to disbandment in 1814. While the local militia subsequently existed in little more than name, the sons of the Anglican landed gentry sought a military career. Lord George Paget and T. L. Hampton Lewis of Henllys distinguished themselves in the Crimean war. When the militia force was revived in 1853, officers encountered reluctance and indiscipline among the rank and file. No more than ten turned up for annual training at Beaumaris the following year. Three companies of Rifle Volunteers raised at Aberffraw, Amlwch and Menai Bridge in 1860 were all disbanded within three years. Artillery Volunteers at Holyhead and Beaumaris had disbanded by 1873, leaving only the Royal Anglesey Engineers Militia. For one reason or another, soldering held little appeal for the *gwerin* of Anglesey – so different to the example of the *émigré* Hugh Parry of Bryngwran, who, in fighting for the Union side in the American Civil War, proved to be one of 'Anglesey's bravest'. Attempts to revive the volunteer movement in the 1880s failed, possibly because of Nonconformist disapproval. The only place in the county to raise a company of volunteers was Cemais by 1887, inspired by the leadership of Captain (later Colonel) Owen Thomas. Composed of farmers and labourers, the 108-strong K Company Cemaes Rifle Volunteer Force formed a unit of the 2nd Volunteer Battalion, Royal Welch Fusiliers. In a shrewd move that overcame local prejudices, Thomas, of impeccable Independent stock, had persuaded a local preacher and chapel officials to enlist.

Progressive steps were taken to combat crime. Apart from the traditional parish and borough constables no effective county police force existed at the beginning of the century. At a time of unemployment and high food prices following the end of the Napoleonic wars anxious property owners in the main towns set up private societies to maintain law and order. Associations for the Prosecution of Felons at Amlwch, Beaumaris and Holyhead offered rewards and threatened legal proceedings. In 1817 a reward of five guineas was given for information leading to the apprehension and conviction of those 'feloniously breaking and entering any house'. Population growth and a greater incidence of crime by mid-century prompted discussion that led to the establishment of a professional police force. The fifteen-strong Anglesey County Constabulary was formed in 1857. Over the years more officers were recruited, and though Anglesey had one of the smallest forces in Wales it proved to be one of the most efficient. Captain D. W. Griffith and Lt. Col. W. H. Thomas, the first two chief constables, drew on their military background to instil strict discipline. Policemen were treated as if they were army soldiers and fined for the merest transgression – in one case 6 shillings for smoking on the horse-drawn Beaumaris to Menai Bridge bus. By 1892 Anglesey had eighteen police stations, complete with either a lock-up or cell. They were not always needed. To reduce the number of undesirable vagrants on the island, Inspector Edward Owen took a pragmatic approach, dipping into his own pocket to pay the penny toll and see them over to the other side of the Menai Suspension Bridge! Anglesey retained its independence as a police authority until 1950, when three county forces merged to form the Gwynedd Constabulary.

Whether as retribution or a deterrent, severe punishment awaited the criminal regardless of the nature of the offence. Two men sentenced to six months' imprisonment for looting a wreck at Aberffraw in 1823 received, upon release, an additional public flogging. Anne Williams of Llanfechell was convicted of housebreaking in 1842 and sentenced to ten years transportation to Australia; aged but nineteen, she knew no English. Six weeks imprisonment with hard labour was handed out in 1869 for the theft of a hat worth one shilling. Anglesey victims of crime evinced little Christian charity and proceedings were initiated for the most trivial offence – such as against two little boys who stole 2 pence – though the magistrates often showed commendable humanity in dismissing the case. At a cost of £6,500 a new purpose-built county jail was erected in the middle of Beaumaris in 1829, which came to be regarded as one of the best in Britain. Serving time inside its grim walls were prisoners like Gaynor Jones, sentenced to one month's hard labour for stealing a quart of milk, and Thomas Williams, imprisoned for three months for killing a hare and three pheasants on Lady Dinorben's land. The usual punishment for inmates was picking oakum, breaking stones, or monotonous work on the treadmill. Only two public executions took place at Beaumaris. William Griffith was hanged for the brutal attempted murder of his wife in 1830, the first execution since 1786. Extra constables had to be drafted in lest the crowd of 3,000 attempt a rescue. Convicted of killing his father-in-law, the last to be hanged was Richard Rowlands in 1862. Though enlarged a few years later, prisoner numbers fell to less than ten, and following the closure of the jail in 1878 they were transferred to Caernarfon.

Each parish remained responsible for its poor, and out of the local rates provision was made for the old, infirm, unemployed, widows and orphans. Most of the old endowed charities of Anglesey were small, and many had been allowed to lapse through maladministration or petty corruption. Indeed, income from charities for the relief of the poor – which supplied bread and clothing – were being added to the poor rates. Care in the community had become largely the concern of women, and for small sums of money they provided lodging for paupers as well as undertaking diverse domestic chores such as cleaning and washing. Alleviating poverty proved a costly business, and by the 1830s ratepayers, especially in Amlwch, resented the mounting rate burden. Reform came with the Poor Law Amendment Act of 1834. Parishes were grouped into unions, but instead of a single island unit, fifty-three parishes would compose the Anglesey Union, leaving fifteen attached to the Bangor Union and six to the Caernarfon Union. Elected Boards of Guardians then supervised administration. No able-bodied labourers would receive assistance unless they entered a workhouse. As intended, this proved to be a deterrent in Anglesey; no applications were made for aid and no workhouse was erected for some time. The sick, the old and the orphaned still received poor relief and children often had trade apprenticeships to give them a start in life. The new system might be more efficient, but it failed to curb poor-rate increases: between 1841 and 1847 the annual expenditure rose from £17,268 to £18,222. Responding to criticism, the guardians were finally compelled to build workhouses at Llannerch-y-medd and then Valley, completed in 1870 at a cost of £3,000. Women and children comprised the largest group, many of whom entered 'in rags'. Tramps and vagrants were regularly admitted – 130 at Valley in 1878 – but such was the rigid discipline that men often rebelled violently.

Inadequate medical attention exacerbated the health problems. Doctors were fortunately available for the workforce at Parys Mountain and the Holyhead harbour project. Unable to afford doctors' fees, the poor would have to resort to traditional herbal remedies or seek advice from the local pharmacist. Women had long practised as midwives and community healers; at Beaumaris in the 1830s Catherine Williams charged a few pence to apply leeches as a method of treatment. A dispensary opened at Llangefni in 1825; Beaumaris had a 'druggist' and Holyhead its 'apothecaries' hall'. Certain Anglesey families were gifted with medical skills. Evan Thomas of Llanfair-yng-Nghornwy and his descendants achieved wide fame as 'Meddygon Esgyrn Môn' (the bone-setters of Anglesey); Hugh Owen Thomas became the pioneer of British orthopaedic surgery. Sickness and infectious diseases meant that people were perpetually living in the shadow of the graveyard. There was still a high infant mortality rate: 30 per cent of the deaths recorded in the Holyhead burial register of 1853 were of children under five. Outbreaks of cholera proved deadly – forty-two perished at Holyhead following the epidemic of 1849. Another twenty-seven died in 1866. Also that year 170 Anglesey people died of tuberculosis. Maintaining the philanthropic record of the Plas Penrhos family, W. O. Stanley became a generous benefactor of the hospital opened on Ynys Halen (Salt Island), Holyhead, in 1871, which became known as the Stanley Sailors' Hospital. Friendly societies made provision for sickness, old age and bereavement based on working-class self-help: eighteen were registered in Anglesey in 1876, dropping to thirteen by 1910. The Druidical Friendly Society at Llannerch-y-medd, the Llangefni Friendly Society, the Mechanics' Friendly Society at Amlwch, like most others, operated as small-time localized benefit clubs. The majority were handicapped by limited funds, in contrast to the lasting success of the Oddfellows, one of the largest societies in Britain. Not until the late 1870s did public health legislation begin to take effect; Dr E. Parry Edwards, the first county medical officer of health, was appointed in 1876.

Even when the face of Anglesey was changing more rapidly than any time before, the lot of the common people remained as difficult as ever. Impoverished families experienced life at its grubbiest; their squalid environment seemed to belong to an earlier age. Most houses were in a dilapidated state. The typical labourer's cottage was the 'square box' type consisting of one or two rooms, often with an earthen floor and thatched roof. Toilet facilities were primitive and refuse heaps accumulated in the road outside, endangering public health. Few places had an adequate water-supply or system of sewerage disposal. Water was usually drawn from surface wells, and as at Amlwch and Llangefni they were liable to contamination. Tourist-minded Beaumaris in the late 1870s was said to be in need of improved sanitary conditions with outlets 'carried further into the sea'. Even by the 1890s little regard was paid to sanitation or drainage at Amlwch, Llannerch-y-medd, or Cemais, which also had pretensions as a tourist resort. Changes came, if only very slowly. Holyhead had made an early start. In 1866 the Holyhead Water Company supplied the town, and water was later piped from Llyn Traffwll. An excellent sewerage system had also been installed. From 1894 elected urban district councils began to tackle public health problems more efficiently. Menai Bridge UDC for one set about providing a satisfactory sanitation and refuse collection, though it faced difficulties providing a sufficient water-supply. At long last, the needs of the lower classes began to receive due recognition. Yet much more had to be done to secure basic living standards; the struggle for social justice continued to present a real challenge.

VI

The Twentieth Century and Beyond

Many of the advances that shaped the modern world made their appearance in Anglesey very early in the century, though their full effects would not be felt for some time. The county entered the motor age in 1903 when EY I, belonging to Sir Richard Henry Williams-Bulkeley, was registered as the first car number plate. It provided a prestige symbol for the wealthy; Henry Cyril Paget, the fifth Marquess of Anglesey, splashed out on a superior French car. The motor-car also fitted the image of public figures such as Sir John Morris-Jones and the Revd John Williams – who saved his blushes by instructing his chauffeur to park some distance away from the chapel. Given the unsuitability of the main post-road for the new traffic, an initial speed restriction of 10mph was imposed. The county council undertook subsequent highway improvement schemes; new bridges were built at Aberffraw and Llangefni. Car ownership proliferated rapidly among professional and business people, so that the number of motor licences rose from 45 in 1908 to 7,747 by 1937. The Anglesey County Constabulary had acquired a patrol car two years earlier. Bicycles, motor-cycles and public transport offered ordinary people the means for cheap road travel. A private company at Cemais had registered a motor-bus in 1912. Operators such as the Bangor Blue Motors, Holyhead Motors (Mona Maroon) and Llangoed Red Motors served parts of Anglesey prior to the Crosville Company taking control over most local bus services in 1930. To cope with the increasing traffic the structure of the Menai Suspension Bridge was strengthened between 1938 and 1941; weight restrictions were lifted and tolls abolished. These developments transformed towns and villages alike, making even the remotest corners of the island accessible. But much of the rural past lingered: horse-drawn carts were still in common use as late as the 1960s. Large crowds of Anglesey people also witnessed early progress in aviation. From Holyhead, Captain Vivian Hewitt made the first successful (75-minute) flight across the Irish Sea in April 1912.

Electricity offered a new form of power to replace gas in the lighting of streets, public buildings and select private houses. A steam-driven generating station at Holyhead enabled the urban council to install electric light in the town as early as 1906. A similar plant run by a private company allowed Menai Bridge to convert to electricity in 1913. But when the

Menai Bridge Light Company ran into serious financial difficulties the urban district council took over the failing enterprise in 1922. From 1931 the North Wales Power Company began to distribute electricity supply to the island along overhead lines. Soon Holyhead and Menai Bridge were taking electricity from the grid and by 1936 Llangefni, Beaumaris and Amlwch had been connected to the system. A private undertaking, the Holyhead and Anglesey Telephone Company, operated the county's first telephone service at the turn of the century, before the Post Office took control in 1912. The following year Llanfair Pwllgwyngyll became one of the few villages in Britain to have a telephone exchange.

Photographic images of Edwardian Anglesey reflect the sharp social contrasts: a gentry family in their finery taking afternoon tea on the terrace were a world away from ill-clad wretches awaiting handouts of food. Disparities verged on the obscene. The fifth Marquess of Anglesey, a flamboyant wastrel, found an annual income of £110,000 insufficient to finance his gilded life. Experienced farm hands existed on 10–12s a week. Agriculture and transport (ships and railways), the principal occupations, were founded on a precarious economic base, and the working class faced a choice of low wages, unemployment or migration. All the while the well-heeled middle class came to enjoy greater material comforts. Contemporary business directories list a substantial number of shops that stocked a wide range of goods. Customers at Amlwch in 1910 had a choice of thirty-one grocers. Multiple stores, notably Boots, Maypole and Lipton, soon began to gain ground. Commercial success on a grand scale was usually associated with those shrewd individuals who had made their fortune in England. David Hughes became a byword for the wealth amassed by numerous Anglesey-born builders on Merseyside. Sometimes they took care to remember their native community. The village hall David Hughes had financed at Cemais in 1898 would inspire Sir John Prichard-Jones, head of Dickins and Jones, Regent Street, London, to donate £20,000 towards building an institute and alms-houses at Newborough in 1905.

News of the great religious revival sweeping south Wales in 1904 soon reached Anglesey. Men from the Llanfair Pwllgwyngyll district who found employment in the Glamorgan coalfield returned home that Christmas spiritually enthused. Religious meetings were held locally. Similar stirrings had been experienced at Brynsiencyn and Dwyran, and during December the revivalist fervour spread to the main towns. In January 1905 a Rhondda minister, the Revd R. B. Jones, led a mission. Following a series of meetings hundreds of converts were recorded in the local press and Anglesey declared 'almost an island for Christ'. All this had been achieved prior to the appearance of the central figure, Evan Roberts 'the revivalist'. Invited by the Methodist monthly meeting, it was the Revd John Williams who organized his missionary tour. For almost a month between 6 June and 3 July manual work came to a virtual standstill. It was said that farmers and shopkeepers left everything to attend the religious meetings. Admission tickets had to be issued for chapel meetings at Amlwch and Llannerch-y-medd. And as the congregations became too numerous for any chapel, services were held in the open air. Large crowds came together, many having cycled from neighbouring villages. At Cemais, Evan Roberts stood on a hay cart to preach to 2,000 people. Over 3,000 assembled at Llanfachreth, 6,000 at Llangefni, 7,000 at Llanfair Pwllgwyngyll and up to 10,000 at Holyhead. There was even a gathering within the precinct of Beaumaris castle, and for the first time a parish church opened its doors, though the bulk of the congregation at Llanddona were Nonconformists.

Events were accorded unprecedented newspaper coverage. Altogether, it is calculated that (allowing for duplication) between 90,000 and 100,000 attended the twenty-eight meetings held in Anglesey. Never before had the island experienced a religious awakening on this scale. Observers noted how the power of prayer and hymn singing, rather than preaching, drew enthusiastic crowds of mainly young people from lower middle and working-class backgrounds. Amid extraordinary scenes of frenzied spiritual rejoicing dozens of converts came forward. Each denomination would benefit: 716 entered the Baptist denomination, while the Calvinistic Methodists won almost 1,700 additional communicant members to reach a peak of 13,059 in 1906. Around a 100 new members were admitted to the Methodist chapel at Llannerch-y-medd; Bethesda chapel, Amlwch, welcomed 60. Numbers attending the Sunday schools increased and Bible sales went up rapidly. Much was made of the immediate social consequences. Taverns were emptied. Two Anglesey women, Sarah Matthews of Amlwch and Lady Reade of Carreglwyd, Llanfaethlu, had already achieved prominence as temperance reformers attempting to curb the serious problems of drunkenness and disorderly behaviour on the island. Branches of the North Wales Women's Temperance Union were established in the county, leading to several more coffee houses and temperance cafés. Soccer, too, lost its appeal; Llanfair Pwllgwyngyll Rovers disbanded. Children took to whistling hymn tunes in the street.

Nevertheless, it was not a uniform success story; Evan Roberts reportedly made little impression in Menai Bridge and Brynsiencyn. Peripheral crowds often proved restless or merely curious. In no time the fire of religious enthusiasm had burnt out, with considerable backsliding as chapels failed to keep hold of the newcomers. Hundreds had remained unaffected, or else quickly reverted to their old ways. Indeed, more poachers were prosecuted during the revival years than before. Unashamed immoral behaviour on the night of Ffair y Borth (Menai Bridge fair) horrified the young Revd E. Tegla Davies. Both the tavern and local football ground quickly recovered their popularity. As many as 1,500 drunkards faced court proceedings in 1908. The Anglesey League was re-formed during 1912–3, to be followed by an official reorganization of north Wales soccer in 1921–2 when the Division 4, Anglesey Area came into existence. The revival did nothing to relieve the real sufferings of the poor. Before long new forms of escapist popular entertainment offered a counter-attraction to weekday religious services. Large audiences enjoyed the 'latest pictures' at Holyhead cinemas in 1909. The Hippodrome, where smoking was permitted, assuaged Nonconformist sensibilities by promising to screen films with 'no vulgarity'. More damaging had been the suggestion that revivalist emotion acted as an aphrodisiac. The illegitimacy rates for Anglesey in 1906 (13.3 per cent) and 1907 (12.9 per cent) were the highest in Wales. It seemed that the spectre of the 1847 Education Report had returned to stalk the island. But to dwell on the negative aspects is to devalue the lifelong change experienced by countless individuals – *plant y diwygiad* (children of the revival), who would loyally serve their chapel to the end. What is beyond dispute, however, is that *Diwygiad '04–5* proved to be the last revival of its kind, marking the high point of religious influence on society.

Distant military campaigns had already touched Anglesey at the turn of the century. One of the first local militia volunteers to fight in the Boer War in 1899 was Colonel Owen Thomas. He made a name for himself in South Africa when he formed a distinctively Welsh cavalry regiment, the Prince of Wales's Light Horse. Fighting alongside him were a few Anglesey men who had made the army their career; the clock tower at Llangefni was erected in memory of Lt G. Pritchard-Rayner, Tresgawen, who died in South Africa. Whereas the Boer War remained a remote conflict, events in Europe would have profound implications. Once Britain entered the First World War in August 1914 the cry of jingoistic patriotism that swept the land was given voice in Anglesey by its most eminent public figures. Berating German militarism, John Morris-Jones, the leading Welsh scholar of his day, issued a 'call to battle'. Two of the island's foremost divines, the Revds John Williams and Thomas Charles Williams, who secured the backing of the Anglesey Methodist monthly meeting, devoted their rhetorical talents to bless the concept of a 'just war'. What they sought to overturn was the gospel of peace nurtured by Nonconformity itself, and only recently reinforced by an extraordinary religious awakening. Young men brought up in the ethos of the chapel were not easily persuaded to take up arms. But no one of note came forward in Anglesey to counter the pervasive hawkish propaganda.

Owen Thomas, at least, remained true to his beliefs. He immediately left London (his business base as managing director of an East Africa land development company) to act as chief recruiting officer for the county recruiting committee set up in Anglesey. In a series of public meetings he shared the platform with the Revd John Williams, Ellis Jones Griffith and others. Despite their efforts there were very few volunteers and little prospect that they could form an Anglesey battalion of 1,000 men, especially at harvest time. To realize his ideal of a 'Welsh Army', David Lloyd George, however, recognized the potential usefulness of charismatic Welsh-speaking Nonconformists in breaking down the barriers that existed in rural society. Characteristically, he manipulated Owen Thomas's promotion to Brigadier-General and the Revd John Williams's appointment as chaplain with the rank of honorary colonel. Thomas organized further recruiting meetings and military marches throughout north Wales, accompanied by Williams – resplendent in full military uniform and matching clerical collar that he wore even in the pulpit. Thousands of Welsh recruiting leaflets were handed out at local hiring fairs. Strong psychological pressure was applied to goad and shame young men into the army, while both leaders gave assurance that they would accompany them to France. Recruitment levels rose.

By February 1915 Owen Thomas could praise the response in Anglesey. He claimed that over 4,000 had enlisted (no doubt an exaggeration), though there were still another 2,000 eligible for service. Most entered training with the 14th (Anglesey and Caernarfonshire) battalion, part of the first brigade of the Welsh Army Corps stationed at Llandudno under Owen Thomas. More success followed. Having recruited a total of 10,000 men for what was retitled the 38th (Welsh) Division, he could justifiably claim that his military mission in north Wales had been accomplished. No other person had done more to draw volunteers from Welsh-speaking Nonconformist communities prior to conscription. At the St David's day review on Llandudno promenade in 1915 Lady Boston presented him with a service sword on behalf of the Anglesey Ladies Recruiting Committee. But as his men prepared to make their way to the front, Owen Thomas was informed that the military authorities would not allow him to lead his brigade because of his age and lack of military expertise. More bitter disappointment followed when he was removed from his subsequent training command at Kinmel Park camp on spurious charges. This scandal prompted vigorous protests throughout north Wales headed by Anglesey County Council. In the end nothing dented his integrity. A knighthood in 1917 offered some consolation, but for the 'Warrior of Mona' the Great War dealt a series of devastating personal blows, made all the more tragic with the loss of all three sons in military operations.

Anglesey, meantime, had been given a taste of the war. Coastal trade suffered serious disruption and seafaring communities began to count the losses. A group of Anglesey crewmen interned at Hamburg a few days after the declaration of war, faced a long stay in Germany. Holyhead became a naval base in 1915; armed forces' personnel utilized the massive Station Hotel as an administrative centre. Airships from the Royal Naval Air Service (RNAS) station, Mona, conducted anti-submarine patrols and provided escorts in the Irish Sea shipping lanes. But unrestricted submarine warfare later caused havoc; no fewer than twenty vessels were sunk off Anglesey in the first quarter of 1918. The Beaumaris-born master of one stricken oil-tanker was taken prisoner on a U-boat. To meet the threat, an Irish Sea Hunting Flotilla of destroyers and motor-launches were deployed at Holyhead, and the situation slowly improved. At Kingsbridge army camp, Llan-faes, the Royal Anglesey Royal Engineers, the former militia force, provided specialist training. Members of the Anglesey Volunteer Reserves undertook guard duties on both bridges over the Menai Straits. Echoes of the European conflict could be heard in the voices of refugees and prisoners of war. Anglesey received 300 Belgian refugees; those billeted at Menai Bridge had constructed the 'Belgian promenade' along the fore-shore by early 1916. German prisoners, among them a number kept at Gwyndy, were engaged on harvest work and drainage schemes at Malltraeth Marsh.

Civilians directed their energies to the war effort, raising funds through the War Savings Association and other activities. Lloyd George's premiership received unquestioning support, and little opposition was expressed. Sales of the anti-war journal *Y Deyrnas* were much lower in Anglesey than other north Wales counties. Of the seventy-one copies distributed in one month in 1917 more than half circulated in Llangoed. Among the few conscientious objectors, the Revd Ben Meyrick, a recently ordained Baptist minister at Pen-sarn, was sentenced to two years' hard labour in October of the same year. His cause aroused little sympathy on the island.

Platform recruiters remained at home. While the likes of John Morris-Jones and the Revd John Williams pursued their interests in worldly comfort, young Anglesey men faced danger and death. Pathos pervades the personal diary kept by Pte T. R. Owen, Coedana, who endured the horrors of trench warfare and incessant shelling on the Somme shortly before he was killed in September 1918, aged twenty-three. Local newspapers reported the course of the struggle and the sacrifices made. War losses totalled well over a thousand, an unprecedented death toll, though no precise figure can be given. In all, 955 Anglesey men who served in the army between 1914 and 1918 had been killed, most on the Western Front. Many others died at sea. Civilian casualties were minimal. Holyhead war memorial lists 287 names, including those of four women – three of whom were stewardesses on the sunken passenger vessels *Connemara* and *Leinster*. Amlwch lost sixty-one men. Sir Owen Thomas was subsequently called upon to unveil a host of war memorials across the island. At Llangefni county school thirty-eight former pupils were commemorated. As families mourned the dead, many survivors returned home bearing physical and psychological scars; Plas Llanfair and Tresgawen became temporary nursing homes for convalescent soldiers. Among the numerous Anglesey men decorated for bravery, two received the highest military accolade. For his 'most conspicuous bravery' in Palestine in 1917, Dr John Fox Russell, Holyhead, of the Royal Army Medical Corps, was posthumously awarded the Victoria Cross. Amlwch seaman William Williams served on disguised armed merchant Q-ships used to decoy German submarines. He won the Victoria Cross for his courageous part in the sinking of the coastal minelayer UC-29 whilst aboard the *Pargust* off Ireland in 1917.

A shadow was cast over the armistice in November 1918 by the influenza pandemic known as the 'Spanish flu'. As it spread across the island schools closed for a fortnight. Rampant at Holyhead, the deadly nature of the scourge claimed a father, mother and two children. Again the following February hardly a community in Anglesey escaped its recurrence. All this added to the suffering that war had brought to innumerable homes.

The war had presented a direct challenge to established religious beliefs. Congregations thinned, more so as the conflict dragged on and more young men of military age were conscripted. Because many ministers chose to work as chaplains or serve in the YMCA and Royal Army Medical Corps there was even a shortage of preachers on Sundays. Understandably, various aspects of the war caused individual heart-searching. The sight of a Nonconformist minister in military uniform was abhorrent to many and the Revd John Williams's war-mongering angered grieving mothers. Ever-increasing casualty lists compounded the disillusionment and doubt, leading in some cases to a complete loss of faith. Yet to all appearances, Nonconformity in Anglesey did not suffer an immediate crisis. However loud the complaints might be about religious apathy and decline at local level, there was no catastrophic drop in total chapel membership after 1918. The number of Calvinistic Methodist communicants remained constant at around 12,500 until the mid-1930s. Chapels, in general, continued to be the centre of weekday social life based on prayer meetings, singing and literary festivals, and the Band of Hope. What Nonconformity faced was a steady erosion of traditional values. Wartime conditions, ominously, encouraged a growing interest in secular entertainment – the cinema, dancing and whist-drives. Sunday newspapers also made their first appearance in many homes. A long-term religious decline was predicted in the fall in Sunday school membership. From a peak of 11,810 in 1906, the number of Methodist Sunday school attendants dropped to 9,906 in 1918, and 6,898 by 1938. While concerned religious leaders espoused moral renewal, it was balanced by recognition of the underlying shift in public attitudes. Naturally enough, all yearned for international peace. The work of the Welsh League of Nations Union received an enthusiastic endorsement: by 1929 it had 88 branches and a membership of 3,387 in Anglesey.

On the home front women had made a vital contribution to the war effort. Female labour was drafted to fill the manpower shortage created by military requirements. Altogether, about 2,700 women worked on the land in Anglesey during the war years, including those who had enrolled in the Women's Land Army. As the food shortage became worse, leading to rationing, more value was placed on the production and preservation of foodstuffs. Promoters of the Women's Institute, founded in Canada, who had no luck in Britain hitherto, finally gained the ear of 'a man of action'. Col. R. Stapleton-Cotton of Plas Llwyn Onn, Llanedwen, a pioneer of co-operative marketing schemes, including the Anglesey Egg Collection Depot (later transformed into the Anglesey Farmers' Society), saw the potential for an organized community effort. He convened the meeting held at Graig, Llanfair Pwllgwyngyll, in June 1915, when the decision was taken to set up a branch of the Women's Institute in the village – the first in Britain. Members were soon discussing the best means of improving the food supply. Talks and demonstrations on cookery, food conservation and gardening featured regularly, and visiting speakers covered subjects as diverse as poultry rearing, reincarnation (reported to be a controversial topic!) and Bolshevism. In 1921 the branch secured a former army hut from Kimnel Park as its meeting place. Erected next to the tollhouse, it remains to this day. As a non-sectarian, non-political organization the movement spread far and wide during the interwar period. Delegates from twenty institutes attended the first council meeting of the Anglesey Federation in 1930. Female horizons were broadened, but mainly within the parameters of domestic and voluntary community work.

Female political emancipation had only figured marginally, initiated by English pressure groups. As early as 1874 delegates of the Manchester National League for Women's Suffrage addressed a public meeting at Holyhead. Very little interest was taken until later societies engaged in vociferous protests to demand the vote for women. Liverpool members of the Women's Freedom League first showed the flag in Anglesey in June 1909, in Newborough of all places. An inaugural gathering at Bod Iorwerth, the house of Bessie Jones (born in Liverpool, her occupation is not stated in the 1901 census), led to a public meeting in the village, followed by a rowdy open-air meeting at Holyhead that came to an abrupt end. Militants, who resorted to more violent methods in 1912, with David Lloyd George as the main target, discredited the suffragette cause. It produced a counter movement in the form of the National League for

Opposing Women's Suffrage that established branches at Holyhead and Valley the following year. Even the non-militant National Union of Women's Suffrage Societies (NUWSS) had to tone down its message to attract wide support; the NUWSS branch at Menai Bridge came under the auspices of the larger Bangor branch. Only the most committed women, drawn from the middle class, involved themselves in party politics. By 1913 the Women's Liberal Association had enrolled 120 members at Holyhead.

All political activity was suspended for the duration of the war. Limited post-war employment opportunities restricted women, once again, to their traditional role in the home. Otherwise, domestic service, nursing and teaching remained the principal female occupations before offices and factories offered alternative work. Though Anglesey would have a woman MP in 1929, very few women played a political part in local government. In keeping with the family tradition of public service, A. M. Davies, eldest daughter of Richard Davies, Treborth, fittingly enough, became the first lady alderman in north Wales when she was co-opted to the county council in 1919. The first two women to be elected as councillors were M. E. Prichard (Holyhead) and M. E. Owen (Llangoed) in 1934, followed by Lady Kathleen Stanley (Holyhead) three years later. Rarely did women surface in public life. It was 1958 before Anglesey had its first woman high sheriff in the person of M. C. Burton of Beaumaris. For the rest of the century the county council remained essentially a man's world; equal opportunities did not mean equal participation. Of the thirty-seven councillors on Ynys Môn Borough Council in 1996, just three were women.

Agriculture had entered a period of unprecedented prosperity during the war. As the U-boat menace took its toll of allied shipping the loss of food imports intensified dependence on home production. Prices for all farm products rose rapidly. By utilizing outside labour, farmers could also save on wages: 148 boys and girls of school age worked on Anglesey farms in 1916. Areas of grassland were ploughed up to grow more cereals and under the Corn Production Act of 1917 farmers received guaranteed prices. The Anglesey War Agricultural Committee was given a quota of 18,000 additional acres, bringing the total arable area to about 75,000 acres. Tractors were first used at this time, lessening the dependence on horsepower. A good third of the island's working population remained in agriculture, but the changes seemed only to benefit the farmers. It caused particular resentment among working families struggling to scrape a living. Trade unionists meeting at Holyhead in October 1916 protested strongly against the high food prices. Given the social gulf already existing between masters and men in rural Anglesey, the antagonism within the ranks of the farm-workers – who were direct witnesses to the profiteering – soon developed into social conflict. Middle-class Liberalism had triumphed over gentry rule in the previous century; now it was the turn of the *gwerin* to assert their challenge through the medium of a rural trade union movement that took a remarkable political direction.

Undeb Gweithwyr Môn (Anglesey Workers' Union) had been established in 1909. As a localized rural union, unique in Welsh labour history, it could trace its origins to the farm-workers' revolt inspired by Ap Ffarmwr. Four who provided the initial leadership – John Hughes, George Jones, Edward Pritchard and Thomas Rowlands – were veterans of the 1890s. Appropriately enough, the first branch was formed at Aberffraw, but as in Ap Ffarmwr's day the farm labourers were slow to respond and only six branches had been set up in the first year. All the same, Undeb Gweithwyr Môn was officially registered as a trade union in 1911. Next came its registration as an approved friendly society under the National Insurance Act. This gave the union a new lease of life so that by 1913 it had 922 members and J. Fred Jones as full-time secretary. With a membership of only 97, the labour section paled in comparison. Support from a few middle-class Liberals proved essential at all stages but added to the internal strains. Those who harboured socialist beliefs, and who advocated the formation of a Labour Party in Anglesey, were critical of the Anglesey Liberal Association for neglecting working-class interests. Independent Labour Party (ILP) activists from Caernarfonshire had already addressed the first socialist public meeting in the county at Llangefni on 29 September 1909. Tradition ascribes founder membership of the ILP in Anglesey to Lewis Thomas, a Llangristiolus postman. Breaking free from Liberalism, however, proved difficult; even the two Undeb Gweithwyr Môn members who stood unsuccessfully in the county council elections of 1913 retained Liberal Party afflliations. Down to three branches, the war caused further disarray, leaving the labour section in a parlous state.

The 1917 Act had also set up statutory machinery for the regulation of wages. Both sides of industry were accorded equal representation on district wages committees and this presented the workers with a unique opportunity. For labour activists the organization of 3,200 or so farm-workers became an urgent priority. In Anglesey, W. J. Jones, 'Brynfab', inherited the mantle of Ap Ffarmwr – but with much greater effect. An avowed socialist, who had worked at the Dinorwig slate quarry before becoming a Brynsiencyn shopkeeper, he proved to be an inspirational orator who instilled fresh spirit into the labour section of Undeb Gweithwyr Môn. In his Ford Model T car, Brynfab toured the island to address meetings shoulder to shoulder with the earlier leaders. Redolent of a religious revival, rural Anglesey was soon in ferment. By February 1918 the union claimed twenty branches and over 1,000 members. Farmers became fierce in their opposition. Recalcitrant workers were threatened with army service and union officials collecting membership payments faced particular venom. In the circumstances, the movement welcomed fraternal support from railwaymen, schoolteachers and ministers of religion as it endeavoured to widen its scope to enrol urban workers and craftsmen. Demonstrating this new strength, the union held *Gŵyl Lafur* (Labour Day) celebrations at Llangefni in May. At the end of the year the number of branches reached forty, boosting membership to 2,597 (thirty-five of whom were women). Ardent members of the 240-strong branch at Llannerch-y-medd had purchased their own building in the high street.

Wearing their own union badge with defiant pride, Undeb Gweithwyr Môn members sought a better future. Beyond improved wages and working conditions, there was urgent need to tackle social problems. Life continued to be a grim struggle for the island's poor. Up to 20 per cent of the population in some villages were dependent on outdoor parish relief before the system of Poor Law guardians was abolished in 1929. The state of housing remained a scandal. In 1914 the secretary of the Welsh Housing Association declared that cottages in rural Anglesey were in a far worse condition than those he had seen in the 'filthy slums' of Canton, China. Small, damp, badly ventilated, insanitary and overcrowded, they proved a health hazard. Combined with an inadequate diet, their occupants fell victim to tuberculosis, diphtheria and other infectious diseases. Problems relating to basic health and hygiene among Anglesey schoolchildren were highlighted when school medical examinations revealed the worrying levels of poor physique, tooth decay and defective eyesight. Children suffering from tuberculosis were sent to the Penhesgyn Open Air Home established in 1908, seven years before the Cefni hospital at Llangefni began to treat TB patients. As the war ended the struggle for improved living conditions intensified. Labour leaders felt that local authorities should be applying greater pressure on the government to build more working-class homes. An ambitious political agenda thus aimed at direct labour representation on the county council and other public bodies. More significantly, the prospect of running a Labour parliamentary candidate was being raised.

Trade unionism had also made rapid strides in the port of Holyhead – principally the Dockers' Union, the Sailors and Firemen's Union and the National Union of Railwaymen. Drawing on the strength of 2,500 members in six affiliated unions, the Holyhead Trades and Labour Council, formed in 1913, also talked of seeking parliamentary representation. Ellis Jones Griffith held little appeal; not once did he further workers' interests in the House of Commons. His unexpected appearance at the *Gŵyl Lafur* in May 1918 only elicited feeble cheers, a clear portent of the changing political climate. That summer the Anglesey weekly newspaper *Y Wyntyll* (founded in 1903) relinquished its Liberal connections to become a forum for trade union and labour interests before being discontinued in 1925. Talks between Undeb Gweithwyr Môn and the Holyhead Trades and Labour

Council had resulted in a joint election committee linking rural and urban workers. Hailed by Brynfab as the biggest 'revolution' in the history of the county, the Anglesey Labour Party, to all intents, came into being – though it did not officially affiliate with the Labour Party until 1924. Various parliamentary candidates were mentioned, but lacking a political fund it was decided to approach Sir Owen Thomas, who agreed to stand and pay the electoral deposit of £150.

In many ways the 1918 election in Anglesey was a curious contest. Both candidates supported the Lloyd George Coalition. Though a 'Labour' nominee, Owen Thomas made little mention of the Labour Party programme, least of all land nationalization. If invited, he would have stood in the name of the Anglesey Farmers' Union. With some leading Undeb Gweithwyr Môn figures remaining in the Liberal camp, traditional political loyalties cut across trade union allegiance. Joining them were local Farmers' Union and Conservative Association members who heeded the call to vote for the official Liberal Coalitionist. In the end, however, the result would hinge on the personality of the respective candidates and the efficiency of their supporting organization.

Ellis Jones Griffith's parliamentary career had once appeared secure. Robustly imperialistic and pro-Boer War at the time of the 1900 election, he reflected popular opinion to be returned unopposed. In both 1906 and January 1910 elections he built up a substantial majority against weak Conservative opposition, and was again unchallenged in December 1910. But complacency and disillusionment subsequently weakened the Liberal cause. Griffith's commitment to compulsory military service in 1916 went against basic Liberal principles. He made little effort to garner working-class support. The Anglesey Liberal Association fell to its worse state for forty years; even the secretary had defected to Labour. Owen Thomas, on the other hand, had a long record of public service in the county, which won respect among all classes. He had close links with both the farming community and farm-labourers' movement dating back to the 1890s when he was a prominent Liberal. In addition, countless families admired his wartime role and personal sacrifice. True, Owen Thomas largely financed his own campaign, but in providing most of the thirty-seven local sub-agents, Undeb Gweithwyr Môn organization played a pivotal role given the increased electorate. And fittingly, now that women over thirty had the vote, they included Mrs J. Eames, wife of a Gwalchmai activist. When Holyhead reportedly plumped for Ellis Jones Griffith on a 3:1 ratio, loyal core support in Undeb Gweithwyr Môn rural strongholds helped secure 9,038 votes for Owen Thomas, giving him a slim majority of 140. It was a debt he acknowledged with a donation of £50 to union funds.

Just as middle-class Nonconformists made their mark on history in the 1868 election, the return of Sir Owen Thomas in 1918 could rightly be projected as a triumph for the nascent class-conscious *gwerin* of Anglesey. Its political significance was confirmed when he took up the Labour Party whip in the Commons. Alone of all the Welsh rural constituencies, Anglesey had a Labour MP to join those from the mining seats in south Wales. Whatever his political sympathies, or lack of them, Owen Thomas was the only Labour member who could not claim a personal connection, either by social background or occupation, to the working class. For a time it was possible to gloss over the contradictions. Though a lacklustre MP he voted consistently in the interests of the labour movement and expressed constituency concerns. To provide work for the growing number of unemployed in Anglesey he called for the reopening of the Parys Mountain copper mine and the implementation of a scheme to deepen the inner harbour at Holyhead. But it was not long before his uneasy relationship with militant socialists at Westminster led him to resign from the party. He became an Independent Labour MP in October 1920, and subsequently a label-free Independent on his own terms. Brynfab denounced his action as the 'greatest let down' the labour movement had suffered.

Galvanized by its parliamentary success, the labour movement had earlier mounted a political challenge in the county council elections of 1919. But only three were returned: Lewis Thomas captured Llangristiolus to join unopposed candidates at Aberffraw and Holyhead. This overwhelming defeat confirmed that electors had voted for the man in 1918 rather than a political brand. The old Liberal guard remained secure in the Shire Hall. At least a number of Labour gains were notched at the urban council elections in Holyhead, and Undeb Gweithwyr Môn was well represented on both Aberffraw and Gwalchmai parish councils. The union's hour of influence would soon pass. Though it won an important concession for the farm labourers with the granting of a Saturday half-holiday, in practice it depended on the employers' good will. An initiative to set up co-operative stores in Anglesey achieved only a modest success. Despite the surge in membership to 3,111 by the time of the second *Gŵyl Lafur*, workforce numbers on the island could not sustain a viable level in the long-term. Undeterred by Brynfab's hostility, the majority of workers decided to cast in their lot with the powerful Workers' Union. All told, forty-six Undeb Gweithwyr Môn branches were absorbed *en bloc* on 1 September 1919. It also meant automatic affiliation to the Labour Party. The Revd Richard Morris, Independent minister at Llannerch-y-medd, then relinquished his pastoral charge to act as full-time secretary of the Anglesey Workers' Union (as it became known). At first, amalgamation could be justified. The labour section benefited from the financial strength of the Workers' Union and membership rose to an all-time high of 3,246 by March 1920. Yet, there were indications that the movement was losing political momentum. Unlike the previous round, Labour made no organized bid to fight the county council elections of 1922.

The 1922 general election would generate another strange amalgam of political allegiances. Standing as an Independent candidate with official Labour support, Sir Owen Thomas also received the endorsement of the Anglesey Conservative Association. Two prominent Tories acted as his chief election officials, and, as before, he financed his own campaign. Against him stood Sir R. J. Thomas, eldest son of William Thomas the Llanrhuddlad-born Liverpool shipowner, who had set up his own shipping company. Previously Coalition Liberal MP for Wrexham, he was now a National Liberal candidate backed by leading Nonconformist ministers as well as Brynfab and the Holyhead secretary of the Sailors' and Firemen's Union. In this topsy-turvy contest, largely shorn of political ideology, Owen Thomas's personal popularity in the rural areas outweighed his opponent's dominion in Holyhead. Polling 11,929 votes he retained the seat and raised his majority to 1,862. But an exhausting campaign added to the personal strain he had suffered over the years. His death early in 1923 ended a singularly eventful career that embodied an Anglesey variant of the Cromwellian mix of farmer, soldier and politician.

At the by-election of April 1923 the labour movement in Anglesey was put to a further test. Once again, the Liberal candidate was Sir R. J. Thomas. In E. T. John, Labour had a candidate of genuine convictions, but lacking a personal following (he had only recently moved to Plas Llanidan) he was not likely to win. The margin of defeat did cause surprise; Anglesey reverted to Liberalism with 11,116 votes, crushing the combined Labour and Conservative totals. Residing at Garreglwyd, his Holyhead mansion, Sir R. J. Thomas had lavished his generosity on the port – as much as £150,000 by his own calculation. Among a range of philanthropic favours he founded the Lady Thomas Convalescent Home for Discharged and Disabled Soldiers and Sailors. At a time of unemployment he always ensured that job vacancies within his enterprises were first offered to Holyhead people. Political opponents could justifiably claim that the town had sunk to the level of a pocket borough. Allowed a walk-over at the general election later that year, with official Conservative support he again trounced Labour in 1924. Lady Bulkeley, president of the Anglesey Conservative Association, opined that socialism undermined 'the religion and morals of young people and children'. But circumstances allowed Sir R. J. Thomas little opportunity to further his career in the House of Commons. Troubled economic times hit the shipping industry with disastrous consequences for his company and its many investors and employees in Anglesey. In 1928 he announced his political retirement prior to the forthcoming election; the following year he filed for bankruptcy.

Agriculture had slumped as Britain entered a period of economic decline. From 1921 farmers no longer received guaranteed prices and the statutory wage rates were scrapped. During the difficult years that followed both farmers and labourers suffered greatly. Agricultural prices fell to their lowest point since 1915. Drastic wage reductions saw the basic weekly rate cut from 45s to 28s; many farm hands faced unemployment. Trade unionism experienced a dramatic reversal of fortunes. The Anglesey Workers' Union dispensed with the services of the Revd Richard Morris in 1923 and at least twenty branches were closed. Subsequent recruitment campaigns had little success. Down to eighteen branches by 1926, it was admitted that the majority of rural workers were now outside the union. The rural revolt of the *gwerin* had failed. Trade unionism never exercised meaningful power in Anglesey after this time; the abortive General Strike in 1926 made little impression outside Holyhead, where the railwaymen came out and the port was closed. When the Workers' Union amalgamated with the Transport and General Workers' Union (TGWU) in 1929, the measure of autonomy previously granted to the Anglesey Workers' Union was lost. Undeb Gweithwyr Môn Approved Society continued to function independently as a friendly society providing basic social security for around 2,000 members until the implementation of the National Insurance Act of 1946. Its dissolution meant the loss of a name replete with unique historical associations linked directly to the vision symbolized by Ap Ffarmwr some sixty years earlier.

Post-war economic realities also ushered changes at the upper reaches of rural society. Poor returns, high death duties and taxes hastened the break-up of the great estates. By 1922 most major landowners in Wales had sold parts of their property; the Bulkeleys received an astounding £200,000 for Baron Hill lands in Anglesey. Farms were sold mainly to tenants, so that between 1909 and 1941–3 the proportion of owner-occupied holdings in the county rose from 12 per cent to 32 per cent (by 1970 it would reach 54 per cent). Plas Newydd had faced a self-inflicted crisis earlier in the century. Shortly before his death in 1905, the fifth Marquess of Anglesey incurred liabilities amounting to £544,000. Much of it had been extravagantly spent on clothes, jewellery, theatre productions and motor-cars (consistent with his 'mad' reputation, he could often be seen careering along Anglesey roads racing the Irish mail train). Yet, the owners of the Plas Newydd estate held on until 1932 before selling their farms. In the event, a process begun in fifteenth-century Anglesey would be dismantled, further loosening the grip of the landed gentry class. Though some would continue to figure in public life as high sheriffs and lord lieutenants, the old order was passing. The seventh Marquess of Anglesey lost his county council seat in 1967, and along with Lord Boston and Lord Stanley he would be removed from the House of Lords in the cull of hereditary peers. Many a *plasty* reflected their fate. Plas

Penrhos has been demolished. Baron Hill stands derelict. Plas Newydd avoided such ignominy when its owners expediently handed control to the National Trust. Henllys was transformed into a country house hotel. Against the trend, the Meyrick family still reside at their ancestral Bodorgan home.

As a safe Liberal seat, David Lloyd George coveted Anglesey for his youngest daughter Megan. An observer of politics from its epicentre at Downing Street, Megan Lloyd George could not have had a better apprenticeship for her own ambitions. With both parents vigorously pulling strings to secure her nomination, disappointed local opponents understandably railed against the 'unfair tactics' and alleged rigging of selection votes. Disaffected Liberals even threatened to field an independent candidate. In the event, the 1929 election became a three-way contest between the main parties. The local Liberal Association stood in good stead, and following the extension of the female vote, Megan Lloyd George issued a personal appeal to the women of Anglesey. Her father addressed support meetings at Llangefni and Holyhead, taking care to rope in sections of the local press. Great emphasis was placed on Liberal plans to conquer unemployment and replace slum hovels. Breaking new ground at a general election, Megan Lloyd George represented her party in a radio political broadcast. Her Labour opponent, William Edwards, prominent in Anglesey public life since the rural struggles of both labourers and farmers in the 1890s, had only converted from the Liberals in 1923. Given the weak state of party organization elsewhere on the island, Labour hopes rested on trade unionists at Holyhead, where almost a quarter of the electorate was concentrated. But after a hard fight Megan Lloyd George won 13,181 votes, giving her a comfortable majority of 5,618 over second place Labour. Anglesey could claim the honour of electing the first woman MP from a Welsh constituency, a feat optimistically seen as 'the great turning-point for the hopes of Welsh women'.

Making her belated maiden speech in a Commons debate on rural housing in April 1930, Megan Lloyd George spoke passionately of conditions in Anglesey. New homes were beyond what most poorly paid labourers could afford. She condemned the 'squalid, dark, ill-ventilated' hovels, linking bad housing conditions with the death-rate from tuberculosis among women that made Anglesey the second worst county in England and Wales. Also alarmingly high, at 93 per thousand, was Anglesey's infant mortality rate. The county continued to show up badly. Housing conditions remained 'appalling', with overcrowding a serious problem throughout the interwar years. Not surprisingly, a Committee of Inquiry Report in 1939 noted the 'consistently high' incidence of tuberculosis; over seven years (1930–6 inclusive) Anglesey had the third highest death-rate from TB in England and Wales. Its insanitary cottages were again deemed worse than those in a Chinese city – this time, Shanghai.

The report was equally scathing in condemning the county council for its 'apathetic' attitude. Labour's paltry representation had settled on the sidelines; independent councillors, usually returned unopposed, dominated proceedings. The average expenditure on public services was among the lowest in Wales, and little progress had been made in the provision of working-class housing. Nothing could justify such negligence when the lives of so many were at stake.

Megan Lloyd George's strong radical beliefs enhanced her popularity within the county. And as the constituency Labour Party decided not to contest the 1931 general election she was able to hold off, with a slightly reduced majority, the formidable right-wing challenge from Albert Hughes (aided by a few disgruntled Liberals), who almost doubled the Conservative percentage of the vote. In the deteriorating economic climate of the thirties, her campaign focused primarily on the unemployment crisis that blighted Anglesey.

Anglesey could not escape the worst effects of the depression. Since the repeal of the Corn Production Act in 1921 farmers had suffered a period of falling prices. The basic agricultural unit was still the family farm of 50 acres; only 304 of the 4,276 holdings in 1939 were over 100 acres. During the depression years there was a pronounced move from arable to pastoral farming. Most farms now concentrated on livestock rearing, and whereas the cattle population remained constant at about 50,000, sheep numbers reached almost 180,000. All the while the area of permanent grassland increased. Crops only constituted 10.7 per cent of the cultivated land, grown mostly on farms around Beaumaris and Newborough. Despite subsidies and the establishment of marketing boards in the thirties, conditions remained very difficult. In general, the prices for farm products tended to fall more steeply than wage levels and most employers sought to reduce outgoings to the minimum. By cutting their workforce they inevitably contributed to the drift from the land. Between 1929 and 1939 the number of workers employed on agricultural holdings in Anglesey declined from 3,665 to 2,138, a fall of 42 per cent. From this time also, increased mechanization hastened the demise of traditional craft trades such as that of the blacksmith and saddler, further accelerating rural depopulation.

Holyhead counted the high cost of lives shattered by hard times. Already the port had suffered when the City of Dublin Steam Packet Company left in 1920. Since the merger of the London and North Western Railway Company with the London, Midland and Scottish Railway Company, the LMS had monopolized trade activities, virtually making Holyhead a 'one company town'. One of the four ships used for the mail run to Ireland was withdrawn from service in 1923. Then, a six-year trade war with the Irish Free State between 1932 and 1938 dealt a devastating blow to railway traffic and cross-channel cargo services. The crisis caused chronic unemployment. Throughout most of the decade over 30 per cent of the insured population were out of work. Few localities in Wales witnessed the level of 42 per cent reached in 1936–7; at its nadir in December 1936 the monthly unemployment rate stood at 47.7 per cent. A workforce engulfed by poverty and social despair was further demoralized by the means-tested unemployment benefit. Half the houses in the town had been condemned, evoking opinion that many of the slum landlords 'should be shot'. A great number of schoolchildren suffered serious malnutrition. The town was a tuberculosis black spot. Impoverished families became dependent on the goodwill of charitable aid organizations and chapel-run soup kitchens. Times of adversity strengthened community and religious ties. The Holyhead Unemployment Association club arranged social events, and though chapel membership remained constant throughout the thirties there were still more licensed premises than places of worship.

With no other industry to absorb those out of work, unemployment rates in Anglesey were consistently higher than those in neighbouring counties. Between 1931and 1938 only once did it dip below 35 per cent; in 1933 the rate soared to 42.1 per cent. Figures presented a distressing picture of a workforce in desperate straits. By 1939, 2,826 were unemployed. Discounting the main towns, most came from the ranks of the agricultural labourers. For many, especially the young, the only answer was to seek new opportunities elsewhere – mostly in the English conurbations. And out-migration largely accounted for the drop in the island's population: down from 51,744 (1921) to 49,029 (1931), it fell to an estimated 46,500 by 1939, a loss of over 5,200 in twenty years. Over a thousand people left Holyhead as its total slipped to 9,882. The 'terrible state of despondency' reported among families facing unemployment at Menai Bridge enveloped the county. Increasingly, there was a growing expectation of government remedies to economic problems; depressed parts of Britain were identified by 'Special Areas' legislation. Megan Lloyd George consistently advocated more public spending to alleviate the distress. For all her pleas in the House of Commons she was unable to gain special area status for Anglesey, though it fully qualified for assistance in every respect.

Labour's return to the electoral fray in 1935 could have been expected to threaten Megan Lloyd George's position. Henry Jones, a Holyhead railway clerk and seasoned Labour councillor, managed to almost equal the Conservative total of 7,045, yet Megan Lloyd George (standing as Independent Liberal) polled 11,227 votes to maintain, as in 1931, a majority of over 4,000. Many potential Labour voters in the county saw her as a standard-bearer for the political left, who fought hard to tackle unemployment. Even at Holyhead, where Labour had secured a strong presence on the urban district council and initiated council-house building, it was the Nonconformist Liberals who still dominated the town's affairs. When Henry Jones was elevated to county council alderman in 1938, the Liberals captured his seat at the by-election. Since the eclipse of the Anglesey Workers' Union, trade union influence hardly figured outside Holyhead. Denominationalism, especially in its Calvinistic form, took precedence over political party considerations in local government. Though the Calvinistic Methodist 'Reconstruction Commission' had reported on social issues in 1921, the Anglesey monthly meeting could offer nothing of practical value to working people. Despite such shortcomings, most Labour activists remained faithful to their chapel; Henry Jones, typically, was a devout Methodist deacon. But the failure, for one reason or another, of the labour movement to gain an influential voice on the county council allowed the conservative middle-class elements to predominate under the guise of independents, and, as we have seen, neglect their responsibilities to the vulnerable in society.

Nonconformity's inability to initiate social reform no doubt contributed to the growing estrangement of the working class. Chapels might distribute soup and bread, but minds were more likely to be eased by cheap entertainment. During the 1930s all the main towns had cinemas – the Empire, Arcadia or Royal – that screened the latest Hollywood 'talkies' and such like. Beyond that, a wealth of cultural activities cut through the gloom at Holyhead; a choral union, orchestral society, and an amateur operatic society directed by W. Bradwen Jones, one of the most gifted musicians of his generation. The economic depression would further expose stark social contradictions and class inequality. In some respects, sections of the middle class in professional occupations and permanent employment actually benefited. If salaries fell, so too did prices, making it possible to enjoy a good quality of life. Contemporary advertisements show the range of goods and services available to a burgeoning consumerist society. Garages, 'high class' tailors and jewellers, and stores selling goods for the 'ideal home' found it a fertile time. Cars and radio sets could be supplied on 'easy terms'. Radio licences issued to Anglesey residents reached 2,583 by 1937, when the opening of the new BBC transmitter station at Penmon promised a better reception for listeners. For hedonists with money in their pocket the Plas Llanfair Hotel and Country Club offered a ballroom, heated swimming pool and American Bar.

Those following political events abroad also found it a time of grave unease. Public sentiment was strongly pacifist. The North Wales Women's Peace Council had collected 11,118 signatures in Anglesey in 1931 in support of disarmament. Ministers of religion endorsed the Peace Pledge Union and Nonconformist bodies passed resolutions opposing conscription. Anglesey registered an impressively high turnout of 77.1

per cent in the Peace Ballot of 1935. A house-to-house canvass carried out by members of the Welsh League of Nations Union revealed overwhelming support for collective security and a reduction in armaments. All this proved academic when the troubled situation in Europe suddenly deteriorated the following year. In the event, Megan Lloyd George became a vociferous critic of appeasement. Only a few months before the declaration of war in September 1939, the fate of the submarine *Thetis* had provided an omen of the sacrifices to come. After disaster struck her sea trials, leading to a loss of ninety-nine lives, she was beached at Traeth Bychan. Unlike the previous conflict, however, there were no emotive debates and the Nonconformist conscience did not suffer any undue crisis. The public became aware of what to expect and stood united. Anglesey men responded to the compulsory military call up; very few had applied to be registered as conscientious objectors by January 1940. Those exempted from service in the armed forces by the North Wales Tribunal undertook alternative agricultural or hospital work. Controversy came later, when the county council began to dismiss teachers and other employees who had taken an anti-war stand.

On the home front a strong sense of community solidarity prevailed. Civil defence measures were already in place with air raid Precautions Committees responsible for safety procedures. All main towns had official public air raid shelters and air raid warning sirens. Gas masks were issued, children being expected to carry theirs to school daily. Blackout restrictions at night had to be rigidly observed. While blamed for causing fatal road accidents, they proved a boon to local poachers as wartime shortages inflated the price of rabbits on the black market. Petrol rations started immediately, followed by the rationing of essential food items in 1940. This time local price regulation committees provided a safeguard against war profiteering. Battalions of the Home Guard were set up at Holyhead, Llangefni and Beaumaris. Women played their part in a number of community activities: Women's Voluntary Service, Red Cross and the Anglesey Ladies 'Comforts' Committee (that arranged for clothing to be sent to the troops). Combining traditional enterprises such as fruit preservation schemes with a more challenging role, some Women's Institute members were marshalled by the Marchioness of Anglesey into a Women's Home Defence squad to be instructed in the use of firearms and hand grenades. Other Anglesey women enrolled in the Women's Auxiliary Police Corps.

Immediately upon the declaration of war Anglesey saw its first influx of evacuees. Women and children would be dispersed throughout the island, though about 1,500 of the 3,400 children evacuated from Liverpool would return by December. Eyebrows were raised at Llanfair Pwllgwyngyll when a mainly rough illiterate lot, lacking in table manners, landed in their midst. Merseyside women found it difficult to adapt to their new environment; frustrated by closed public houses on Sundays, mothers billeted at Menai Bridge willingly returned home to brave the 'Blitz'. Incorporating the children of Catholic parents into Nonconformist households could be problematic, and their presence allowed bigotry to surface at Holyhead. Aside from the extra burden placed on the local education authority (it requested financial assistance from the Liverpool LEA), there were fears that monoglot English children would have an Anglicizing influence in schools. But by March 1942 it was reported that Liverpool teachers in special premises were educating 926 of the 1,382 evacuated children in the county. Holyhead county school ran a double shift system whereby local children received instruction each morning and pupils from a Liverpool school attended an afternoon session. In due course a fair number of the remaining evacuees had successfully assimilated into local society, learning Welsh and attending Nonconformist chapels. Bilingual testaments were issued at a Benllech Sunday school.

As had happened during the First World War, the urgent need for home-produced grain meant government subsidies to agriculture. The Anglesey War Agricultural Committee asked farmers in the county to plough up an additional 10,000 acres of grassland, raising the area under cultivation to 24,500 acres by 1940. Within a year the quota had been raised again, so that more than 41,000 acres would be ploughed. As before, labour shortages were partly filled by women and children. Farmers trained Women's Land Army volunteers, and in May 1942 a WLA hostel opened at Menai Bridge. School holidays were arranged to coincide with the harvest. Not that Anglesey schoolchildren needed official permission to help out on local farms; taking advantage of wartime conditions their 'very bad' attendance record deteriorated even further. Additional quotas brought the total acreage of arable land to 52,500 by 1944. Sufficient grassland was left to support dairy cattle, and to deal with increased milk supplies the Milk Marketing Board opened a creamery at Llangefni in March that year. But farmers were reluctant to meet further ploughing quotas, protesting against the inadequate supply of labour and the new farm prices fixed by the government. Minimum wages for workers had doubled, but this time it did not lead to the unionization of farm labourers. The TGWU area organizer made little headway in Anglesey during the war, nor during the rural recruiting drives of 1947–9. By 1965 the number of full-time agricultural workers was down to 954.

The darkest days of 1940–1 brought home the terrible reality of war to Anglesey people. In May 1940 the SS *Scotia* was withdrawn from the Irish mail-passenger service to assist in the military evacuation from Dunkirk. Hit whilst carrying French troops on 1 June, seventeen crewmen from the Holyhead area were lost when she sank. The bravery of her captain, W. H. Hughes, was recognized with the award of the Distinguished Service Cross. Soon, German bombers based in northern France were involved in raids on Anglesey itself. The first bombs fell at Holyhead in October; several houses were demolished yet no one was killed or seriously injured. As a strategic target, the port was reportedly attacked on eleven occasions. Though it did not suffer civilian casualties the damage to property, including Bethel chapel (later rebuilt at a cost of £6,000) was considerable. As the island lay in the path of Luftwaffe raids on Liverpool, many of the bombs that fell in 1941 were dropped at random by aircraft jettisoning their load when chased by RAF fighters; hence the damage to nursery greenhouses and a chapel roof at Pentre Berw in January and property at Llanfair Pwllgwyngyll in March. Crew members of a Heinkel bomber shot down near Bodffordd were buried at Holyhead. When allied ships and aircraft came to grief, help was readily at hand. Richard Evans, who later went on to win two RNLI gold medals for heroic feats at the helm of the Moelfre lifeboat, took part in the rescue of the crew of a torpedoed steamship in the Menai Straits in 1940, and the aircrew of a crashed Whitley bomber three years later.

In little time Anglesey found itself placed on a war footing. On a bleak site at Tywyn Trewan, the former haunt of the robbers of Crigyll rocks, an aircraft fighter station was constructed to provide defence cover in the northwest sector and protect shipping in the Irish Sea. Named RAF Valley, it became operational in 1941. To overcome the incessant problem of sand, peat was later dredged from nearby lakes – a process that led to the uncovering of the rich archaeological findings at Llyn Cerrig Bach. Unbeknown to the workers they had been using an Iron Age chain to haul out lorries stuck in mud! When the main danger from German aircraft receded by late 1943, RAF Valley became a transatlantic staging post for USAAF heavy bombers. Over 5,000 made the journey, a record 518 American aircraft landing in March 1945 to take part in the final allied bombing operations of the war. Another airfield was built at the former RNAS station, Mona, and used by the Flying Training Command to prepare air gunners and bomb aimers. At the third, much smaller, airfield at Bodorgan radio-controlled target drones took off to provide aerial targets for Royal Artillery gunners stationed nearby at the Tŷ-croes army camp. Holyhead served as a naval base for minesweepers, and after the fall of Holland ships of the Dutch Royal Navy were stationed at the port. Resurrected fears of an invasion via Ireland had resulted in the construction of military pillboxes to defend Holyhead harbour, potential beach landing sites, as well as the three RAF stations. Army units occupied both Plas Penrhos and Baron Hill mansions, and the latter was used as a military hospital.

Military construction projects boosted Anglesey's stagnant economy. They offered not only welcome employment but also higher wages to farm-workers and gardeners. Moreover, essential wartime industries were set up to take advantage of the island's relatively safe geographical position. A. W. J. Wells established a factory at Holyhead that produced precision components for aircraft under a government contract. Saunders-Roe Ltd relocated from the Isle of Wight to Friars, Llan-faes. Between 1941 and 1945 over 300 American-built Catalina flying boats were modified and tested to meet RAF operational requirements for coastal patrol against the German U-boats. It was not merely local employment; some Anglesey girls were conscripted to work in factories in England.

The war effort helped to maintain public morale. People were prepared to endure the hardships and support the various National Savings campaigns. With one exception, Anglesey far exceeded its appeal target for the annual 'war savings' week: £570,222 was raised for 'war weapons' (1941), £428,471 for 'wings for victory' (1943) and £443,931 for 'salute the soldier' (1944). Only in 1942, when £332,836 was collected during 'warship week', did it fail to attain the set target that included a Beaumaris sub-district sum earmarked for the minesweeper HMS *Beaumaris* (which bore the arms of the borough). No casualty lists had appeared in the local press this time to sap morale. Losses, it turned out, were not as high as in the Great War. New names would be added to town and village memorials, with the greatest number, 140, at Holyhead. The Commonwealth War Graves Commission lists 233 casualties from Anglesey, more than half of whom were seamen serving in either the merchant or Royal Navy. But a sample comparison with the local war memorials points to a higher overall figure of well over 300.

Most patterns of life on the island had been disrupted or further exposed to change during the war years. External influences inevitably steered people's outlook and habits from the old ways. English daily newspapers provided the latest news of the war. Cinemas continued to offer the most popular form of mass entertainment (on the radio there was a dearth of Welsh-language programmes). Local dances became a regular social occasion. The hundreds of servicemen of various nationalities stationed at military locations mixed with locals in such heady delights as the 'Yankee swing ball' held at the Llangefni town hall. Traditional interests competed for adherence. Concerts and local eisteddfodau still provided enjoyment in village halls. Unlike the years 1915–19, when proceedings were postponed, Eisteddfod Môn held an annual one-day festival throughout the duration of the war. Audiences also warmed to Welsh drama productions staged by amateur groups; Bodffordd had no fewer than three drama companies. Gŵyl Ddrama Môn (Anglesey Drama Festival) was launched in 1942. As with the potentially disruptive effects to Welsh culture, old religious certitudes were also being severely challenged. Nonconformist ministers felt their pastoral authority had diminished, threatening moral standards. The undermining of individual faith was evidenced by the fall in chapel attendance – as at Amlwch, Bryn-du, Llanfaethlu and Llanrhuddlad. Other chapels adapted to the situation, to embrace evacuees and even prisoners of war who worked on local farms. German POWs attending chapel service at Caergeiliog received a German copy of the New Testament.

Hard on the heels of the VE-day celebrations came the general election of 1945. The Anglesey Liberal Association had earlier gone about reviving its sixty-odd branches for what became a straight fight with Labour. No Tory candidate could be found in time. Megan Lloyd George, standing as a 'Liberal pure and simple', highlighted her wartime governmental experience, her championing of welfare reform, Welsh self-government, women's rights, and, crucially, the importance of retaining wartime industries in Anglesey. Cledwyn Hughes, her opponent, was a young Holyhead solicitor in the radical tradition (his father, a Methodist minister in the town, had been a loyal Liberal supporter), prominently involved in Welsh cultural movements. Now, post-war concerns predominated. He saw Labour as the only progressive party capable of providing a social security system, much-needed council housing and basic public utilities. Holyhead, he averred, faced a bleak future unless transport was nationalized. Farmers were promised increased subsidies. Short of resources, Labour's campaign suffered badly; they had a poor local organization and an acute shortage of cars needed to spread the message across the island. Anti-socialist Tories were said to have supplied most of Megan Lloyd George's motor-car fleet, though a formal pact was denied. In the end it was a close contest: 12,610 votes to 11,529. Whereas the great Labour landslide failed to engulf Anglesey, Megan Lloyd George's slender majority of 1,081 offered encouragement to the constituency Labour party.

As in the case of her predecessors, Megan Lloyd George's success was more about personality than a platform of policies. But at Westminster life within a miniscule Liberal party became increasingly fractious. Maintaining her leftward political drift, she welcomed the National Insurance and National Health Service Acts of 1946 for the benefits they brought to ordinary people, but stopped short of full-blown socialism. Even so, rumours persisted that she would soon join the Labour party. As it was, her willingness to defend the nationalization of public utilities guaranteed a Conservative opponent at the next election. In the meantime, Megan Lloyd George spoke up for Wales and Anglesey. Putting emphasis on local needs, she campaigned for more factory-based industries, council housing, better water supplies, a new hospital, and, presciently, the conversion of the RAF base at Valley into a civilian airport (instead, it provided advanced training for jet fighter pilots). This put her in a strong position for re-election in 1950. Labour mounted a confident challenge; Cledwyn Hughes, who had raised his political profile as county councillor and Holyhead town clerk, was supported by a sturdier local organization. Constituency party membership had by now reached a high point of 987. An almost static vote made his defeat all the more surprising. The poor Conservative showing indicated that many Tories had voted tactically to keep Labour out; Megan Lloyd George's majority rose to 1,929.

No such good fortune came the following year. The Labour government appeared vulnerable, and with O. M. Roberts, an energetic Conservative candidate, urging his followers not to vote tactically, the die was cast. In raising the Tory vote from 3,919 to 6,366 he scuppered Megan Lloyd George's chances. Attracting but 55 more votes, Cledwyn Hughes was therefore able to snatch victory with a 595 majority at his third attempt in 1951 to become Anglesey's first genuine Labour MP. Her long reign finally over, Megan Lloyd George declined to stand again in Anglesey. Cledwyn Hughes went on to hold the seat untroubled in seven subsequent contests. Never once did his majority fall below 4,500; at the 1966 election he polled 14,874 to secure 55 per cent of the total vote. Constituents could take pride in a distinguished ministerial career that saw him join the Cabinet as Secretary of State for Wales and then Minister of Agriculture. When he decided not to contest the 1979 election he was elevated to the Upper House, adopting the title Lord Cledwyn of Penrhos. A few years later he became Labour leader in the Lords. A true Anglesey man, Cledwyn Hughes's identification with the finer strands of Nonconformity, socialism and nationalism made him a genuinely popular figure with an extensive personal following. Much to his credit, he lived up to his principles. He remained deeply committed to the causes he had raised in his House of Commons maiden speech: social and economic progress in Anglesey, legislative devolution for Wales and the preservation of the Welsh language, international peace and improved living standards across the globe.

Previous electoral surprises could hardly match the shock result of the 1979 election. Overturning a Labour majority of almost 6,000, Keith Best, a Sussex barrister and former Parachute Regiment captain, won a spectacular victory for the Conservatives. His 15,100 votes – a swing of 15.2 per cent – even exceeded the totals achieved by Megan Lloyd George and Cledwyn Hughes. For the first time since the eighteenth century Anglesey had returned a Tory MP. A party that long suffered from its perceived association with 'English interests' triumphed with an unlikely English candidate. For Labour, who fielded the former Cardiganshire MP Elystan Morgan, and Plaid Cymru it was a devastating psychological blow. Anguished nationalists feared for Anglesey's heritage. No doubt the Conservatives had profited from the inflow of mainly English settlers that appeared to twin Benllech with Brighton. But Keith Best, who involved himself in community work, and who cut a dash with his dynamic election campaign, also successfully tapped the significant conservative element that had long existed in Anglesey society; after all, there was no greater Tory than the Methodist John Elias. As in the 1880s with G. Pritchard-Rayner, John Eilian Jones, the colourful National Eisteddfod chair and crown winner, had made a strong showing in 1966 to take the Conservative vote to 9,576. In learning Welsh, Best made every effort to endear himself with his constituents. Re-elected in 1983, he became, however, the unfortunate architect of his own downfall. Found guilty of obtaining multiple British Telecom shares by deception in September 1987 he stood down before the next election. Conservative difficulty was Plaid Cymru's opportunity.

As a political movement Plaid Cymru had made laborious headway. A year after its foundation in 1925, the party had three members in Anglesey. Only when the Llangefni branch was formed in 1931, with the solicitor-poet Rowland Jones as its first secretary, did it begin to make its presence felt. One of the first to gain political representation was G. J. Williams, who won a seat on Menai Bridge UDC in 1932. Pressure on the county council led to a resolution in favour of giving 'more prominence' to the Welsh language (though, in practice, Welsh was not commonly used in council meetings until the mid-1990s). In 1937 the party was able to harness the upsurge of patriotism that followed the release from prison of the three Plaid Cymru members who set fire to the RAF bombing school at Pen-y-berth, Llŷn. Cledwyn Hughes, in his pre-Labour days, had thought it 'timely and appropriate' to establish a Plaid Cymru branch at Holyhead. Within three years (1936–9) the number of branches in the county leapt from two to nine. It was at the suggestion of the Revd John Pierce, a stalwart of the Llangefni branch, that a national petition was launched in 1938 seeking equal status for the Welsh language in court proceedings. By the end of the following year 24,672 people in Anglesey had signed in support. But while other north Wales counties were being pressed to select parliament candidates to follow Caernarfonshire's lead, Anglesey evidently lagged behind.

As the war ended, Gwynfor Evans, shortly to become party president, reactivated interest when he addressed a series of meetings in Anglesey in 1944. Once again, the premier branch was at Llangefni. Here, in June 1951, Megan Lloyd George, Cledwyn Hughes and Gwynfor Evans shared a platform in support of the all-party Parliament for Wales campaign. Only in 1955, later than a number of other constituencies, did Plaid Cymru venture to contest the parliamentary seat, when J. Rowland Jones, a young history research student, attracted 2,183 votes. Dr R. Tudur Jones managed to push the Liberals – now doomed to irreversible decline – into fourth place in 1959 when he increased the total to 4,121 votes. But humiliating results in the sixties were a severe setback for the party. Later events would soon change the political landscape of Wales, leading to a nationalist resurgence. During the next decade two highly respected Welsh language campaigners, John L. Williams and Dafydd Iwan, raised Plaid Cymru's credibility as a political force. In 1979 the party recorded 7,863 votes. A disastrous Labour showing in 1983 (when the vote slumped to 6,791) lifted Plaid Cymru into second place, with 13,333 votes to the Conservative total of 15,017. Following Keith Best's downfall, the Ynys Môn constituency became a key marginal at the 1987 election. Only Plaid Cymru fielded the same candidate, and with over twenty-five local branches underpinning its party machine, Ieuan Wyn Jones emerged as the main challenger. Understandably, every chance was taken to present the contest as a two-horse race, allowing those seeking political change to vote tactically. Beyond that, Plaid Cymru came to be seen as not merely the defender of Welsh culture, but also the party to voice the economic concerns of a peripheral constituency.

Once again, Anglesey sensationally switched political direction to give Ieuan Wyn Jones victory with 18,580 votes. To some, the island's fickle electorate had displayed another mood swing; uniquely, it became the only parliamentary seat in modern times to return an MP from each of the main parties. To others, Anglesey had reasserted its Welshness, belatedly joining Caernarfon and Merioneth constituencies to make Gwynedd a Plaid Cymru stronghold. Withstanding the Conservative challenge in 1992, and a revitalized Labour party that shot back to second place in 1997, Ieuan Wyn Jones held on to the seat, albeit with reduced majorities. For all this, Plaid Cymru success only yielded modest gains in local government. Of the forty seats on Ynys Môn County Council, Plaid Cymru had but 7 to Labour's 6 in 1997, with independents still forming the largest group. While the county council endorsed the 'Yes' vote at the Devolution Referendum that year – Lord Cledwyn of Penrhos served as honorary president of the Ynys Môn 'Yes' branch – public opinion on the island was polarized to the extent that the 57 per cent turnout split almost evenly to 15,649 'Yes' votes and 15,095 'No' votes. Plaid Cymru again performed impressively in the first National Assembly election of 1999. Ieuan Wyn Jones won 16,469 votes, a majority of 9,288 over his nearest rival representing Labour, to combine both Westminster and Assembly roles.

When Ieuan Wyn Jones stood down for the 2001 general election, Labour took advantage of internal divisions within Plaid Cymru and the adverse publicity that the party had attracted on the matter of inward migration. After a tight contest Albert Owen was able to wrest the seat with a slender majority of 800. Yet again changeable in its political affections,

Ynys Môn thus became a highly marginal constituency. Local government, where egos clash and factionalism reigns, has proved even more perplexing. Plaid Cymru councillors would join their Labour counterparts to form an uneasy coalition group to run the county council in defiance of their party's high command. Further humiliation came in the National Assembly election of 2003, when the Tory candidate inspired a recovery to slash Ieuan Wyn Jones's majority to 2,225, and relegating Labour to third place. But at the 2005 general election Labour fortunes took a turn for the better. Albert Owen, and independent-minded and moderate rebel backbencher in the House of Commons, solidified his position with 12,278 votes as Labour edged ahead with a slightly increased majority. Plaid Cymru's intensive campaign to recapture their prime target seat had badly stalled – its prospects notionally thwarted by the third place Independent candidate, although as a former Tory National Assembly member he attracted support mainly at the expense of the Conservatives.

Always of great concern was the extent of Anglesey's economic problems. Unemployment had been a recurring theme in post-war electoral contests, and as MP, Cledwyn Hughes, in conjunction with the local authorities, fought hard to expand the island's industrial base. A. W. J. Wells set a pattern at Holyhead when he switched to the peacetime production of clocks and plastic toys. But in 1955 the 7.1 per cent unemployment rate was four times the Welsh average. By 1958, when it reached almost 13 per cent, the county 'stood out as the new depressed area in Wales'. Government subsidies had been of great benefit to farmers, but mechanization and the shift back to livestock farming led to a 20 per cent fall in the numbers engaged in agriculture – down from 2,927 to 2,300. The building industry also suffered badly, leaving a third of the workers attached to the trade out of work. To a large extent, Anglesey was a victim of geography; it lacked the location advantages and transport links enjoyed by areas of northeast Wales. There seemed to be little likelihood of attracting large-scale industrial development to the island; and when attempts were coupled with a proposal in 1957 to settle 'overspill' population from Birmingham, the potential threat to Anglesey's Welshness provoked an outcry spearheaded by Plaid Cymru. It meant, too, that young people would have to migrate to find work, thus slowing population growth.

Transport offered a major source of employment, especially in the Holyhead area where British Rail was the largest single employer. New cross-channel ships to Ireland had entered service in 1949, and to meet the demands of the age a car ferry service began in 1965. Port facilities were enlarged to handle both passenger and container traffic. The increase in freight tonnage turned Holyhead into the third largest ferry port after Dover and Portsmouth by 2000. Modern high-speed superferries meant that Dublin was only 99 minutes away. Recently a £14.5m plan for a fifth terminal was endorsed to cater for the astounding growth in cargo and car crossings. After the war Saunders-Roe Ltd had switched to light engineering projects – constructing the world's first aluminium high-speed patrol boat for the Royal Navy and making motor-bus bodies mainly for export. Subsequent company mergers led to the building of various other naval craft; depending on contracts, upwards of 900 were employed by the early 1960s. The military establishments at Valley and Tŷ-croes provided both maintenance and civil administration work.

As part of the county council water scheme a central reservoir near Llangefni had been completed in 1951. The Cefni works would guarantee almost 80 per cent of the island's water supply and help sustain agriculture and industrial development. One direct result was the establishment of the Associated Octel chemical plant (later Great Lakes Chemical Ltd) at Amlwch that extracted bromine from seawater. Most of its employees were local people, but at just over 3,000, the town's population had halved since the peak of 1831. Another reservoir, Llyn Alaw, was created in 1966 to provide a new water supply for Anglesey's industries and growing population. Classified as an area of high unemployment under the Distribution of Industry Act, government grants and loans were made available to industrialists to set up firms, usually on trading estates in the main towns. Government advance factories were also established at Holyhead and Llangefni. Increased job opportunities by 1960 had enabled women to find work in low-paying industries such as clothing: Mona Products Ltd at Menai Bridge employed 75. Whether in connection with engineering, electronics, manufacturing or clothing, the total employed was severely limited. By 1968 only about 2,500 found work in the industrial units. Many factories remained vacant, and little more had been done to stimulate industrial development at Amlwch. The number of unemployed in the county was in excess of 2,000. Educational qualifications had opened better career prospects for women. From the 1970s a higher proportion were employed in the service sector – public administration, education and health. Illustrative of the rising female presence in the labour market, women made up 47 per cent of the registered workers at Beaumaris in 1977. Wide pay differentials, however, still persist as a source of gender inequality.

For the first time since the heyday of the Parys Mountain copper mines, the 1960s would also see Anglesey enter another ambitious phase of industrialization that transformed the economic infrastructure. Major capital projects offered new opportunities. At Wylfa, the Central Electricity Generating Board built a nuclear power station with Magnox reactors that began operating in 1971. It provided employment for over 2,000 during construction work, and several hundred subsequently, a high proportion from the local workforce. In the wake of the Chernobyl disaster Wylfa became a subject of controversy. Plans for a new Wylfa 'B' station with a pressurised water reactor were strongly opposed, and later the operators received a fine for breaching safety regulations. Electricity from Wylfa supplied the Anglesey Aluminium operation at Holyhead, a joint £80m venture headed by the mining conglomerate Rio Tinto, which also commenced in 1971. This huge smelting plant emerged as the island's largest enterprise, now employing 550 workers. Another major international company, Shell, built an offshore terminal near Amlwch that piped oil from Rhos-goch to the refinery at Stanlow, Cheshire, until 1987.

Once the construction phases at Wylfa and Anglesey Aluminium had been completed, however, the county again crept to the top of the jobless league. By 1977 the unemployment rate of 14.9 per cent was almost double the Welsh average. Indeed, the figure of 2,557 was reported to be the highest since 1929. Tough times for industry generally would also force a number of businesses to close during subsequent years. High rates of unemployment continued to pose problems up to the close of the century. Despite the increase in freight traffic, unemployment at Holyhead, a traditional black spot, stood at 15.6 per cent in 1995, one of the highest in Wales. A year later the jobless figure in Anglesey had climbed to 3,286.

Changes that had occurred since the 1960s, nevertheless, boosted the upward trend in post-war population back to the level last seen in 1921. While there was less dependence on agriculture and Holyhead port, enhanced job opportunities in other industries also saw key workers brought from outside. Combined with Anglesey's increasing popularity as a retirement haven, totals rose from 51,705 in 1961 to almost 60,000 a decade later. But after reaching a peak of 69,149 in 1991, the population fell to 66,828 by 2001. It was expected that improved communications would further aid economic revival. When fire seriously damaged the tubes of Britannia Bridge it was reconstructed to accommodate a road deck above the railway track by 1972. With the completion of the new 20-mile A55 'expressway' across the island in the new century, opportunities were offered to inward investors and start-up businesses. Quite what impact it will have on Anglesey's fragile economy remains to be seen. Already thousands of daily commuters drive across the two traffic-congested bridges to work on the mainland (giving rise to talk of a third crossing). Reversing a centuries-old trend, some unemployed islanders even travel to Ireland to take up jobs. Salvation is sought, in part, in the implementation of the European Union Objective One programme and the injection of new funds to create and safeguard jobs on the island. In reality, factory closures and weak economic activity places Anglesey amongst the poorest areas of Wales, and with the ageing Wylfa power station also due to close in 2010, employment prospects appear grim.

Industrial developments, taken together with reservoirs, airfields, housing, schools and roads, meant the loss of nearly 20,000 acres of agricultural land by the 1980s. Large-scale afforestation, carried out by the Forestry Commission, is confined to the sand-dune area near Newborough and the slopes of Mynydd Llwydiarth. Agriculture still retained its importance, with farming interests stoutly defended by the National Farmers' Union and the Farmers' Union of Wales, which had established its first branch at Llanfechell in 1956. Opposition to the aluminium smelting works and oil terminal, however, proved unsuccessful. Though many benefited from government grants under Farm Improvement Schemes in the 1950s, mechanization and the amalgamation of uneconomical units led to a steep fall in the number of agricultural holdings. As small holdings authority, the county council became the second largest landowner. By the end of the century the total was down to 1,200. Most were small family farms of between 20 and 100 acres, many run part-time. Far fewer would be engaged in agriculture, and for the rural community this would have deleterious social consequences. Today, livestock farming predominates, with prize livestock exhibited in Sioe Môn, the county agricultural show at Gwalchmai. Overall, sheep outnumber cattle by 200,000 to 50,000. Sheep enterprises are geared to producing fat lambs, cattle to beef production and dairying – over eight million gallons of milk were produced in the 1980s. A high proportion of the acreage is therefore devoted to permanent grass, relegating cereal crops – barley, oats and spring wheat – to a minor position. Falling incomes mean dismal times for family farms. Uncertainty in some cases can present new challenges. Diversification into other sectors such as tourism, and the success of agri-food processing plants, offer partial hope to a rural economy badly in need of regeneration.

Tourism plays a substantial role in Anglesey's economy. Attracted by the outstanding natural beauty of the coastline, visitors have long turned places like Benllech, Moelfre, Cemais, Trearddur, Rhosneigr, Menai Bridge and Beaumaris into popular holiday destinations. So much so that a high proportion of homes around the coastal areas are second homes: by the 1980s there were roughly 2,500. Nowadays every aspect of tourism is marketed. Among the diverse attractions are the historic sites, heritage trails, museums, nature reserves, a sea zoo, butterfly farm, and of course the village with the famous long name. Relatively few outside business concerns are involved. The trade is characterized by owner-occupied hotels, guesthouses, caravan and camping sites. At the close of the century the tourist industry employed 2,600 people and contributed £180m a year to the local economy. Recent road improvements have made the island even more accessible to holidaymakers. Maximizing Anglesey's tourism potential presents a number of challenges, not least the safeguarding of its cultural heritage and environment. Aspects of the island's landscape and natural history have been captured by two eminent artists: Sir Kyffin Williams, and Charles Tunnicliffe – whose studies of bird life are on view at Oriel Ynys Môn, Llangefni.

Local government administration offered increased employment opportunities, especially at the main county council buildings in Llangefni, the island's administrative capital. Following local government changes in 1974 Anglesey lost the independent status it had enjoyed since 1536 when it was absorbed into a larger regional authority, the new county of Gwynedd. The Ynys Môn (Isle of Anglesey) Borough Council came into being. Further reorganization enabled Anglesey to regain its separate autonomous identity in 1996 with the creation of an all-purpose unitary authority, the Ynys Môn County Council. At the first elections 45 per cent of the candidates were returned unopposed. For better or for worse, the council remained firmly, as it had been for most of the century, under independent political control. Unfortunately, its reputation was somewhat marred by allegations of sleaze, corruption and misdemeanours relating to planning and housing. A series of controversial disclosures and damaging official inquiries in the 1980s and 90s weakened public trust.

As agents of change, the local authorities were instrumental in promoting social progress. Beyond question, one of the most significant developments of modern times had been the welfare state reforms. In the case of housing, old unfit stock was pulled down – 720 houses were listed for demolition at Holyhead in 1955 – and investment made in a programme of modern council estates. Llangefni UDC, which had one of the best housing records, became the first in north Wales to provide rented properties for government officials. In 1954 Beaumaris Borough Council was awarded a medal for the best designed housing estates in Wales. Holyhead UDC opened a six-storey block of council flats on Newry fields in 1965, dubbed a 'little skyscraper'. Between 1974 and 1981 the Ynys Môn Borough Council built over 900 new council houses. Well before this, essential public utilities had also been provided to improve standards of life. Following nationalization, the electricity supply was extended to most parts of the island by the Merseyside and North Wales Electricity Board (MANWEB). Uniquely in England and Wales, the Anglesey County Council (Water) Act of 1944 had designated the county council as a water authority empowered to take over the eight existing undertakings, beginning with the Holyhead Water Company, some 165 public wells, and to commence with the construction of new reservoirs. By 1964 every community on the island was supplied with piped water.

Improvements in social conditions were accompanied by healthcare services. The first clinics were established at Llangefni and Menai Bridge in 1918; the county had a complete midwifery service two years later. The

National Health Service would provide a range of benefits. Free medical and hospital treatment relieved ordinary people of many of their fears. Vaccinations against tuberculosis, diphtheria and the like would reduce the overall incidence of deaths from infectious diseases. The welfare of children was well provided: free school meals, free dental and medical inspection. Anglesey, in 1935, had been the first Welsh county to provide daily milk in all schools. The county council struck a progressive note in the fifties in more than one sphere. However, its decision to add fluoride to the public water supply as a means of improving dental health provoked controversy. But despite opposition to 'mass medication' the fluoridation experiment began in 1955 within the district served by the Gwalchmai reservoir. Soon after Welsh Water stopped the practice by 1992, there were complaints that tooth decay among Anglesey children was on the increase.

As in the past, there are extremes of wealth and poverty. Along certain stretches of the coastal strip the affluence is tangible; a 'millionaire's mile' overlooks the Menai Straits between Menai Bridge and Beaumaris. Large parts of the island, in contrast, face economic decline and multiple deprivation deepening the divide between rich and poor. Half of Anglesey's forty electoral divisions are ranked among the 40 per cent most deprived in Wales. Two of the poorest, Morawelon and town ward, are at Holyhead. Evidence of dereliction can be seen within the centres of Holyhead, Llangefni and Amlwch, while many villages have a drab appearance. No different to other regions, Anglesey has its share of contemporary ills. People housed in disadvantaged communities suffer unemployment, low incomes, poor living conditions, child poverty, ill health, crime and anti-social behaviour. Symptomatically, drug abuse became very prevalent in towns and even rural villages. In 1994, when the Gwynedd Drugs Advisory Service operated 'drop in' centres in the main towns, Anglesey had the highest number of heroin referrals.

Religion appeared unable to give answers to social problems or comfort to the less fortunate. Anglesey was no longer soaked in Nonconformist values. Attendances at places of worship followed a pattern of continuous decline. By the 1990s the Independent and Baptist denomination could only muster some three thousand members between them. The once powerful Calvinistic Methodists crumbled at a catastrophic rate: between 1947 and 1967 membership fell from 11,477 to 8,718. As a microcosm of this sustained downturn, Holyhead had eight Methodist chapels in 1983, yet Hyfrydle chapel alone could seat the entire local membership of 663. By 2002, the total number of communicants had plummeted to 3,304; barely 500 attended Methodist Sunday schools on the whole island. Indicative of the decline in traditional Sabbath observance was the outcome of the septennial plebiscites on the Sunday opening of licensed premises in Wales. The majority in favour of remaining 'dry' tumbled from 10,353 in 1961 to 1,743 by 1975, so that it was hardly surprising that Anglesey turned 'wet' in 1982. As chapel-going lost its meaning, dwindling congregations forced some to close. By the end of the century, on the other hand, there were nine Roman Catholic churches on the island. The Mormons, too, have a place of worship at Gaerwen.

The contrast between the first and last decade of the century could not be starker. Sustained by a mere handful of ministers and clergy, organized religion was no longer a power at the heart of Anglesey's communities. The impact of two world wars had weakened individual faith. The earlier obsession with temperance, disestablishment and narrow Sabbatarianism (that even frowned upon whistling on a Sunday) at the expense of urgent social issues harmed Nonconformity in the long run. Equally detrimental was rural depopulation and the decrease in the number of Welsh speakers. Above all else came the change in social attitudes from the late 1950s. Post-war years of austerity gave way to welcome improvements in living standards, but in the television age more and more households lay greater store on the material goods that secured a better quality of life. Pop music and new freedoms heralded a generational shift in values. Having long overcome the sectarian animosities, the relentless tide of secularization in modern life further eroded the reverence once held for religion. With the breakdown of traditional moral values, Anglesey has now one of the highest proportions of single-parent families.

Changes in education since the beginning of the century would make it progressively easier for children from less advantaged backgrounds to better themselves. The 1902 Education Act abolished the school boards and established a state system whereby the county council became the local education authority (LEA) responsible for both primary and secondary education. But the proposed rate-aid to struggling church schools aroused Nonconformist fury. Anglesey was up in arms as the traditional vendetta between church and dissent flared once more. Radical Nonconformist leaders addressed protest meetings to mobilize public support. Anglesey County Council intimated that it would not willingly accept administrative responsibility. Ellis Jones Griffith and the Revd David Rees, Llangristiolus, were prepared to suffer imprisonment rather than pay the 'unjust rate'. At a Llangefni conference Nonconformists resolved to contest the 1904 county council elections on this issue. Sweeping success for the Liberals gave them a popular mandate, but unlike some other Welsh authorities the Anglesey County Council did not follow an aggressively militant path. It decided that the twenty-three 'non-provided' (mainly National) schools would be maintained by parliamentary grants, and rate-aid channelled towards the forty-three 'provided' (former board) schools.

Mercifully, this explosion of sectarian dissension finally ended the church-chapel controversies that had riven education for so long. Lord Stanley of Alderley, the Liberal Anglican who served as first chairman of the LEA, encouraged a new 'friendly spirit'. The basis was laid for a new unified system. But as most of the antiquated church and board schools had been allowed to deteriorate to an unsatisfactory condition they were very bleak beginnings. Considerable expenditure, spread over a lengthy period, had to be directed towards structural repairs and improvements to the newly designated 'council schools'. Surviving National schools would struggle on – Sir George Meyrick was loath to surrender Llangadwaladr school – until financial constraints forced their transfer to the LEA, or final closure. Only eleven 'non-provided' schools were left by 1928. A decade later the number had fallen to nine, so that with fifty-four council schools the LEA controlled a total of sixty-three primary schools. When new housing developments necessitated the provision of larger buildings many were remodelled or replaced. The post-war school building programme began with the opening of Beaumaris primary school in 1951; built at a cost of £82,000 it incorporated the latest modern design. In addition, there were the three county secondary schools. New permanent buildings had been opened at Llangefni in 1900 and Holyhead in 1904. Along with the old-established grammar school at Beaumaris, they too benefited from David Hughes's charity.

An 'education ladder' had been raised; the challenge now was to help children climb that ladder. Since the county schools charged an annual tuition fee, able children from poor families could only proceed to secondary education by means of 'free places' or scholarships. Admission was dependent upon passing the annual entrance examination. As only 51.4 per cent 'free places' were available in 1931–2, the Anglesey LEA pressed the Welsh Department of the Board of Education to raise the allocation. If the county council was negligent of health and housing at this time, it proved strikingly alive to educational advancement. By 1936, 100 per cent 'free places' became available, but many working-class parents still lacked the means to pay the cost of books, uniform and travel. Almost all the pupils came from local primary schools. And head teachers invariably concentrated on the select scholarship class at the expense of the less academic pupils, who would be stigmatized as 'failures'. Within the county secondary schools very little had changed. Instead of developing commercial and technical education adapted to local needs the curriculum served a middle-class social purpose – preparing pupils for a professional career. As most were destined to find work outside Anglesey, the cream of the county was for export. Though secondary education remained highly selective, it underwent a remarkable period of expansion. Within the three existing, but severely overcrowded, schools the number of pupils more than trebled between 1914 and 1939, from 372 to 1,241. A fourth school, at Amlwch, opened in temporary premises in 1940.

In the wake of the Hadow Report (1926) the idea of 'secondary education for all' began to gather momentum. But the concept of separate county and 'central' schools (for non-academic pupils) was rejected by the Anglesey LEA in favour of 'multilateral' schools that catered for children of differing abilities and needs, irrespective of social background. Only at Holyhead did they think it practical to set up a central school – at St Cybi. Leading the crusade were Dr Thomas Jones, Amlwch, the enlightened chairman of the LEA, and E. O. Humphreys, appointed Anglesey's first director of education in 1935. From this time on they became engaged in a long and difficult struggle for a revolutionary reorganization that would secure 'equality of opportunity' for all Anglesey children. As things stood, approximately 60 per cent of those of secondary school age remained in all-age primary schools, leaving but 40 per cent to go to the county schools. Not a man to falter, E. O. Humphreys displayed unshakable resolution as an all-powerful, if dictatorial, educational administrator committed to the egalitarian ideal. It meant overcoming entrenched middle-class attitudes preoccupied with academic standards, plus the customary penny-pinching elements in Anglesey society. Progress came at extra cost. Secondary schools had to be suitably staffed and equipped to offer a range of academic, technical and practical education.

Reforms under the 1944 Education Act made it possible to implement the long-standing proposals for secondary education in Anglesey. Guided by E. O. Humphreys, the LEA made urgent preparations. During a short interim eight secondary modern schools were attached to primary schools. Then, in 1949, St Cybi central school and Holyhead county school amalgamated to become one 'comprehensive' school, the first in Anglesey. A wide-ranging curriculum was provided, and such was the success that all county schools quickly followed once the selective entrance examination had been scrapped. In 1953 the Anglesey LEA thus gained the distinction of being the first in England and Wales to implement a system of comprehensive schools. New buildings were opened that year at Llangefni, and Amlwch (named to honour Sir Thomas Jones's public service), and in 1962 pupils were transferred from Beaumaris to the new Ysgol David Hughes at Menai Bridge. Anglesey could be justifiably proud of its pioneering role. Whether it was possible to fully realize the high ideals envisaged by early proponents is doubtful, but there can be little argument that comprehensive schools were best suited to circumstances within a small, self-contained rural county. E. O. Humphreys had also prepared plans in 1951 for further education colleges at Holyhead and Llangefni (that specialized in agriculture), ultimately amalgamated on the Coleg Pencraig site at Llangefni. Essentially, he was the one man to provide vision and courageous leadership, yet no educational establishment on the island commemorates his name.

Welsh prevailed as the spoken language of daily life in most parts of the island. John Morris-Jones had transcribed a typical example of *llafar gwlad* (everyday speech) heard among the villagers of Llanfair Pwllgwyngyll back in 1889. Moreover, he was convinced – rightly, no doubt – that Anglesey people spoke the most perfect Welsh. A quarter were monoglot Welsh speakers in 1931, though the number would swiftly drop from 23.9 per cent to 9.6 per cent during the next twenty years. Outside influences had hardly begun the process of erosion, yet the purity, preservation and development of the language – *iaith bereiddia'r ddaear hon* (the sweetest language of this earth) – remained foremost in Morris-Jones's academic mind. First as a lecturer, then Professor of Welsh Language and Literature at the University College of North Wales, Bangor, he worked to standardize the spelling of Welsh, culminating in his authoritative books, *A Welsh Grammar, Historical and Comparative* (1913) and *The Orthography of the Welsh Language* (1928). As founder of the 'Bangor School' of poetry, eschewing the bombastic language of the Victorian era, he also introduced a 'new purity of diction and clarity of style' into Welsh poetry. *Cerdd Dafod* (1925) contains the fruit of his study of the rules of prosody. Ranked among the greatest authorities on the Welsh language, what he achieved as scholar, poet and eisteddfod critic directly influenced the literary renaissance of the early twentieth century.

As a member of the first LEA, Morris-Jones was in a position to promote the teaching of Welsh in primary schools. In 1904 he co-authored a report advocating that the younger children be taught in the mother tongue. By adopting the scheme, the LEA committed itself to a Welsh policy. Reporting on his visit to Carreg-lefn school in 1910 the inspector noted: 'Welsh, the home language of the children is systematically taught and Welsh History lessons given in Welsh secure attentive listeners in the highest class.' But in practice much depended on the attitude of the headmaster and staff. The era of the 'Welsh Not' had passed, still English remained as the main language of instruction, with only token Welsh lessons. It was certainly the case at Holyhead. The poet R. S. Thomas lamented that English was the language of his school, save on St David's day. Small wonder a Board of Education report in 1938 found that 80 per cent of the Anglesey children who did not speak Welsh were in Holyhead schools. The Anglicization of the town had gathered pace; in another decade or so Welsh ceased to be the language of the school playground. In rural schools, such as at Llandrygarn, the language of the classroom might be more suited to 'a school in central London', but at least Welsh was heard on the yard outside. By the same token, pupils were cut off from their cultural roots. The 1938 report also pointedly criticized the fact that there were children in Anglesey who knew nothing of Goronwy Owen.

Differences between the professed LEA language policy and actual practice aside, Anglesey could still be counted as a Welsh citadel. At the start of the 1950s 84 per cent of children between five and eleven were reported to be Welsh-speaking. It was just over 60 per cent at Holyhead and the surrounding district, while Beaumaris had become so Anglicized that the percentage fell to 35. Each secondary school had been allowed to develop its own language policy – of a sort. Welsh remained a subject that could be dropped at an early stage. At Llangefni, Welsh grammar received great prominence simply because the headmaster, S. J. Evans, was himself the author of several textbooks. But endless parsing and analysis dulled the mind, whereas little effort was made to foster interest in Welsh literature. In truth, the energies of the LEA had been focused on the pursuit of the comprehensive ideal at the expense of the Welsh language. With no scheme for teaching Welsh, indifference prevailed. Nowhere was Welsh the everyday medium of school administration. Various memoirs decry the total disregard shown by Welsh-speaking headmasters and teachers who spoke only English to their pupils. A system given common consent by administrators and parents alike would not be changed overnight.

Monoglot Welsh speakers were a mere 5.6 per cent of Anglesey's population in 1961. No Welsh child would remain monoglot for long. Indeed, the plight of the language became a matter of concern when it was disclosed that the number of Welsh-speakers in primary schools had fallen to 72 per cent by 1961. With it came the uncomfortable truth that some parents saw little value in passing the language to their children. As many as 234 pupils spoke English as their first language even though both parents were Welsh-speaking. Attitudes changed once the seriousness of the situation was grasped. Positive action began in the mid-60s with the establishment of independent, voluntary *ysgolion meithrin* (nursery schools) at Holyhead, Benllech, Llangefni and Amlwch. By 1977 there were twenty-three such groups on the island; Llanfair Pwllgwyngyll would have the largest group in Wales in 1983. The LEA had already appointed a language organizer and in 1974 Ysgol Morswyn, a Welsh-medium primary school, opened at Holyhead. Soon after the new Gwynedd County Council adopted a bold bilingual policy in education, Welsh became the principal medium at Anglesey's fifth comprehensive school established at Bodedern in 1977. By this time only 25 per cent of secondary school pupils at Holyhead spoke Welsh as their first language, contrasted to 76 per cent at Llangefni. Efforts to teach Welsh to children from non-Welsh speaking backgrounds would prove largely disappointing. In 1994 the percentage of Anglesey children fluent in Welsh at primary school level stood at 56.4. Only for 35.2 per cent was Welsh the fluent language of the home.

The psychological legacy of generations of English-based schooling was but one factor in the decline of the language. In 1961 the percentage able to speak Welsh was 75.5. Further critical changes came in the 1960s and 70s when external cultural influences intensified, compounded by the high volume of in-migration. Between 1971 and 1977 some 12,000 incomers settled on the island, 70 per cent of whom came from England. As MP, Cledwyn Hughes had been anxious to get the balance right between Anglesey's need for new industries and fears of accelerating the process of Anglicization. But economic development inevitably meant the introduction of outside workers. The growing attraction of the tourist-orientated coastal communities as a retirement spot has reconfigured their linguistic base. At Trearddur, Moelfre, Bryn-teg and Llanbedr-goch over 40 per cent of the inhabitants had been born outside Wales. Almost a third of the people in Llanbedr-goch in 1991 were over the age of 65, with 70.7 per cent monoglot English-speakers. At the same time, a flagging economy has contributed to a significant 'brain drain' of young people leaving the island in search of better opportunities – a trend predicted to increase. Even for many with jobs, comparatively low incomes mean they are unable to compete in the housing market as property prices soared ahead.

Predictably enough, all this helped push the percentage of Welsh-speakers down to 62 by 1991 (with a further two per cent drop in 2001). Over 30 per cent of the population were born outside Wales. Such large numbers limited the opportunities for local inhabitants to speak their language in a day-to-day context. Welsh-speakers visiting the county could now expect a regular reply of 'no Welsh'. The few places to retain a high concentration of Welsh speakers were located in the central parts of the island, especially at Llangefni and Bodffordd. Contrary to what the Revd John Williams prophesied at the beginning of the century, Mynydd y Garn, Llanfair-yng-Nghornwy, will not be the last refuge of the Welsh language on Anglesey. The threat to the Welsh heartland and the dangers of further loss are immediately obvious. If Welsh is to survive as a living community language, strategic initiatives that guarantee affirmative action have to be taken. Ironically, the proposed holiday complex at the former Tŷ-croes army camp in 1987 was rejected not because of the adverse effect it might have on a thoroughly Welsh locality, but for concerns relating to the preservation of the environment.

Welsh culture remained sharply defined throughout many vicissitudes. The eisteddfod, and the island's literary, musical and drama tradition continued to foster native talent. In 1957 the Eisteddfod Môn Bardic Gorsedd celebrated its fiftieth jubilee. Formally organized in 1911, when the inimitable W. Charles Owen, 'Llew Llwydiarth', began his long association, the institution produced National Eisteddfod bardic winners such as Rowland Jones, 'Rolant o Fôn', and Tom Parri Jones. No fewer than forty-two choirs entered the Anglesey eisteddfod at Gaerwen in 1937. Of the twenty-five or so local eisteddfodau held during the 1950s, those at Bodffordd, Marian-glas, Llandegfan, Llanddeusant and Talwrn still flourish. From the turn of the century John Jones, 'Telynor Môn', Llannerch-y-medd, and his three sons, maintained a remarkable tradition of harp playing in Anglesey that dates back to the thirteenth century and which continues today. The tenor Ifor Owen Thomas, and latterly Gwyn Hughes Jones, have performed in the world's opera houses. Ceinwen Rowlands of Holyhead became one of the foremost sopranos of her time. More recently, the singing duo Tony and Aloma and Aled Jones have enjoyed popular success. Literature of the period encompassed the romantic and the modern. Two notable writers, W. D. Owen and G. Wynne Griffith, drew on traditions in Anglesey's past – smuggling in the case of *Madam Wen* and *Helynt Coed y Gell*. The short stories of W. J. Griffith and the autobiographical volumes of Ifan Gruffydd provide an engaging portrait of a rural life that has passed. Human relationships of a more contemporary nature are explored in the novels of Jane Edwards.

Before the advent of television, local amateur drama companies flourished. Llannerch-y-medd drama society made a name for itself way beyond the island; in 1943 a group from the tiny hamlet of Rhoscefnhir carried off a premier prize at the National Eisteddfod. Llangefni drama society drew from the talents of a Welsh learner, George Fisher, who in addition to writing and directing plays inspired the establishment of 'Y Theatr Fach' (the little theatre) in the town in 1955. Hugh Griffith of Marian-glas had already made his way to the Royal Academy of Dramatic Art in London and he became a distinguished stage actor prior to crowning his roguish screen performances with an Oscar in 1959 for best supporting actor in the film *Ben Hur*. Closer to home, on stage, radio and television, Welsh-language audiences gained more from the contribution of his sister, Elen Roger Jones; also the consummate talents of Charles Williams and Hywel Gwynfryn, both popular household names. In a changing society traditional cultural activities might be in retreat, yet heartening efforts are still being made to maintain and promote the Welsh language. Whereas *Y Clorianydd* ceased publication in 1969, volunteer-run *papurau bro* (community newspapers), among them *Papur Menai* and *Y Glorian*, took its place. As a Welsh-medium counterpart to the Women's Institute, Merched y Wawr began to set up branches in the county in 1967; thirty years later the movement had a membership of 638. Mostly in connection with the schools, Urdd Gobaith Cymru registered over 2,600 members in the county in 1997. The fulfilment of cultural aspirations sets an enduring stamp on a society facing further change. For all those involved, Anglesey's past contribution can provide inspiration.

An evocation of the past inevitably rests upon certainties embedded in personal affections. Attachment to place is arguably stronger in Anglesey than in other regions of Wales in that it is strengthened by a well-defined natural boundary and a pride in the distinctive historic status accorded to *Môn, mam Cymru*. Such sentiment creates a greater sense of identity beyond the initial bond to a place of birth and upbringing. It also gives rise to the fierce independent spirit that has characterized native islanders over the centuries. Attachment to people is carved from a memory of generations who shared that community. And it is bound closer by a deeper knowledge and understanding of social continuity and inherited values. Attachment to language can be considered as emblematic of the link with a collective past. It is an integral part of Anglesey's rich heritage, rooted in two millennia of island history.

Select Bibliography

Anthony, H., *Menai Bridge and its Council* (Menai Bridge, 1974).

Carr, A. D., *Medieval Anglesey* (Anglesey Antiquarian Society, 1982).

Cowell, J., *Edwardian Anglesey, A Pictorial History*, vol. 1 (Llangefni, 1991), vol. 2 (Llangefni, 1992).

Eames, A., *Ships and Seamen of Anglesey 1558–1918* (Anglesey Antiquarian Society, 1973).

Evans, G. N., *Social Life in Mid-Eighteenth Century Anglesey* (Cardiff, 1936).

————*Religion and Politics in Mid-Eighteenth Century Anglesey* (Cardiff, 1953).

Hope, B. D., *A Curious Place. The Industrial History of Amlwch (1550–1950)* (Wrexham, 1994).

Hughes, D. L. and Williams, D. M., *Holyhead: The Story of a Port* (published by the authors, 1967).

Hughes, M., *Anglesey Remembers. Some of its Eminent People* (Llanrwst, 2000).

———— *Anglesey 1900* (Llanrwst, 2002).

Hughes, R., *Enwogion Môn, 1850–1912* (Dolgellau,1913).

Hughes, T. A., *'Tamaid i'w brofi' o 'lwch mân Llan'achmedd'* (Llangefni, 2001).

Islwyn, D., *Hydref y Rhos* (Caernarfon, 1983).

Jones, B. L. (ed.), *Gwŷr Môn* (Cyngor Gwlad Gwynedd, 1979).

Jones, D. and Thomas, G. (eds), *Nabod Môn* (Llanrwst, 2003).

Jones, G. T. and Roberts, T., *Enwau Lleoedd Môn* (Cyngor Sir Ynys Môn, 1996).

Jones, R., *Dic Tŷ Capel* (Caernarfon, 1995).

Jones, R. T., *Tân ar yr Ynys* (Caernarfon, 2004).

Jones, W. E. (ed.), *A New Natural History of Anglesey* (Anglesey Antiquarian Society, 1990).

Lynch, F., *Prehistoric Anglesey* (2nd edn, Anglesey Antiquarian Society, 1991).

Owen, H. (ed.), *Braslun o Hanes M.C. Môn 1880–1935* (Liverpool, 1937).

———— *Hanes Plwyf Niwbwrch ym Môn* (Caernarfon, 1952).

———— *History of the Anglesey Constabulary* (Anglesey Antiquarian Society, 1952).

Owen, W. (ed.), *Bwrw Cyfrif 'Rôl Canrif* (Llanrwst, 1999).

Parry, R., *Enwogion Môn* (Amlwch, 1877).

Pretty, D. A., *Two Centuries of Anglesey Schools 1700–1902* (Anglesey Antiquarian Society, 1977).

————*Rhyfelwr Môn. Y Brigadydd-Gadfridog Syr Owen Thomas, A.S., 1858–1923* (Dinbych, 1989).

Price, E., *Megan Lloyd George* (Caernarfon, 1983).

———— *Lord Cledwyn of Penrhos* (Bangor, 1990).

Pritchard, J., *Methodistiaeth Môn* (Amlwch, 1888).

Ramage, H., *Portraits of an Island. Eighteenth Century Anglesey* (Anglesey Antiquarian Society, 1987).

Richards, M. (ed.), *An Atlas of Anglesey* (Anglesey Community Council, 1972).

Richards, E., *Yr Ardal Wyllt* (Y Bala, 1983).

———— *Potsiars Môn* (Caernarfon, 2001).

———— *Pregethwrs Môn* (Caernarfon, 2003).

Roberts, G. (ed.), *Wel Dyma Fo ... Charles Williams* (Penygroes, 1983).

Roberts, W. H., *Aroglau Gwair* (Caernarfon, 1981).

Rowlands, E. W., *O Lwyfan i Lwyfan* (Caernarfon, 1999).

———— *Masts and Shafts. The Story of the Town and Port of Amlwch 1793–1913* (2000).

Rowlands, J., *Copper Mountain* (Anglesey Antiquarian Society, 1966).

Steele, P., *The Anglesey Guide. Môn Mam Cymru* (Porthaethwy, 1990).

———— *Beaumaris: The Town's Story* (Porthaethwy, 1996).

Taylor, A., *Beaumaris Castle* (4th edn, Cadw, Cardiff, 1999).

Wiliam, D. W., *Llwynogod Môn ac Ysgrifau Eraill* (Penygroes, 1983).

Williams, E. A., *The Day Before Yesterday. Anglesey in the Nineteenth Century* (translated and published by G. Wynne Griffith, 1988).

Williams, H. Ll. (ed.), *Braslun o Hanes Methodistiaeth Galfinaidd Môn 1935–1970* (Dinbych, 1977).

Williams, R. Môn, *Enwogion Môn, 1850–1912* (Bangor, 1913).

Yates, M. J. and Longley, D., *Anglesey. A Guide to Ancient Monuments on the Isle of Anglesey* (3rd edn, Cadw, Cardiff, 2001).

Local Periodicals
Môn
Transactions of the Anglesey Antiquarian Society and Field Club

Newspapers
Y Clorianydd
Herald Môn
Holyhead and Anglesey Mail
Holyhead Chronicle
Y Wyntyll

Unpublished Theses
James, G., 'Llanfair Pwllgwyngyll: astudiaeth o gymuned wledig ym Môn c1700–c1939'. M.Phil. University of Wales (Bangor), 1997.

Job, A. G., 'Agweddau ar syniadau cymdeithasol a'r farn gyhoeddus ym Môn rhwng y ddau ryfel byd'. M.Phil. University of Wales (Bangor), 1990 .

Owen, A., 'The port and town of Holyhead during the Depression of the 1930s'. M.A. University of Wales (Bangor), 1987.

Williams, O. A., 'Anglesey: towards comprehensive education, 1926–1953'. M.Ed. University of Wales (Bangor), 1985.

Index

Aber 21

Aberconwy 20

Aberconwy, treaty of 21

Aberffraw 1, 2, 6, 9, 10, 12–14, 16–18, 20–2, 24, 26, 29, 34, 41, 56–7, 64, 86, 99, 101–2, 108, 111–12, 116, 125, 128

Aberlleiniog 15, 47

Abermenai 15, 19, 69

Acts of Parliament
 Act for the Better Propagation and Preaching of the Gospel in Wales (1650) 50–1
 Act of Union with Ireland (1800) 77
 Acts of Union (1536–43) 35, 43
 Anglesey County Council (Water) Act (1944) 147
 Anglesey Turnpike Act (1765) 69
 Corn Production Act (1917) 124–5, 132
 Distribution of Industry Act (1958) 144
 Education (1870) 98, (1889) 99, (1902) 149, (1944) 151
 National Health Service Act (1946) 139, 148
 National Insurance Act (1911) 125, (1946) 130, 139
 Poor Law Amendment Act (1834) 113
 Reform Act (1832) 104 (1867) 106 (1884) 107

Aelwyd y Cymro 103

Afan Ferddig 9

Agricola, Julius 6

agriculture 1–3, 7, 18–19, 30, 42, 45, 54, 56, 63–6, 83–7, 117, 124–5, 129–30, 132, 136, 143–6, 152

Alaw, river 14

Almanac Caergybi 62, 74

alms-houses 55, 117

America 63, 76, 87

Amlwch 3, 19, 51–2, 56–7, 63, 66, 68–9, 73, 79–82, 84, 86–95, 97, 99–100, 103–4, 109–15, 117–18, 121–2, 139, 144–5, 148, 151, 153

Amlwch Literary and Scientific Institution 88

Amlwch Port 68, 81, 84, 88, 93

Amlwch Shipping Company 68

Anarawd ap Rhodri 12

Anglesey Agricultural Labourers' Union 86

Anglesey Agricultural Society 84

Anglesey Aluminium 145–6

Anglesey Association for the Preservation of Life from Shipwreck 82–3

Anglesey Auxiliary Bible Society 92

Anglesey Coal Company 88

Anglesey Colliery Company Ltd 89

Anglesey Conservative Association 107, 127, 129

Anglesey County Committee 49–50

Anglesey County Constabulary 112, 116

Anglesey (Ynys Môn) County Council 108, 116, 120, 124–6, 128–30, 132–5, 141–3, 146–9

Anglesey County Scholarship 99

Anglesey Drama Festival 138

Anglesey Druidical Society 65

Anglesey Egg Collection Depot 123

Anglesey Farmers' Society 123

Anglesey Farmers' Society (Union) 86, 127

Anglesey Joint Education Committee 99

Anglesey Ladies 'Comforts' Committee 135

Anglesey Ladies Recruiting Committee 120

Anglesey (Soccer) League 111, 119

Anglesey Liberal Association 107, 125, 127, 131, 139

Anglesey Liberal Unionist Association 108

Anglesey Local Education Authority (LEA) 136, 149–53